Widely regarded as the foremost expert on the history of Irish broadcasting, Rex Cathcart is Professor of Education at Queen's University, Belfast, and previously held the same post at the New University of Ulster. He was chairman of the first Educational Advisory Committee of RTE, which planned their educational service, and Regional Officer of the Independent Television Authority. His practical experience has included devising, writing, producing and presenting programmes for BBC, ITV and RTE. In addition to articles in various journals, Rex Cathcart has contributed a chapter on the history of Radio Éireann to *Communications and Community in Ireland* edited by Brian Farrell.

For
Geoffrey, Jean and Brian,
all born in the historic province of
Ulster

The Most Contrary Region

The BBC in Northern Ireland 1924–1984

REX CATHCART

THE
BLACKSTAFF
PRESS

First published in 1984 by
The Blackstaff Press Limited
3 Galway Park, Dundonald, Belfast BT16 0AN

© Rex Cathcart, 1984
Printed in Northern Ireland by
The Universities Press Limited

British Library Cataloguing in Publication Data
Cathcart, Rex
The most contrary region: the BBC in Northern Ireland 1924–84
1. British Broadcasting Corporation. Northern Ireland Region – History
I. Title
384.54'09416   HE8689.9.I7
ISBN 0 85640 326 1 (hb)
0 85640 323 7 (pb)

Contents

Preface

My original interest in the history of the BBC in Northern Ireland was aroused by my experience as the Regional Officer for Northern Ireland of what was then the Independent Television Authority and is now the Independent Broadcasting Authority. From 1967 to 1972, as the public servant immediately responsible for Independent Television in the region, I was made acutely aware of the fact that the communities in Northern Ireland had very different attitudes to, and expectations of, the broadcasting media. In those early years of the current phase of the Troubles, unionists of every hue were enraged at almost any coverage of their opponents and their opponents' activities. Those occupying the middle ground protested against the emphasis on violence, extremism and confrontation. Those across the nationalist-republican spectrum were incensed when they believed aspects of the situation were being ignored or censored. A notable feature of the submissions made by protesting deputations, which I sometimes received on my own, but more often in company with the senior executives of the contractor, Ulster Television, was their tendency to assert that no matter how serious ITV's offence, it was as nothing compared with the BBC's.[1] As one who kept a close eye on all coverage and who knew in some detail how it was achieved in both services, I felt the distinction made by the deputations was one which was only in their minds and bore little relation to what was shown on the different channels of the small screen. In a broad sense, reactions to the coverage of the Troubles were less to be accounted for by the content of the programmes than by the precon-ceptions which the two broadcasting services had managed to engen-der in their audiences over previous years. I therefore began to explore the records and to interview broadcasters, retired and active, with a view to elucidating the historical roles of the BBC and ITV in Northern Ireland. The exercise enabled me to understand the situation more fully and to see my own functions in the ITA in perspective.[2]

vii

My interest in the BBC's history deepened when a mentor and friend, the late Professor T. W. Moody of the University of Dublin, invited me to contribute a chapter on the mass media and Ireland to *The New History of Ireland*.[3] The challenge which this task posed gave a new purpose to my research. My first draft of the proposed chapter was circulated among historians and broadcasters and provided the background in some of their published papers.[4]

In 1974 I was asked to contribute to the celebration of the fiftieth anniversary of the BBC in Northern Ireland and as a consequence, a short historical survey was published in the *Listener*.[5] At the same time I wrote a ninety-minute feature for radio, together with other ephemera. In 1983 I was approached and asked if I would consider writing a more extended essay for the sixtieth anniversary. What follows is the result. It is, of course, an independent work. Nevertheless, in writing it I have had the fullest co-operation of the BBC executives in Northern Ireland, especially the Controller, James Hawthorne, and the Secretary, Virginia Hardy. Dick Hewitt, Head of BBC Data, London, has put the resources in his charge at my disposal, at least in so far as convention allows. I would also like to acknowledge the assistance of librarians and archivists in the BBC Written Archives Centre, Caversham; in Broadcasting House Library, Belfast; in the Library of Radio Telefís Éireann; in the Central Public Library, Belfast; in the Public Record Office, Northern Ireland; in the National Library, Dublin, and in the Library of the Queen's University, Belfast.

It is important that I should indicate here the limitations of my work and so anticipate inevitable criticisms. In the first instance, this is not an institutional history of the BBC in Northern Ireland. Many aspects of the BBC's operations in the region receive scant attention. My prime concern has been to explore the way in which the BBC, founded and developed in a society which enjoyed a large degree of political and social consensus, has coped with a profoundly divided society. The political and cultural dimensions have been grist to my mill, the stories of engineering and of administration, for example, have not.

For more than forty years the BBC's efforts in Northern Ireland attracted little attention outside the region. The British national press occasionally took notice of unionist protests against network coverage of Northern Ireland but that was all. An indication of the slight significance attached to the Northern Ireland region was the fact that Asa Briggs in his monumental history of the BBC devoted some 200 lines in all to the region in 2,926 pages.[6] The upsurge of agitation and violence in 1968, however, changed perceptions when Britain's political backwater suddenly thrust itself onto the television screens of the world. Now with hindsight we can see that the problems for broadcasters which surfaced then were there from the beginning. The intrinsic interest of the most contrary region of the BBC has only been highlighted by the current long-running crisis.

The second limitation of my work arises from the nature of the documentary sources on which I have worked. Most of the records I have consulted were written by senior executives in the BBC. These were certainly the people who determined policy, but the 'top-down' view inevitably distorts the assessment of the way in which regional production staff as a whole responded to the local situation. Most programme initiatives come from producers and not from Controllers or Heads of Programmes. Consequently some producers contributed significantly to the drive to broaden the scope of broadcasting in the region, to liberalise it politically and culturally. I suspect that I have done these producers less than justice. It must be said, however, that had they not met with a willingness to accede to their programme proposals there would have been little advance.

The records proved to be inadequate in a number of respects. I therefore found the interviews which I conducted with past and present members of the BBC staff in Northern Ireland invaluable. I am very grateful to all who agreed to talk with me.

In conclusion, I wish to thank Mrs Brenda Johnson and Mrs Audrey Henderson for the trouble which they took in rendering my idiosyncratic hieroglyphics into a typescript. I would like above all to thank my son Brian for the care with which he cast a professional eye over my sometimes difficult prose and saved the reader from many infelicities and obscurities.

Rex Cathcart
The Queen's University of Belfast, 1984

Introduction

When the British Broadcasting Company began broadcasting in Belfast on the evening of 15 September 1924, there were some thirty people on the staff, including the station's orchestra. Most of them worked on the first floor of a linen warehouse which had been converted into offices and a studio. The studio was linked by telephone cable with a transmitter installed in an electricity generating station a mile or so away. From there the engineers were able to provide a signal for those living within a radius of thirty miles.

Sixty years later the BBC in Northern Ireland is a much changed organisation. There are six hundred staff and the BBC has taken over not alone the linen warehouse but the entire site of the industrial complex of which it formed part. The 1924 scene has been totally erased and two large purpose-built buildings with their service areas constitute Broadcasting House, Belfast. Today, the engineers operate a range of transmitters across the region which ensures that the whole of Northern Ireland receives the BBC's radio signals and the signals for its two television channels as well.

The BBC has grown not only in size but in social significance. In the beginning it was a commercial enterprise of such doubtful viability that even two years after the opening night Belfast shopkeepers were still hesitating to change the Company's cheques.[1] Now, as a public corporation, it is accepted as one of the most important institutions in Northern Ireland.

The growth of the BBC in the region parallels its development elsewhere. What has made it different in Northern Ireland is the political context within which it has operated. Northern Ireland was created at the behest of two thirds of its population and against the expressed wishes of the remaining third. The attitudes of the disaffected third have not altered significantly with the passage of time. The BBC has had to cope with this divided society. The manner in which it has done so at any one time has been determined in part by the changing nature of broadcasting and in part by the varying

1

stances of the broadcasters in Belfast and in London towards the political system in Northern Ireland.

In the beginning the impact of the political situation on programmes was minimal. In 1924 listening to radio was an exciting experience for most people. They were still struck with wonder that sound could be received over the air and into the home. They were not particularly discriminating and were often less concerned with the programmes than with seeing who could pick up the most distant stations. The equipment too distracted people from the programmes, for even the most expensive was so primitive that getting it to work was a hobby in itself. In this situation broadcasters sought earnestly to attract listeners by filling the air with music and talk. Their purpose was to entertain. The programmes might attempt to improve the audience; they certainly were never meant to disturb it. Controversy and the controversial were strictly banned.

Radio was not even a significant source of news; the newspaper proprietors had seen to that. Short, carefully laundered, bulletins were prepared from news agency copy. The BBC had no news service of its own; it could not have its own correspondents. The concept of investigative journalism, as far as broadcasting was concerned, was more than thirty years away. It was not surprising that Westminster politicians, who kept broadcasting apolitical, did not regard it as a serious medium of communication. Their counterparts in Northern Ireland shared their opinion.

In spite of the style of the time, broadcasters were soon affected by the Northern Ireland situation. The second Station Director, Gerald Beadle, had served in Durban, Natal, before he was called to Belfast. He summed up the two experiences:

Northern Ireland had one important characteristic in common with South Africa in that both were peoples divided against themselves; an unhappy state of affairs in both countries and one from which the broadcaster cannot escape.[2]

Beadle was writing about the period from 1926 to 1932. A little later, in 1936, a senior BBC executive was sent from London to examine the divided society of Northern Ireland and to assess it from the broadcaster's point of view. The report of Charles Siepmann, Director of Regional Relations, is remarkable, not least for its broad analysis of the characteristics which made Northern Ireland different from any other BBC region.

2

The bitterness of religious antagonism between Protestants and Catholics invades the life of the community at every point and for our purposes conditions almost everything we do. Of the total population roughly a third is Roman Catholic and the remaining two thirds Protestant. Party alignments in politics, appointments to the public service and the commercial and cultural life of the community are all affected. In the official life of Northern Ireland the Roman Catholic by virtue of his religious faith is at a discount. Roman Catholicism for purposes of party politics means fusion with the Free State and the political existence of Ulster is of course based on the determination to oppose such fusion at any price. Politics and public administration conditioned by religious faction have about them an Alice-in-Wonderland-like unreality. A system of government developed by and for a great nation has been imposed upon a province the size of Yorkshire and a population a little larger than that of Glasgow. An imposing parliament house has been built with administrative offices attached at an inconvenient distance from the town. An equivalent of a house of commons and a house of lords and of the British civil service system have been instituted in a province which could be as well administered by a couple of commissioners and the normal machinery of local government. The government is in effect that of a loyalist dictatorship. Constituencies have been so devised as where possible to split the Roman Catholic vote. There is virtually no opposition. A civil authority special powers act makes possible the arrest and indefinite imprisonment of any citizen without trial at the discretion of the authorities. Ministers of State commit themselves in public statements to partisan provocation of the Roman Catholic's religious susceptibilities. More than one responsible person told me that the recent riots were not unconnected with such provocative outbursts by Cabinet Ministers.[3]

Siepmann was referring to the 1935 riots which occurred as a result of an Orange march in Belfast on the Twelfth of July and which led to eleven deaths, hundreds being injured and many families, mostly Catholic, being driven from their homes. The BBC seemed to be above all this, as indeed it endeavoured to be in relation to every aspect of the sectarian division in Northern Ireland. It reported the riots in its brief local evening news and refrained from any analysis or explanation of the facts. This was the normal practice in BBC bulletins of the time. A unionist politician was incensed and demanded that the Stormont government take over broadcasting.

During the recent disturbances they all had an example of the attitude adopted by the BBC in regard to riot news, when they had been told in a description of the occurrences on the Twelfth of July that 'a riot had arisen', no mention being made of the fact that the Orange procession had been attacked. Thereafter the BBC was almost silent on the subject. How much better would it have been if the Inspector-General or the Commissioner of Police had been able to come to the microphone every three hours and reassure the people as to the real position.

The speaker indicated that a government broadcasting service would have another attraction. It would be 'a great vehicle for counter-propaganda to the republican stuff which comes over nightly from Athlone' (the transmitter of the state service in the Irish Free State).[4] Unionists resented deeply the interpretation of events put out by Radio Athlone and wished to have the means to reply.

Siepmann's analysis of the political situation in Northern Ireland, 'a loyalist dictatorship', might suggest that the proposal for a government takeover of the BBC would have been sympathetically received by the unionist establishment. The reasons why not were outlined by one of the two unionist morning papers in Belfast. The *Northern Whig* devoted a leader to countering the proposal. It began by drawing a distinction between the British and Irish broadcasting services:

> The British Broadcasting Corporation, which derives its authority from a charter by Parliament, controls the service throughout the United Kingdom, but a separate Government controlled system exists in the Irish Free State. Partly because of limited financial resources, Free State broadcasting is greatly inferior, technically and artistically, to that provided by the BBC. It is also used freely as an instrument of Government propaganda, and the predilections and prejudices of the party in power are unmistakably reflected in broadcasting policy . . .
>
> During the Belfast disturbances last year there was much indignation in Northern Ireland regarding the versions of the events broadcast in the Free State. A suggestion has now been made that, when the present charter of the BBC expires, Northern Ireland broadcasting shall be detached from its control and taken over by the Ulster Government.

The *Northern Whig* leader writer then put two arguments against the suggestion:

> One is that broadcasting is primarily a medium of entertainment, not of propaganda; the other is that the broadcasting of news is part of the function of the BBC, and the maintenance of a reliable news service does not depend upon a change in control . . .
>
> To place broadcasting in Ulster under separate control, whether of the Northern Government or of a corporation corresponding to the BBC,

4

would have far-reaching consequences from the stand point of the general programmes. The Province would lose the advantage of the immense resources of the BBC, and it would be necessary to build up locally an entirely new organisation . . . the continuance of the present system, under which the United Kingdom is a single unit for broadcasting purposes is eminently desirable. If the day should ever come when Northern Ireland had a broadcasting service inferior to that of the Free State, the local station, for discriminating listeners, would simply cease to count.[5]

There was another argument for maintaining the status quo. It was one the local BBC was inclined to use in self-justification. Northern Ireland, it went, 'is, to some extent, isolated from the neighbours with whom it shares common loyalties and interests, and must rely on broadcasting to strengthen and maintain the contacts with British opinion which it desires'.[6]

The view of the BBC in London was somewhat different and found expression in Siepmann's report previously quoted:

Broadcasting in Northern Ireland is necessitated by political consider-ations. It is not justified by any extent of indigenous programme resources.[7]

He had in mind the fact that nowhere else in the United Kingdom was the BBC obliged to provide a regional service, which produced local programmes, for one and a quarter million people. The operation was a costly drain on central resources. The deficit between the income from licences sold in the region and local expenditure was considerable. The population made no great effort to pull its weight, for the proportion of licence holders was lower than in any other region. In fact, more copies of the *Radio Times* were sold in Northern Ireland in any week in the mid-1930s than licences were held, suggesting that there were quite a few 'radio spongers' around. The arrival of detector vans in the late 1930s changed that.

Broadcasting House in London tended to regard the BBC in Northern Ireland as the BBC in Ireland. It was a means by which the network could tap the whole island for programme material. This was its one merit. The BBC in Belfast, however, began to resist this view of its role. Influenced by the local political situation, its top executive, the Regional Director, George Marshall, adopted an unfriendly attitude to the state south of the border. He expressed his position clearly in 1937 when he objected to a programme on 'The

5

Irish', produced in the BBC's Northern Region, in the following terms:

> ... In the first place, to label the programme 'The Irish' is to include the region which I represent, and I immediately become interested. My first reactions would have been that the very title itself was highly undesirable, linking under one name two strongly antipathetic states with completely different political outlooks. There is no such thing today as an Irishman. One is either a citizen of the Irish Free State or a citizen of the United Kingdom of Great Britain and Northern Ireland. Irishmen as such ceased to exist after the partition. If it is intended to devote a programme exclusively to the Irish Free State, the programme should be labelled as such ... I would suggest that consultation might be desirable, so as to avoid giving offence to this province.[8]

The implications of this analysis could be far-reaching, especially as the sensitivities Marshall was concerned about were those of the unionist majority in Northern Ireland. He pressed the issue of consultation in London and eventually secured a BBC directive during the Second World War which required that all programmes which dealt with Ireland, north or south, had to be cleared with him. Many BBC executives and programme-makers in Britain became very concerned that BBC policy towards the twenty-six-county state, Éire, was being determined by the Ulster connection and they resented the directive. It had to be modified when the war ended.

The tension between the BBC elsewhere and the BBC in Northern Ireland continued in various forms after 1945. Broadcasting House in Belfast never failed to cast a wary eye over all BBC coverage of Ireland. It did so as a form of self-protection against outbursts of unionist rage occasioned by network programmes. New sources of friction, however, arose with the profound changes in post-war broadcasting styles. Dialogue and debate became the order of the day; controversy was encouraged and the microphone and camera were brought into the political arena. The BBC developed its own extensive news service with its own correspondents. Interpretative and investigative journalism was encouraged and consequently current affairs programmes became an important element in the schedules. Liberalisation proceeded apace in Great Britain; it was much slower in Northern Ireland. Yet the price of the link with the network was that it had to happen. Change did occur and when the Region Controller, Robert McCall, was asked in 1958 by the BBC Board of Governors to describe his region, he did so as follows:

Broadcasting in Northern Ireland has a number of special stresses with which to contend. The majority and the minority of the population are divided by fixed ideas based on religous belief and political ideal. Both belief and ideal are strongly held and ingrained. As a result, an impartial BBC comes under careful scrutiny from both sides since open discussion of two sides of problems, except in the Northern Ireland parliament, is rare outside of broadcasting.

For some years past the BBC in Northern Ireland has concentrated on its public service responsibility of getting both sides together round the microphone and this, so far, has proved successful though it has been a slow process. Roman Catholic now airs his views with Protestant; Nationalist and Labour man join in argument with Unionist.

Our relations with the Government of Northern Ireland are good, though there have been occasions when the Government has seen fit to protest about programmes carried on the Northern Ireland wavelength from elsewhere. On the whole it is fair to say the Government regards the BBC in Northern Ireland as representing the country fairly to the rest of the United Kingdom, though some of its supporters take a less broadminded view of such things as Irish music (Republican propaganda) and the use of swear words in plays.

The Ulster audience is sensitive about sound broadcasting and television being a potential source of evil to their way of life. The recent series of World Theatre plays evoked expressions of embarrassment and anger. Frequent protests about drink in drama programmes are made publicly. These critics cannot be dismissed as 'cranks'. It is a fact that there is a strain in the majority of the Ulster Protestants which governs their way of life. They regard such problems as prostitution and perversion as being unmentionable.

This is a small community which is inclined to feel 'cut off' from the rest of the United Kingdom and is jealous of the maintenance of such traditions as it had at the time when these traditions led to its isolation from the rest of Ireland.

There are many differences between Northern Ireland and the rest of Britain. The weather, the partially separate Government and the considerable local pride mean that the BBC must take account of the special necessity for regional broadcasting. Agriculture, gardening, sport, news, a local magazine, our own balance of religious services, our own variant in local terms of the 'Any Questions' discussion, even, in the near past, Northern Ireland election broadcasts, form part of the Ulster broadcast pattern.

It is a rewarding variant of the BBC pattern as a whole and has been supported by Management throughout our development. In Northern Ireland there are over two sound only licences for every television licence. Audience Research figures show a remarkable preference of the listener

7

for locally originated material. An Ulster play can get twice the audience of plays from elsewhere. The same is true of religious programmes, discussions, talks, and even light entertainment.[9]

The BBC in Belfast moved forward slowly taking its provincial-minded audience with it. The BBC network advanced apace and it was inevitable that eventually the difference between the two rates of progress would lead to a clash. When an investigative journalist, Alan Whicker, descended on Belfast in 1959 and prepared a series of film reports on Northern Ireland, his jaunty metropolitan outlook in the first programme provoked very angry reaction from unionists but most significantly from a 'former BBC employee':

> We have in the TV staff in Ormeau Avenue a highly informed and trained team whose job it should surely be to provide items on Northern Ireland for the national network when these are needed, rather than the sensation seeking visitors from Lime Grove who have from time to time descended on the province, producing the kind of programme for which our Regional Controller has had to apologise . . .

The writer mentions the natural disgust of Northern Ireland viewers,

> . . . who are told afterwards that the producer has not followed the advice of the men on the spot. In Ormeau Avenue all are aware of the political and social niceties involved and respect them in their own programmes. This no doubt is dismissed as mere provincialism.[10]

The disposition of the local production team was to present to Britain an image of Northern Ireland designed to improve its touristic potential and to concentrate on progressive developments in the region.[11] This was what the unionist government and population wanted, not exposés. Critical reporting of Northern Ireland tended to provoke such uproar and so much official displeasure that journalists and commentators in London were inhibited in their coverage. Peter Black, for long television critic of the *Daily Mail,* drew attention to 'one of the unwritten laws affecting current affairs at the time: be careful what you say about bullfighting and Northern Ireland'.[12] The outcome was that in the 1960s the network current affairs teams did not probe the situation which was developing in the region and which led to the civil rights campaign in 1968. Lord Annan's Committee on Broadcasting criticised the BBC for this failure when it reported in 1977.[13]

8

Within Northern Ireland itself the BBC had since the 1950s dedicated itself to fostering dialogue between the communities and developing a consensus. It had accentuated positive advances in this direction but failed to indicate the underlying factors which had prevented real changes in the relations between the communities. Broadcasting House, Belfast, undoubtedly contributed to the promotion of the false confidence which those who occupied the middle ground felt in the Unionist Prime Minister, Terence O'Neill, and in his capacity to deliver reforms.

So in Northern Ireland and in Britain the BBC did not prepare the population for the crisis which the civil rights marches precipitated. In 1969 the violent consequences of the profound political division in Northern Ireland exploded onto the small screens and radio bulletins of the world without forewarning.

The immediate outcome for the BBC in Northern Ireland was described by the Controller, Waldo Maguire:

> The small news staff in Belfast was quite unable to cope with the massive demands for news coverage as well as with the big increase in local news – up to an hour a day in television on BBC Northern Ireland. Extra staff – including some of the most senior television news staff in London – and extra equipment to supplement the limited resources of the BBC's smallest region, were flown in.[14]

With the influx of network personnel it might have been thought that network attitudes and procedures would have prevailed. They did not. One reason was given by a network reporter:

> All over the world the BBC have given extensive coverage of riots and civil unrest, but, having photographed, recorded, reported and analysed the scene, they have been able to go home and forget it. For the staff of N.I.Region, this was not possible. When they left the building they did not turn their backs on a state of civil strife, they went home to live with it. There were barricades, petrol bombs, and armed patrols in the streets. There were vigilantes and barbed-wire entanglements along their routes to and from work . . . [15]

Another, more compelling, reason for modifying network attitudes and procedures was given by the Controller Northern Ireland:

> . . . if you are reporting violence, arson and street fighting in a foreign country, you have to do so with accuracy and responsibility; you don't have to take into account the direct effect which the words or pictures

9

may have on the behaviour of your audience. But the effect of its broadcasts on its own audiences in Northern Ireland is something which the BBC cannot ignore at times of acute crisis. It has to recognise that the broadcasting of violently opposed views, passionately and offensively expressed, could have direct and immediate consequences on the streets of Belfast and Londonderry. So we have this dilemma. We have a duty to our audiences throughout the United Kingdom to present the news fully and fairly, to explain the background to the violence, and allow the expression of all significant points of view. At the same time we have a duty to ensure that our news bulletins and programmes do not avoidably inflame, and worsen the disorder.[16]

The dilemma only existed because the BBC insisted on treating the United Kingdom as a unitary system. A simple resolution could have been achieved if the Northern Ireland region had opted out of network news and current affairs items which referred to Northern Ireland. This was politically unacceptable.

The dilemma of whether or not to modify network news and current affairs coverage in the interests of the Northern Ireland situation was eventually to lead to the fairly stringent editorial procedures which are practised today. The procedures are, however, only one side of a BBC strategy for coping with the region's severely divided society. The other side of the strategy is the determined effort in programme and institutional terms to reflect faithfully the different and differing elements of which Northern Ireland's society is composed.

For sixty years the BBC has endeavoured to provide a broadcasting service in a region which is totally unlike any other in the system. For sixty years broadcasters have been confronted with a society devoid of consensus while they were presumed to operate with institutional values which derived from a society blessed with a measure of consensus. The task created tensions for the broadcasters in the region and on the network. It continues to do so. An account of their difficulties over the sixty years provides the interest in the story of the BBC's most contrary region.

1

Broadcasting Comes to Belfast

Broadcasting emerged as a practical proposition in Britain at the same time as legislative arrangements were being prepared for the partition of Ireland. In the course of 1920, Marconi's Wireless Telegraph Company carried out the first experimental transmissions of music and talk in these islands, while the British Government was fashioning the bill for the Government of Ireland. The broadcasts, which were permitted under temporary licences from the Post Office, aroused widespread public interest. Radio manufacturers and amateur wireless enthusiasts pressed the Post Office to allow a permanent service to be established. Post Office officials stalled for a year, influenced by the naval and military lobby which was concerned that the frivolous use of wavelengths would interfere with serious communications. During that year the Irish War of Independence continued and was concluded with the Anglo-Irish Treaty.

As 1922 opened, the Irish Free State came into existence and the British Postmaster General still 'had under consideration the extent to which the broadcasting of matter (including music) of interest to persons possessing radio-telephone receiving sets, and designed to promote the sales of such sets, can be permitted in this country'.[1] In April, he handed over the Post Office in the twenty-six counties to the new Irish Postmaster General. In May, he resolved to allow a number of broadcasting stations to be set up in Great Britain and encouraged the leading manufacturers, including Marconi's Company, to consider how this might be done. In June, Marconi's Wireless Telegraph Company wrote to the Irish Postmaster General requesting a licence 'for the erection and exploitation in Dublin of a broadcasting station, that is to say, a wireless station which would broadcast concerts, speeches, etc., to members of the public possessing the necessary receiving instruments'.[2] The Irish Postmaster General proved in no hurry to make a decision on the application. He had a strong disposition to regard broadcasting as a

11

recreational activity and as a consequence to place it low among the priorities in the construction of the new nation state. He went along with the advice of his Post Office officials, which was to observe what happened in Great Britain.[3]

People in Northern Ireland were obliged to do the same. The Post Office in Northern Ireland was under the control of the British Postmaster General and the power to legislate in the fields of wireless telegraphy and wireless telephony was reserved to the Imperial Parliament. Officials in the Ministries of Home Affairs and Commerce in Belfast were disconcerted to discover that this was so.[4] They wished to control and limit, possibly to ban, the sale and ownership of wireless equipment. This was for security reasons. Political stability had scarcely been achieved since the northern administration had been set up in the previous year. Wireless equipment in the hands of those opposed to the new regime could be used to monitor police and army communications and as a means of intercommunication among themselves for subversive purposes. During the summer of 1922 the situation became critical. Civil war broke out in the Irish Free State and its impact was felt in Northern Ireland. The ownership and possession of wireless equipment was made illegal by the southern government. In the north, the government was not able to follow suit. It could, however, prosecute under the Special Powers Act persons who improperly used wireless equipment. It soon discovered too that under the Restoration of Order in Ireland Act, 1920, which was still in force, it could oblige the Postmaster General only to issue licences for wireless equipment to persons whom it recommended.[4]

All in all then 1922 was not a propitious year for the development of broadcasting in Ireland.

Ireland and Irish people had featured in various ways in the circumstantial background to broadcasting. The pioneer of wireless communication, Guiglielmo Marconi, had an Irish mother. She was Annie Jameson, daughter of a family closely related to the distillers of the famous Irish whiskey. It was she who persuaded Marconi to go to England in 1896 to try his fortune there, after he had failed to interest the Italian government in wireless telegraphy. It was largely Jameson money that provided the capital to launch Marconi's Wireless Telegraph Company in London in 1897 and, not surprisingly perhaps, the company's first managing director was a

Jameson cousin, a successful engineer in his own right. Subsequently in 1905, Marconi strengthened the Irish connection by marrying Beatrice O'Brien, daughter of Lord and Lady Inchiquin.[5]

Such family ties were peripheral to the advance of wireless telegraphy. Ireland was, however, the scene of some of Marconi's important experiments. It was here that he gave two of the first demonstrations of the practical use of his apparatus. In June, 1898, he was commissioned by Lloyds of London to show how wireless could improve the means by which news of ships entering the north-western approaches reached them. It had been the custom to convey information about the sighting of ships from Rathlin Island to the mainland by flag signals, but visibility often made it difficult or impossible to read the signals. Marconi's engineers established a radio link between a lighthouse on the island and Ballycastle, Co Antrim, so that when observers on the lighthouse caught sight of a ship they informed the receiver in Ballycastle and from there the details were telephoned to London. In July, 1898, Marconi himself accepted a commission of a somewhat similar nature in Dublin. From a transmitter installed on board a steam tug he reported the results of the Royal St George's Regatta from a vantage point at sea in Dublin Bay. In previous years, mist had often made it difficult for journalists to observe the events from land. Marconi signalled the names of the winners after each yacht race to a receiver on land and from there they were telephoned through to the offices of the local newspaper which had paid for the experiment. The paper was enabled to scoop its rivals.[6]

Marconi had thus shown that wireless telegraphy could solve problems of communicating over short distances when visibility was poor or nil. He next turned his attention to long distance communication. Although it was from Cornwall that he first succeeded in reaching North America with radio, it was in Ireland he built a permanent commercial station designed to provide a trans-Atlantic telegraphic service. He chose Clifden, Co Galway, as the site. The Clifden station was very busy sending and receiving messages in Morse from 1905 until 1922, when it was blown up by Republican 'irregulars'. It was never rebuilt because technical advances by then had eliminated Ireland's geographical advantage.

Marconi had always believed that the prime use of wireless telegraphy would be in marine communication, where it could end the isolation of ships at sea. In the years before the First World War, wireless equipment was installed in many naval and merchant vessels. The consequence was that a new career opened up for young men as wireless operators. Marconi's company would have liked to maintain a monopoly in training them but public and private educational establishments entered the field. In Ireland, for example, the municipal technical colleges in Dublin and Belfast offered courses. As a consequence a pool of people with a professional interest in wireless began to grow.

Enthusiasm for radio was not confined to those who intended to make a career of it. The equipment and its use were at such an early stage of development that there was ample opportunity for valuable experimental work to be carried out in university, and even in school, laboratories.[7] Members of the general public too bought components and built sets. They endeavoured to make contact over the air with other amateurs and vied with one another to see who could make the most distant contacts. The emergence of wireless telephony in the years immediately before the 1914–18 war stirred even greater interest. Instead of having to encode and decode messages in Morse, there was now the possibility of direct conversation over the air. Professional and amateur enthusiasts in Dublin were impelled to come together and to form a wireless club in 1913.

During the war the private ownership and use of wireless equipment was made illegal for security reasons. Nevertheless, research and development went ahead for military purposes. In addition, many men gained experience of radio through service in the forces. When hostilities ceased, the basis had been laid for a major advance in the peaceful uses of wireless communication.

Marconi's company remained in the forefront. In 1919 his engineers established a temporary station in Ballybunion, Co Clare, and succeeded in transmitting a human voice westwards across the Atlantic for the first time. Spurred on by this achievement, the company built a more powerful station at Cheltenham; from there Marconi's engineers conducted regular experimental transmissions. They were dependent on reports from wireless operators scattered all over the world for information about the strength and the distance reached by their signals. In order to attract attention it became their practice to read lists of British railway stations over the air. This eventually proved boring to the engineers and they made a decision to invite some of the more musically talented among their

Marconi colleagues to play and sing over the air instead. The positive reaction among professional and amateur operators who received the signals proved newsworthy. Tom Clarke, a former signals officer with a lively interest in wireless telephony, who had become assistant to Lord Northcliffe, proprietor of the *Daily Mail*, saw the opportunity for a publicity stunt. Northcliffe was easily persuaded to sponsor a song recital by Dame Nellie Melba from Chelmsford. She performed and her 'voice was heard by listeners all over Europe and at places as far away as St John's, Newfoundland'.[8] Broadcasting in these islands had begun.

The Marconi Company went on experimenting through the summer of 1920. Its executives were not completely convinced that broadcasting represented the way forward for them. In collaboration with the Press Association they experimented with a news dissemination service. A number of newspaper offices throughout the United Kingdom were linked to London by radio. The *Belfast Telegraph* provided the Northern Ireland contact. On 25 July 1920 'the live news of the day' was transmitted from Chelmsford for the first time. The transmission was received and taken down in shorthand by a *Belfast Telegraph* journalist. It began with an account of a fire that day in Fleet Street. The fact that this particular lead-story only provided six lines of copy for that evening's *Telegraph* was not significant.[9] What mattered was that a new means of communication had shown its capacity to disseminate news rapidly and efficiently. It was soon apparent, however, that there was no reason why the dissemination should not be direct to the public: an outcome which the newspapers were to oppose vigorously.

Radio manufacturers were persuaded by the Marconi Company's experience and by the information which they were receiving about the contemporary scene in the United States that broadcasting would open up a large market among the general public for wireless receiving equipment in the form of assembled sets, construction sets and components. They began to apply to the Post Office for permanent licences to broadcast. The growing number of radio enthusiasts among the general public also pressed for a broadcasting service. The Post Office, however, came under very strong counter-pressure from the naval and military establishment. The armed services resisted broadcasting because it wasted wavelengths but more importantly because the unsophisticated nature of the wireless transmitting and receiving apparatus at the time caused serious interference with their communication systems. The Post Office indicated in December, 1920, that it would grant no more of the temporary licences which enabled manufacturers to carry out experimental broadcasts.

The Postmaster General, F. G. Kellaway, took a long time to reach decisions about a permanent service. In the end he responded positively to the pressures of the manufacturers and the wireless societies. He disclosed his plans in May, 1922. The country was to be 'divided into areas centreing approximately on London, Birmingham, Manchester, Newcastle-on-Tyne, Cardiff, Plymouth, Glasgow or Edinburgh, and Aberdeen, one or more transmitting stations being allowed in each'.[10] A meeting of representatives of firms engaged in the manufacture of wireless apparatus was called in order to discuss arrangements. The representatives when they met concluded that 'the total number of stations should probably be limited to eight to avoid interference and consequent chaos. It was recognised that the provision of a suitable daily programme at the various stations would be expensive and that it was important in the interests both of the public and the manufacturing industry that the continuity of the service and the maintenance of a high standard in programmes should be ensured. The best means of attaining these objects seemed to lie in co-operation among the firms concerned, and it was suggested that one or possibly two groups should be formed which should become responsible both financially and otherwise for the erection and maintenance of the stations and the provision of suitable programmes.'[11] In the event one group was formed. The 'Big Six' among the manufacturers agreed to found an independent company and to provide its capital. The Post Office, which had strongly encouraged this development, granted the new company, the British Broadcasting Company, a monopoly of broadcasting. The smaller firms were given the right to become shareholders and they took advantage of it.

The BBC began transmitting programmes on 14 November 1922. The proposed eight stations 'were soon in working order, but naturally large tracts of country were left with facilities only available to those who were in a position to buy comparatively powerful, and therefore expensive, apparatus. The Company early announced its willingness to extend its operations so as to make that which was broadcast receivable in the greatest possible number of homes'.[12] This involved catering for the owners of cheap crystal sets which were effective only within thirty miles at most of a broadcasting station. The BBC was therefore proposing to build more stations in areas of dense population and thereby to multiply its audiences and the sales of licences considerably.

The original plan for eight stations made no provision for Northern Ireland. Its omission may have been due to an oversight but more likely it was in recognition of the difficult political position there. The Northern Ireland administration, created to control six counties in which a third of the population totally opposed its existence, had scarcely achieved stability in the summer of 1922. The very limits of the territory under it remained to be determined by a border commission and those in opposition were convinced the outcome of the commission's recommendations would render Northern Ireland a non-viable unit, both politically and economically. In the meantime civil war broke out in the twenty-six counties of the Irish Free State and the six north-eastern counties in Northern Ireland could not be immune from its influence. In the circumstances wireless equipment, even when it was in the hands of politically reliable persons, represented a security risk because it could be seized by subversive forces. The Ministry of Home Affairs in Belfast was not able, however, to ban ownership and use because it had not the power to do so. Indeed, the Ministry of Commerce found itself unable even to control the importation of such equipment from Great Britain by retailers. Any attempt to do so and to seek special conditions for Northern Ireland within the United Kingdom was regretfully regarded as undesirable because, as one senior official in that Ministry put it, 'it will undo a great part of the propaganda which we have been doing for months on the subject of the stability of this part of the world.'[13] The northern administration was therefore obliged to allow the ownership of wireless receiving sets to grow. In the circumstances these were the expensive multivalve sets which alone were capable of picking up signals from the BBC in Great Britain and from continental stations.

By the spring of 1923 it was possible for some radio enthusiasts to meet in Belfast and form the Northern Radio Association (Ireland). The prime mover and inspiration of the Association was its first elected president, Captain Norman Inglis. He had been committed to wireless for some time. Immediately before the 1914–18 war he

17

owned an amateur wireless station which had a transmitting range of fifty miles. He joined the 36th (Ulster) Division and served in France as a signals officer and instructor. He was the author of manuals on wireless telegraphy. Inglis seems to have had one purpose in mind in founding the Association and effectively he used it as a front to that end.[14] He wrote on behalf of the Association to the BBC requesting that the Board of Directors consider the claims of Belfast for a broadcasting station. He himself was convinced that his action was on behalf of the small man, who could only afford a crystal set.[15] The BBC was sympathetic to this cause and so on 14 November 1923 the Company's managing director, John Reith, later to become Lord Reith, reported to the Board that 'a scheme was being prepared for broadcasting from a station in Northern Ireland'. Somewhat enigmatically the minutes add, 'The position of broadcasting in the Irish Free State was considered but it was decided that this was outside the licence granted to the BBC'.[16]

On 17 December 1923 the BBC sought permission from the Postmaster General to erect a station in Belfast. The Postmaster General enquired of the Government of Northern Ireland whether it would wish to impose any special conditions if permission was granted. Two special conditions were laid down which the GPO communicated to the BBC:

(1) That the right to stop transmission at any time, if such a course is considered necessary or desirable in the public interest, is reserved to the Government of Northern Ireland.

(2) That the station is restricted to the use of a transmitting wavelength of between 300 and 400 metres.

The BBC questioned the wavelength limitation and suggested that it should be broadened to between 300 and 500 metres. The Post Office stated that this was not possible because it had been agreed that the proposed Dublin station would use 485 metres.[17]

During months of behind-the-scenes negotiation, the owners of valve sets in Northern Ireland made representations to the BBC that it should not set up a local station. They were convinced that its signal would interfere with their reception and ruin their pleasure in listening to other more important and worthwhile BBC stations. The BBC paid no attention to their resistance, although in the event many valve set owners were in fact to find their reception affected.[18]

The BBC at last felt it could make a public announcement and so

18

on 14 February 1924 Belfast learned it was to have a radio station. It would not simply relay programmes from other stations but would originate local programmes and have a full staff of its own. It was not until a month later that the Post Office gave final confirmation that the proposed station could go ahead, with a power not to exceed 1½ kilowatts; the wavelength 435 metres could be used but not 485 metres. The call-sign allotted to Belfast was to be 2BE.[19]

Captain Inglis, who had initiated the development, welcomed the BBC's announcement in a press interview and stated that the Company had been in contact with him about possible sites for the station and studios. The BBC's Assistant Chief Engineer, H. Bishop, arrived in Belfast immediately after the GPO's final confirmation had been received.[20] He looked around and decided that the East Bridge Street Electrical Power Station with its twin 187-foot-tall chimneys provided a suitable site for the transmitter as there was enough space available and the transmitting aerials could be slung between the chimneys. The BBC, on his advice, acquired the first floor of a former linen warehouse at 31 Linenhall Street, for studio and office space. Considerable alterations were necessary, especially in Linenhall Street, and builders worked on them all through the summer of 1924.

At the same time BBC headquarters in London began to appoint staff for Belfast. The first to be appointed was E. Godfrey Brown. Brown was an English musician, well-known and respected in Northern Ireland's musical circles. He had lived in Belfast since 1912, having settled there as director and conductor of the Belfast Philharmonic Society orchestra and choir. His appointment as Director of Music in the BBC was well received by local people. His experience of life in Northern Ireland was to prove invaluable because among the early programme staff he was almost unique in having any at all. Godfrey Brown began to be involved in BBC operations in July but his salary was paid from 1 August. In a letter dated 30 August 1924 he described the first few weeks:

> This station is going to be quite a fine place when finished, with ten commodious rooms and a studio 40′ × 30′. At first it was awful, with plasterers everywhere, and only one table and a chair for us all. Later we borrowed another table: I lent some chairs: a typist, Miss Caughey, came along, and as white as millers, we then began to prosper. We still possess nothing further in the furniture line, and if we had it would soon be spoilt with paint and dirt. Another typist, Miss E. Dales, has begun, and moving our heaped up tables from room to room in an attempt to avoid paint pots

19

on our heads and the awful noise of knocking, we are doing our best to comply with Headquarters' rules and regulations . . .[22]

Godfrey Brown's initial task was to recruit an orchestra. He found his leader in Scotland: E. A. Stoneley came from a 'well-known Manchester musical family, and made his first public appearance at the age of five. He studied at the Paris Conservatoire, and was one of the best known soloists in Scotland'.[23] Other players were 'drawn from the best orchestras in England'.[24] The Belfast station was for some time unusual among BBC stations in having a harpist: she was Pauline Barker who came from the Carla Rossa Opera Company.[25] In all there were seventeen members of the orchestra, plus an accompanist, Captain T. O. Corrin. Corrin's stay was short because he left after a year to become an inspector of music in Northern Ireland schools.

Godfrey Brown was soon joined by the new Station Director, Major Walter Montagu Douglas Scott. Scott was an old Etonian and cousin to the Duke of Buccleuch. He was interested in music and drama and had a certain facility with modern languages.[26] His senior assistant was to be Major Edmund J. Thomson, MC, another Scot, who had considerable experience of amateur drama. His junior assitant was Tyrone Guthrie who had just come down from Oxford where he had distinguished himself in undergraduate drama productions and who was in later life to become one of the greatest directors of the English stage. None of these men had any previous experience of broadcasting but there was nothing unusual in this, in those pioneering days.

The team began to plan programmes and to develop a schedule, conforming to instructions laid down in a letter from Arthur Burrows, the BBC's Director of Programmes. The supposition was that local programmes would be complementary to a selection of programmes taken down telephone lines and a submarine cable from other BBC stations. These were known at the time as simultaneous broadcasts (SBs). A normal commercial submarine cable was used at first while a special cable was being laid from Scotland to Antrim. Unfortunately for the Belfast staff these technical arrangements were unsatisfactory for some time and so Belfast – 2BE – was left to its own devices and resources for most of the schedules.

With regard to the basic ingredients of the schedules, Burrows wrote:

Experience shows that different localities have different musical interests.

We have no data to work upon in the case of Belfast, but we imagine that a fairly light type of programme will be welcome. Your task, therefore, will be to provide a light type of entertainment, without departing from a high moral tone and good musical standard. In this connection, you must make a point of warning every humorist, in as tactful a manner as possible, that a wireless audience includes women and children and others unaccustomed to broad humour. Nothing must be transmitted by wireless that will offend sensitive folk, and in the event of particularly tragic material being broadcast it may be advisable to warn invalids and others to put down their 'phones for a specified period.[27]

Most talks were to come from London but there would remain space for some local talks. 'These talks must not contain any material that can be classed as direct or indirect advertising, and under no circumstances may they contain political matter.' All talks were to be submitted to the Station Director in manuscript form sometime before the date of delivery, and all unsuitable material, if any, was to be eliminated. Local talks presented the station with an opportunity to respond to and stimulate local interests but, apart from Godfrey Brown's rather specialised experience of the concert-going public of Belfast, none of the staff had any knowledge of the audience they were proposing to serve. Major Scott was obliged to establish a local committee to suggest topics and speakers.

The position with regard to news bulletins was difficult. The newspaper proprietors and editors had succeeded from the beginning in imposing through the Post Office a straightjacket on the BBC in the supposed interests of their papers. The Belfast Station Director was told:

By an agreement with the newspaper organizations, we may not broadcast any narrative which can come within the category of news, except such as is provided in the nightly news bulletins. This means that should you decide on a weekly review of sport, that review may not contain a description or criticism of any event that has occurred on the day of the broadcast. It is difficult to define news as distinct from history. The line of demarcation seems to be provided in a time period possibly of twenty-four hours – at any rate sufficient time to have enabled the press to have published the narrative in question. In addition to the news broadcast simultaneously from London, or 'district' news phoned from London for the particular use of your station, two local news bulletins will be provided nightly by a Belfast journalist, Mr John Sayers of the *Belfast Telegraph* (a nominee of 'Central News'). The fact that local news bulletins are prepared by a professional journalist selected by one of the

21

recognised news agencies does not relieve the Station Director from responsibility. The Station Director or someone nominated by him must always read through these bulletins before they are broadcast, and satisfy himself that they contain nothing unfitted for verbal transmission to men, women, children and invalids, and that the bulletins show no political prejudice. It will be found good policy to eliminate party statements except when made locally by a Cabinet Minister or leader of a parliamentary group. In which case equal prominence must be given on the same or subsequent occasion to the replies from other quarters.

Station Directors will have noticed that the SB bulletins give but the barest publicity to tragedies and other sordid happenings. Neither do they contain much information useful to gamblers. The standard set by the general news bulletins should be followed in the local news bulletin, and improved upon where possible.[27]

Outside broadcasts and Sunday evening addresses by nominees of the churches were to be subject to the closest surveillance. 'You will undoubtedly add interest to your programmes by arranging to broadcast from time to time after-dinner speeches by eminent persons at the principal functions in your area. You must have a guarantee beforehand that these speeches will not be political in character or highly controversial from a religious point of view.' With regard to the Sunday addresses the selection of speakers should be undertaken with the advice of a religious advisory committee. 'To this committee you should invite the recognised leaders of Roman Catholicism, the Church of England or its equivalent and the United Free Churches. The committee should certainly meet at intervals of about four months, and as oftener as is necessary, and should provide you with a list of folk who can be relied on to give a good address entirely free from dogma . . . Special care should be taken in the examination of the manuscripts of these religious addresses.'[27]

The tone and tenor of the instructions to the Belfast Station Director were designed to ensure that the service he provided his listeners with was innocuous, uncontroversial. His staff had, therefore, limited opportunities to produce adventurous programming. The fault lay not in the predilections of the BBC's London executives but in the Post Office which imposed rigorous conditions on them. John Reith found the situation not to his liking and at the same time as the finishing touches were being put to the Belfast studio and offices he was writing optimistically:

The tendency is in the direction of giving greater freedom . . . There is little doubt that sooner or later many of the chains which fetter the greater

22

utility of the service will be removed. It is probable that more debates will be held so that people may have an opportunity of listening to outstanding exponents of conflicting opinions on the great questions political and social which are today understood by a mere fraction of the electorate but which are of such vital importance . . . An extension of the scope of broadcasting will mean a more intelligent and enlightened electorate.[28]

While progress in this respect was made in Great Britain, especially after the Company became a Corporation in 1927, it was long in coming to Northern Ireland. This was undoubtedly due to the fact that until after the Second World War almost all programme staff came from outside the region. In a divided society in which local political passions could be easily aroused the staff remained cautious, indeed timid.

The staff set the opening date for the station as 15 September 1924. On that evening the *Belfast Telegraph,* the unionist evening paper, addressed its leader to the occasion. It welcomed the BBC and gave an account of the local arrangements. It concluded: 'The possibilities will now be brought home to the multitude. Hitherto wireless has been the recreation of the comparatively few in Northern Ireland owing to the absence of a local station. Soon there will probably be fifty crystal set holders for every one possessing the more expensive sets.' The *Telegraph* congratulated Captain Norman Inglis and the Northern Radio Association (Ireland) on bringing the BBC to Belfast. 'This is a proud day for him and the Association, and, indeed, for all Ulstermen, who are delighted to have the first Irish station of the kind in Belfast.'[29]

In 31 Linenhall Street the studio was only made ready on time by an emergency measure. Godfrey Brown recalled that, 'Studios in those days were draped heavily but at four o'clock on the opening day there was not so much as a pocket handkerchief on the floor, ceiling or walls. When the time for broadcasting arrived, however, a miraculous change had taken place. The whole room clad temporarily in sheets was ready for use.'[30]

Tyrone Guthrie was announcer for the evening. After he had opened with, 'Hello, hello, this is 2BE, the Belfast Station of the British Broadcasting Company, calling,' and the national anthem had been played, the station went off the air. There was a technical fault which was eventually remedied and the published programme proceeded with amendments. Apart from a short local news bulletin and some closing words from the Station Director the transmission consisted of about an hour and a half of music. On the following day a Dublin *Evening Telegraph* correspondent reported that the music directed by Godfrey Brown had been excellent:

He had selected a programme of popular items – called so to assure us of the fact. It is an evidence of the standard of musical taste in Belfast that the appeal to popularity embodied so much really good music. There was nothing at which even the highest brows could scoff. The performance of Mr Brown's very capable orchestra did full justice to the items chosen. The male voice choir of the Queen's Island is an admirable combination. We are so accustomed to associate the name of Queen's Island with the 'savage breast' that it is a delightful experience to learn that it is so fully conscious of the charms of music to soothe. It even specialises in pianissimos. Mrs John Seeds, who sang songs by Hugh Wolf, Roger Quilter and others, has a mezzosoprano of fine quality and uses it with perfect judgement. Whatever the future of the Belfast Station may be, its opening experiment proved that listeners-in may confidently expect from its programme music, at least as good, and probably better, than from any of the other stations.[31]

The quality may not have been in doubt but was there anything to mark the performance as distinctively from Northern Ireland? There were only two songs in the evening's music which suggested that the new station was not in Britain. They were Moore's 'Oft in the Stilly Night' and Hughes' 'The Good Men of Eirinn'. It was not this aspect which caught the Dublin *Evening Telegraph* correspondent's attention:

The first words spoken from the new broadcasting station in Belfast last night reached Dublin in a very English accent . . . I had just been listening through Glasgow to the sturdy accent of the Clyde, and expected from Belfast the accent of the Lagan . . . But just at present Belfast is more English than the English themselves, and perhaps the choice of an announcer was motivated by this consideration. Another straw showing the present direction of the Belfast wind was the fact that while the British stations are content to finish their programmes with God Save the King, Belfast began its first programme with what most of its inhabitants regard as that good party tune.[32]

By contrast, a correspondent in the *Northern Whig* who only tuned in for the last twenty minutes asked:

Am I correct in saying that 2BE on this night closed down without the time-honoured 2LO closing announcement, viz., Ladies and gentlemen, at home and abroad on the high seas the King . . . I would suggest that if the Belfast British Broadcasting Station cannot be closed down in the same manner as all other British stations, then close it up altogether. Anyone in Ulster who cannot listen to our National Anthem has no right to be catered for by a British company.[33]

It should be said that the Belfast Catholic and nationalist morning paper the *Irish News* was in no sense as sensitive to the political undertones. It simply reported with enthusiasm:

In countless numbers of houses within the magic circle of the Belfast Broadcasting Station, amateur 'listeners-in' waited with baited breath for the first message from the Director last evening. To say that their vigil was rewarded is to put it mildly, for, according to reports from every district of the city, and from distant parts of the north-east, users of even the cheapest crystal sets were able to enjoy the delightful programme submitted. The clearness with which the various items were heard was commented upon by wireless enthusiasts, who were loud in their praise of the efforts of the officials of the station to provide such interesting programmes as they have arranged for the week.[34]

So the informal opening of 15 September met with a variety of significant reactions. The formal opening on 24 October made much less impact. It was held in the Ulster Hall, Belfast, from where the evening's proceedings were relayed. A range of dignitaries from the new establishment attended and revealed their political disposition by breaking into loud cheers and laughter when the London news bulletin, which was relayed into the Hall, announced the arrest of Eamonn de Valera by the RUC in Newry. The programme included speeches and music; the speakers in succession were Lord Gainford, who was Chairman of the BBC, the Lord Mayor of Belfast, the Governor of Northern Ireland and the Prime Minister, Lord Craigavon. Craigavon amused the audience by suggesting that 2BE stood for 'the second city of the British Empire'. The highlight of the evening was the first performance of a fantasy on Irish folk tunes specially commissioned by the BBC from the Ulster composer, Norman Hay.

John Reith, the managing director, was present and his diary entry for the event reveals another side to the official opening:

The show in the evening went excellently as far as the public were concerned, but there was actually a disgraceful series of muddles, beginning with our not knowing if Gainford's address was to be simultaneously broadcast or not. Also there was a row about precedence in the procession, the Lord Mayor insisting on walking with Gainford and

25

the Governor into the Ulster Hall. Further the programme ran 25 minutes short.

Not surprisingly the entry for the next day, the 25th, reads 'went to the station and made a real row about the previous night'. All in all, his Belfast visit must have raised grave doubts in Reith's mind about the Station Director's efficiency, for his impression of Linenhall Street was, 'the premises are nice, but I found everything in a muddle. Scott is not doing as well as he should'.[35]

Nevertheless 2BE was very definitely on the air and the staff from 15 September was confronted with the necessity of providing programmes for every night of the week, save Sunday for the first couple of months. In the beginning the prospect was more daunting than it was to prove later. The *Radio Times* explained why, at the end of November, music was not being relayed to the Belfast Station. It was because of:

> the difficulties inherent in transmission over the submarine cable. A commercial cable is designed primarily to carry speech, and many of the higher frequencies of the voice were attenuated or lost in transmission over the cable. This is not very serious where speech is concerned, because many of the frequencies can be cut out of the voice while still leaving it intelligible, if not natural. It is different with music, where every frequency, from the highest harmonics of the violin to the lowest note of the cello, should be present in the transmission.[36]

Even when the cable, which was specially laid for the BBC, became available at the end of 1924, it proved unreliable for some time. A heavy weight of responsibility fell on the Belfast Station orchestra. In whole or in part it had to provide much of the schedule in the early months.

Much ingenuity went into ringing the musical changes. The basic repertoire was light classical and operatic music in the great European tradition. Musical evenings were organised under thematic titles: 'Mainly Mendelssohn', 'Musical Comedy', 'A Night of Scottish Music', 'Choral Night', 'Sea Programme', 'A few Excerpts from Grand Opera' and, somewhat unbelievably, 'A Windy Night', devoted to compositions which featured the wind instruments. One night every week the orchestra was augmented by a number of extra players, recruited from the professional ranks of the Philharmonic Orchestra. On such occasions the number of players rose to thirty and a regular symphony concert was possible.

There were 'Irish Nights' when traditional music was featured. The uilleann piper, R. L. O'Mealy, often played.

At first the novelty of the local station preserved the staff from criticism, but 2BE's honeymoon did not last long. Two months after opening night a newspaper correspondent wrote in terms which were to be repeated many times thereafter.

> Why can we not get more London programmes instead of having to listen practically week after week to the same local artistes? If anyone has taken the trouble to look up the programmes it would be interesting to know how many engagements certain people have got within the past year . . . Almost every time I put on the headphones the Station Orchestra seems to be in full swing. There is very little variety in our programmes . . . I have no objection to Englishmen personally, but I should like to know if there is even one Irishman among those at the head of affairs in our local station and have his name. I suggest the appointment of someone who can with authority say what Belfast people do and do not like in the way of programmes.[37]

Monotony and the performance of music which was too highbrow were frequent causes of complaint in the early years but there were technical criticisms too:

> . . . the orchestra is too large and ought to be cut down. Notice how clear, for instance, the Sunday night quartet music comes through compared with the blurred sounds during the week. Also the position of the players leaves much to be desired. One or two players sit too near the microphone, with the result that in loud passages there is merely vibration, but no musical sound.[38]

Some of the criticisms could be exaggerated. The charge that the programmes were always too highbrow was misplaced in a service which had performances from the Yorkville Mouth Organ Band and the Sir Henry Wilson Memorial Bagpipe Band among others.

Drama got off to a hesitant start. As in Britain the Theatrical Managers' Association viewed broadcasting as a threat to the live theatre, so in the case of 2BE the Ulster Players were prevented from taking part in the first play scheduled to be broadcast, *The Drone* by Rutherford Mayne, one of the earliest Ulster kitchen comedies. However the theatre management soon relented and a group of actors began to provide productions, including extracts from the plays of Shakespeare. Among the part-time performers making up the Station Players were Richard Hayward and Charles K. Ayre. Both men were establishing themselves as writers and they began to experiment with the new medium, producing humorous sketches which provided interludes in the interminable music. Hayward was responsible for a series called 'Double-Sided Records' consisting of two vignettes following one another. They were dialogues presented in the Belfast dialect, describing aspects of local life, as 'In the Tram', 'At the Cinema', and 'Seeing them off at the Liverpool Boat'. One of his longer pieces was called 'A Trip to the Isle of Man'.

> This was partly broadcast from the open air – a yard adjoining the station – where a real taxi, bands and unlimited paraphernalia were used. In the studio the equipment included barrel organs, Punch and Judy shows, etc, etc. The author and producer, with his knowledge of the legitimate stage acquired from his very creditable work with the Ulster Players, has set himself the task of solving the problems of radio drama, and perhaps his greatest achievement as a producer is the skilful manner with which he weaves into his broadcast plays suggestive sounds which do literally take the place of scenery as it is known in the theatre.[39]

Charles K. Ayre experimented with the recreation of an Ulster ceilidh on a number of occasions. It must have been difficult to achieve an authentic atmosphere in the studio. According to the *Radio Times* the performance was to include, 'an Irish piper, fiddler, a fluter, singers and "Arther", the crusty, deaf old farm servant who may be prevailed upon to sing one of the traditional "come-all-ye's" of the countryside'.[40] The first ceilidh had been held before the end of 1924 and by then the Station Players had already given a production of W. B. Yeats' *Land of Heart's Desire* over the air.

These and other productions were the general responsibility of Tyrone Guthrie. He was learning the skills in Belfast which were later to be revealed in his classic radio dramas, *The Squirrel's Cage* and *The Flowers are not for you to Pick*. Guthrie spent only two years with 2BE but it left him with vivid memories which he recalled in 1948:

> We were in Linenhall Street, up a dark little stair – a series of poky offices, just cubby-holes, leading off a dark passage, that, in its turn, led to The Studio.
>
> In those days it was considered necessary to prevent the very least suspicion of echo. So the room – a big one, supported by thin cylindrical iron pillars, was completely draped in thick heavy pleats of thick heavy material – even the pillars wore sort of puttees from ceiling to floor. There was a thick, thick carpet and something – I don't remember what – had been done to 'muffle' the ceiling.

The colour of all this was a particularly evil 'off-mustard', with a wide band about a foot from the floor of Greek key pattern in mauve and silver. The light fell from great chamber-pots suspended by muffled chains from the muffled girders in the muffled ceiling – a cold, hard, glaring light.

Three minutes in this chamber of horrors would have meant asphyxiation; so there was a 'plant' which filled it – and us – with ozone. One minute of deep breathing of this ozone was, we were assured, the equivalent of a fortnight at Blackpool; the funny little smell of rotten eggs was merely proof of its invigorating, tonic, bracing excellence. You can imagine the effect upon the spirit of those who had to perform here – the smell, the gross, crass ugliness of it all, the neuralgic glare from the chamber-pots, and, above all, the acoustic deadness. A cheery 'Good day' or a ringing roundelay fell with a dull thud into a sterilized blank; the back-chat of two comedians sounded like one mute telling dirty stories to another mute in the undertaker's parlour.

None the less, we crusaders of the ether were constantly cheered and uplifted by the thought that nobody was listening. Sometimes now I wake at night and blush in the dark to think that, occasionally and by a few, our prentice efforts were heard.[41]

The programme staff, not knowing Belfast and its environs, Ulster people and their predispositions, were very dependent on advice from local committees. They recruited one in the field of religion and another in the broad field of education.

The Religious Advisory Committee first met on 3 November 1924. It was summoned somewhat hurriedly because 2BE had come under attack for failing to provide any Sunday broadcasts. Many letters were written to the newspapers and questions were asked in the Northern Ireland House of Commons. There was a widespread suspicion that it was the churches which were responsible for the ban. In fact the Station Director was merely being cautious, as he had been advised to be. The Religious Advisory Committee approved of arrangements whereby programmes would begin at 8.45 p.m. when people had returned from evening church. There would be a religious address at 9.00 p.m. and not earlier. The address would be 'preceded by hymns and followed by programmes, not extending too late into the evening, of sacred and other serious music fitted to the day'.[42]

There was no Catholic representative present at the first meeting of the Advisory Committee. This was explained at the time as being due to the absence of the Bishop in Rome but it soon became apparent that the absence was dictated by the Church's policy. The reservations about the BBC expressed by the Catholic Church elsewhere in the United Kingdom were reinforced in Northern Ireland by the unwillingness of the hierarchy to co-operate with British-based institutions of any kind. It was not until 1944 that a Catholic representative appeared at an Advisory Committee meeting.

The Advisory Committee noted that the Catholic Church had decided not to provide Sunday evening addresses locally and agreed to arrangements whereby Catholic sermons were taken from other stations instead. In settling the allocation of slots to correspond broadly with the distribution of the religious persuasions in Northern Ireland, the Station Director faced a problem. The number of Anglican addresses available from stations in Britain was far in excess of the number needed in Northern Ireland where the Presbyterian Church was the largest Protestant church. The Committee advised that the right balance could be achieved by relaying addresses from Scotland.

The Advisory Committee proved more liberal than might have been anticipated, for in February 1925, it resolved 'that this Committee offer no obstacle to the relaying or providing of Sunday afternoon programmes on the undertaking that the music should be of a high-class nature, and that it be confined to the hours between three o'clock and five'.[43] The Protestant clergy were persuaded of the beneficial influence of the medium and so granted this concession gracefully. The Church of Ireland Dean of Belfast had, in fact, in a broadcast paid 'an eloquent tribute to the value of wireless in spreading God's message over a troubled world'.[44]

The Educational Advisory Committee first met in November 1924. It was concerned not alone with advancing schools' broadcasting but also with providing advice on speakers and topics for local talks in the early evening. There is no record of who was invited to join but the Committee had no members of the Catholic community on it during its existence. They may have been asked and they may have refused as had happened with the clergy and the Religious Advisory Committee. The principals of the major Protestant grammar schools in the city were members and the Queen's University of Belfast sent Professor R. M. Henry. Dr Rupert Stanley represented the Belfast Board of Education, of which he was Director. Dr Stanley had a keen interest in radio, being an expert in wireless telegraphy and telephony. He was to prove an active member of the Committee.

Earls, Stanley's successor as principal of the municipal college of technology, also attended.

The Educational Committee met with little success in promoting schools' programmes which were relayed from London. Reception was poor and when a demonstration was arranged for teachers it proved a complete fiasco. There was an effort to provide local programmes for schools, including French lessons and English poetry readings. While the grammar school principals insisted that the programmes be transmitted at the end of the school day, at 2.50 p.m., once a week, the Committee felt there was little chance that they would be listened to earlier in the day. It was thought in fact that primary schools would benefit more from radio than grammar schools, but no primary school principals or teachers attended any of the fifteen meetings held during the Committee's existence. Programmes got under way but very few schools listened; certainly none responded to broadcast requests for reaction. Members of the Committee were scarcely any more enthusiastic. Their attendance at meetings was poor and few of them appear to have listened to the broadcasts for which they were responsible.

The Committee's recommendations with regard to the talks for early evening listeners may have resulted in more successful broadcasts. There was a bias towards classical studies in the topics proposed, and in the early months both the Vice-Chancellor of Queen's University, Dr R. W. Livingstone, and Professor R. M. Henry gave series on aspects of Greek and Roman civilizations.

In December 1924 Tyrone Guthrie reported that the Ulster Association had offered to provide speakers for a series of talks on such subjects as Ulster's contribution to the Empire; Ulster's contribution to the breakfast table; the building of a liner; the romance of a flax seed; and Ulster past, present and future. 'These talks would be delivered by prominent public men and would be absolutely free of political bias.'[45]

The first of the series provoked the following reaction from the *Irish Statesman*, edited by the Ulster writer George Russell, known as 'AE':

It is surely unwise for a Company which seeks the support and aims at the sympathy of all sections of the community to broadcast the address which Mr Pollock, the Northern Minister of Finance, delivered as the first of a series of addresses on Ulster, arranged by the Ulster Association. Mr Pollock has not formed his style upon the principle of conciliation, and

31

large parts of his address must have seemed highly controversial (to say the least of it) to those who do not share his political opinions.[46]

There was continuous pressure from the press and elsewhere for talks on Ulster topics and the Educational Advisory Committee's suggestion that a series dealing with Ulster's antiquities should be arranged was acted on. Other dimensions of culture in the province were also touched on, and the Dublin *Irish Radio Journal* of 1 June 1925 remarked, 'There is no mistaking the call of 2BE, and we in Dublin, denied the privileges of our own, appreciate the one Irish broadcasting station in existence. Last week we listened to Mr Sam Henry on Ulster Folk Songs, and the item was a fitting answer to those who suggested that 2BE is merely a pocket edition of the British stations'.[47]

The real test of 2BE's recognition that it operated in a distinctive region with strong cultural traditions was to be the way it handled the festival of St Patrick. In the first year, 1925, all went well. On St Patrick's Eve an Ulster ceilidh was staged in the studio by Charles K. Ayre. On St Patrick's Day itself programmes had an Irish flavour: from 4 to 5 p.m. the orchestra played a variety of Irish music and a baritone, J. H. Chambers, sang songs such as 'The next Market Day', arranged by H. Hughes and 'Trotting to the Fair', arranged by Stanford. From 9.00 to 9.30 p.m. a St Patrick's Day Celebration was relayed from the Belfast Municipal Technical Institute. This was followed by a simultaneous broadcast from London which was taken by all BBC stations and consisted of Irish music, a variety of songs, including some by Percy French, and a couple of interludes provided by Irish comedians. No reaction to the festival's special programmes was recorded, or reported in the press. This was not to be the case in the following year.

When the *Radio Times* published the programmes for 17 March 1926 it was immediately apparent that 2BE's schedule did not include any special productions from the Belfast studio. There was to be a carillon recital from St Patrick's Cathedral, Armagh, and two special St Patrick's Day programmes relayed, one from Dublin and one from London. The total time devoted to Irish programming by 2BE was less than in a number of other BBC stations. A correspondent in the *Irish News* drew attention to these facts, giving a breakdown of all BBC coverage. 'Crystal user' went on:

True St Patrick's Day is to be a bank holiday, and true also Sir James Craig has announced that his Parliament will observe the occasion as a holiday;

but the Prime Minister and every other good Irishman living within the 2BE wavelength will find that these sentimentalities are regarded as out of date by the Olympians who guard the microphone in Linenhall Street. They will have to tune into London, Dublin or any of the other stations for a programme racy [sic] of the time honoured occasion.[48]

From 2BE there was an evening of ballroom dance music!

The Belfast Station Director clearly took fright on reading this letter: the St Patrick's Day schedule was revised. On the Day, readers of Belfast newspapers discovered that more than an hour of Irish music had replaced the dance music. The orchestra had completely changed its programme and two local singers had been brought in to render songs such as 'She is far from the Land', arranged by Lambert and 'Shule Agra', arranged by Somervell.

The problems of the Day were not yet over. Listeners discovered at 9.15 p.m., when the Dublin relay was due, that it was not transmitted. It should have consisted of a half-hour recital by the Irish Army's No. 1 Band under its conductor, Colonel Fritz Brase, formerly of the German Army. No explanation was offered over the air. The *Irish News* columnist who wrote under the title 'The Searchlight' got on to the Belfast Station for an explanation. A BBC official stated, 'We received instructions from London, about half an hour before our own programme commenced that the Dublin programme was not to be relayed. No reason was given and we are yet in the dark as to why we were ordered not to take it'. 'Searchlight' commented: 'On the face of it underhand work was responsible for the cancellation. What person 'got at' the heads of the Broadcasting Co. in London? Is it the policy of the Company to allow itself to be dictated to by a certain individual in Belfast, whose name is known, and who although living in Ireland and making plenty of money out of it, hates everything Irish.'[49] Presumably the BBC official had given a broad hint as to whom he thought was responsible for the cancellation. The identity of the person concerned remains a mystery.

There was no great press controversy over the pattern of events in the BBC in March 1926. In later years Belfast newspapers were often to reverberate with weeks of controversy about the BBC's St Patrick's Day programmes. The 1926 story, however, illustrates a number of facets of the situation which were to prove typical. There was the BBC's insensitivity to local conditions which meant that programmes did not reflect the expectations of considerable sections of the audience, its timidity when faced with determined criticism in the press and finally, the discovery by local interests that they could get their way by passing over the head of the local BBC station and bringing pressure to bear on the centre of power and responsibilty in London. The events of St Patrick's Day 1926 provide a paradigm for the future.

While this is true, it was already clear to headquarters in London that all was not well with the management of 2BE. In the previous December, a senior executive, J. C. Stobart, had been sent over to report on the station. Stobart's general assessment was as follows:

> I have no doubt this is a very difficult station, partly because its resources – artistic and literary – appear to be limited, and partly because the conditions of travel and transmission by land lines render the arrangement of programmes exceptionally difficult. The Belfast people seem to be unresponsive and slow-moving, and full of small jealousies and suspicions. I did not, however, get the impression of a really well-organised station. The staff is pretty strong . . . but I am not at all sure that full scope is given to them for exercising their abilities.[50]

Not surprisingly, there was a continuous stream of criticism of the programmes. This prompted a number of people to call a public meeting on 25 June 1926 to discuss what should be done. The meeting opened with a speaker reading a précis of recent criticisms of 2BE which had appeared in the press. A Mr Scop then contrasted the ways in which complaints were dealt with by Belfast and by London: an organisation with which he was connected had made ten suggestions as to how programming could be improved; London had accepted that the suggestions were reasonable, Belfast had ignored them. Mr Scop then 'asked if Belfast had been relayed by Daventry – the main BBC transmitter – the same as other stations. "If it had not, why had it not?" he questioned. That in itself should be an indication that Belfast was not looked upon as a first-class station and yet officially took that place.' This criticism was unfair, as the situation arose from a technical problem relating to the lines, rather than from any deliberate policy. The meeting ranged over most aspects of the BBC's Belfast operation; a Mr Kilroy made an interesting suggestion that an advertisement in the form of a questionnaire should be published in the press with a view to obtaining a census of opinion.[51] J. G. Blair, one of the organisers of the meeting, said 'the studio was the most unsuitable building probably in the Six Counties. It had iron supports, which caused distortion even before transmission, while the aerial was suspended between iron-lined chimneys, and the current was inconstant'. Finally, the meeting resolved to appoint a committee to draw up a resolution summarising their complaints and to present the resolution to the BBC.[52]

The meeting provoked a comment in the Dublin *Radio Journal:*

> Broadcasting is now a great public concern, and whatever be the local arrangements made regarding it, it can never now be regarded as a private affair, to be managed without regard to the behests of the general public. That, at any rate, is part of the moral to be drawn from Belfast's demonstration.[53]

The management of 2BE, in fact left much to be desired from every point of view. The Station Director was not efficient, as Reith had discovered on his visit to Belfast in 1924. He failed to deal with mail, did not pass on instructions from head office to staff and gave no leadership. There is evidence that it was only the efforts of the Director of Music, Godfrey Brown, which held the place together and got programmes on the air.[54] London at last felt obliged to act and on 16 July 1926 Major Walter Montagu Douglas Scott was relieved of the post of Station Director, Belfast.

During the remainder of that summer 2BE was run by a head office official, D. H. Clarke, who was sent over temporarily for the purpose. He quickly learned that there was a real problem of communication between London and the stations. Memos and letters from head office were curt, impersonal, imperious and seldom showed any appreciation of local conditions. He recommended that their authors should at least be made to identify themselves by signing their missives instead of initialling them. Such a small reform, Clarke maintained, might improve staff relations. Clarke did more for 2BE than that: 'he tightened up the programmes, shortened the intervals between items and generally pulled a rather demoralised station into shape.'[55]

2

2BE Consolidates

The BBC's Managing Director, John Reith, looked to South Africa for his new Station Director in Belfast. Almost two years earlier he had sent a young Englishman to Durban in Natal to set up and run a broadcasting station for the municipality. Gerald Beadle had gone willingly, even though he had only one year's experience in the BBC. He coped successfully, and by the summer of 1926 his contract in South Africa was coming to an end, enabling Reith to write offering him the vacant post in Belfast. Beadle accepted without hesitation.

In later years Sir Gerald Beadle, who was to become Director of BBC Television Broadcasting, recalled the situation he encountered in Northern Ireland and its impact on him:

> The BBC's Northern Ireland operation had been going on for two years, so mine was not exactly a pioneering job; rather it was a task of consolidation, which meant building the BBC into the lives of the people of the province and making it one of their public institutions. When I arrived in Northern Ireland I was made to feel for the first time in my life that I was a person of some public importance, and this was in spite of the fact that the BBC was less than four years old and its Northern Ireland operation was not much more than two. Obviously the BBC's prestige had grown out of all recognition during my two years' absence in South Africa, and I, as its chief local representative, shared the fruits of it. I was invited to become a member of the Ulster Club, where almost daily I met members of the Government; the Governor, the Duke of Abercorn, was immensely helpful and friendly, and Lord Craigavon, the Prime Minister, was a keen supporter of our work. In effect I was made a member of the Establishment of a province which had most of the paraphernalia of a sovereign state and a population no bigger than a moderate sized English county.[1]

Beadle was absorbed into the Unionist regime quite quickly, a process which other heads of the BBC in Northern Ireland were to experience in the future. It was a situation in which any sense of autonomy which the broadcaster might have could be lost. Beadle, being 'young and naive' as he was to say later, succumbed at first.[2]

He resolved within a few months to create 'a closer liaison between the Government and the BBC'. Before he could formally raise the matter with the Northern Ireland Prime Minister, Lord Craigavon, however, he needed advice on the legal position. He therefore wrote to Reith:

> I would like to make my mind clear as to the exact relationship between ourselves and the Northern Government. I understand that the Belfast Station, like all our other stations, is ultimately responsible to the British Government for its actions and that it has no actual responsibilities towards the Northern Irish Government. Nevertheless, I am sure that our position here will be strengthened immensely if we can persuade the Northern Government to look upon us as their mouthpiece.[3]

Beadle was not aware of how sensitive the issue of BBC – Government relations had become during his absence in South Africa. In May 1926 the BBC in London had been faced with a Government take-over during the General Strike. Only after heated debate in the Imperial Cabinet was it decided that Reith should be allowed to continue running the Company during the crisis. He acted on behalf of the Government but managed to ensure that the BBC's news bulletins retained a credibility with the general public which was denied to the partisan daily newspaper published by the Government during the Strike. The crisis confirmed Reith in his conviction that the BBC could best serve the national interest if it was allowed an autonomous role. Later in the year the Government accepted this principle when it provided the BBC with a charter converting it into a 'public utility' corporation.[4]

The General Strike proved a turning point in the early history of broadcasting. An editorial in the Dublin *Radio Journal* at the time indicated its significance:

> Most people have been looking at wireless and broadcasting as a delightful pastime. But all along while they were using it to listen to opera and jazz, to band and to chorus, they were really handling, in frivolous moments, an agency of national and international concern, a new medium and weapon of such possibilities that it became part of the battlefield the very instant this vast conflict began. The opening acts of hostilities included pressure brought to bear on the press with a view to influencing the nature of the news and comments issued. This was resented . . . The government at once invoked broadcasting . . . Here, at any rate, we have clearly defined the high status of wireless broadcasting in the armoury of a modern nation.[5]

It was against the background of the General Strike and the new Charter that a reply to Beadle's inquiry was drawn up in Head Office. It restated Beadle's question and then provided an answer. 'Can you unreservedly place the Station at the service of that Government to be made use of at that Government's direction? No. Moreover, it will be injudicious even to assure the Prime Minister that in the event of a national emergency in Ireland the station would be entirely at his service; this would only be so to the extent which the British Government (by consent sought from Head Office) might approve.' Reith did not sign the draft. He pencilled in a comment instead: 'It might be better to talk over the matter and clear up doubtful points. It is rather involved. We cannot help the Government in a *party* question. We can help them in uncontroversial things. In an *emergency* – this is officially declared by the King in Parliament and if notice is given us (according to Charter) we're not responsible then – they take us over. This did not actually happen in the General Strike, but nearly did. We were allowed considerable discretion. J.C.W.R.'[6]

Head office refused to write to Craigavon directly as Beadle had requested but suggested that Beadle should simply discuss with the Prime Minister the limited range of ways in which the Belfast Station could help him. Later in 1927 Beadle outlined the position in the BBC's *Year Book:*

The broadcasting Station, though in no sense under the control of the Northern government, does to a considerable degree co-operate with it. Announcements of public importance are frequently made at the request of one or other of the Ministries, and the elucidation of new Government regulations is broadcast by Northern Government officials.[7]

In the following year Beadle offered another formulation:

The Government of Northern Ireland, although it exercises no direct control over the Irish Station, enjoys its co-operation in all matters outside party politics.

A notable field in which 2BE gave the Government assistance from the beginning was agriculture. Ministry of Agriculture officials had access to the microphone to speak to farmers, informing them of changes in regulations and in general advising them. Farm prices provided by the Ministry were regularly broadcast.

Beadle, however, remained determined to demonstrate to the Government and to the unionist majority of the population the more comprehensive value of the BBC to them. He propounded a view of the BBC's role in Northern Ireland:

The Ulster Broadcasting Station, situated in Belfast, radiates to its listeners most of the important London programmes, and on occasions programmes are relayed from Scotland, Wales and the North of England. Thus the broadcasting service reflects the sentiments of the people, who have thus retained a lively sympathy with, and an unswerving loyalty to, British ideals and British culture. The chimes of Big Ben are heard as clearly in County Tyrone as they are in the County of Middlesex, and the news of the day emanating from the London Studio is received simultaneously in Balham and Ballymacarett.[8]

Beadle even asserted that, before the BBC came to Belfast, 'The Government of Northern Ireland evidently believed that one of the most efficient ways of fostering the imperial link was through broadcasting.'[9] There is no evidence to substantiate this claim. On the contrary all the evidence suggests that broadcasting was initially viewed by Government officials as an unwelcome nuisance.[10]

Curiously, when Beadle propounded the idea that the BBC 'provides a living contact with the "hub of the Empire" and there are no more enthusiastic lovers of our Empire than the people of Ulster', he described it as the *second* most important function of the Belfast Station. He considered that 'first of all' the Belfast Station was 'an indispensable adjunct to Irish music, Irish drama and Irish life'.[11] Beadle took a broad view of Irish culture and saw no ideological contradiction in promoting it over the air alongside the relaying of programmes from the rest of the United Kingdom. These were the early years of partition and few people had drawn any cultural conclusions from the political division. Beadle was therefore very happy to develop close co-operation with the new Dublin station, 2RN, with a view to mounting Irish programmes of all kinds.

2RN had come on the air on 1 January 1926. It had been reluctantly established by the Irish Post Office as a branch of its own operations. This followed the recommendation of a parliamentary committee which rejected the Postmaster General's plan for an Irish company similar to the original British Broadcasting Company. A state service was preferred because the committee viewed the use of radio 'for entertainment, however desirable, as of vastly less importance than its use as ministering alike to commercial and cultural progress'.[12] In the event the service provided by 2RN in its first years was remarkably similar to that which emanated from the early 2BE.*

Within four months of opening, on 20 April, 2RN and 2BE mounted an ambitious joint programme. Belfast led off with a half-hour of Mozart; Dublin replied with a similar period of 'good' music. Then from 9.00 to 9.30 p.m. 'Mrs Rooney' of Belfast and others presented a variety of Ulster humour; from 9.30 until 10.00 p.m. 2RN offered light music and Dublin humour.

Co-operation built up steadily until Beadle could write in the BBC's 1931 *Year Book:*

> . . . the most important feature of activities in the year under review (1930) has been the increasing co-operation between the BBC and the Irish Free State Post Office which directly administers the Free State Broadcasting Stations. The result can be seen in the many interesting broadcasts which have passed between the centres. Seamus Clandillon, the energetic Dublin Station Director, has given invaluable practical advice on all matters, especially as to artists resident in the South, with the happy result that many of them have found a place in the Belfast programmes.[13]

The British press reported these developments with approval. The *Daily Express,* for example, under the headline 'Broadcasting Partners', told of 'the steadily improving relationships between the British Broadcasting Corporation . . . and the Irish Free State Post Office'. It went on: 'Probably at present the Free State has more to gain than has the British Broadcasting Corporation but Dublin has relayed recently over the border to Belfast some interesting broadcasts, and there are undoubtedly vast untapped sources of good programmes in the Free State'.[14]

From 2RN's own staff, Dr Vincent O'Brien, conductor of the station orchestra, and Terry O'Connor, leader of the orchestra, were invited north to perform. Seamus Clandillon, the director, and his wife, Maighread Ni Annagain, accomplished artistes in their own right, gave a programme of Irish folksongs from the 2BE studio in September, 1931. Colonel Fritz Brase, the German director of music in the Irish Army, conducted symphony concerts given by the augmented BBC Wireless Orchestra on a number of occasions. The traffic was by no means confined to musicians. Actors and actresses from Dublin's Abbey Theatre Company were invited to play leading roles in 2BE drama productions. Hubert Maguire and Mary

* See Appendix I.

Sheridan, for example, played in *The Building Fund* by William Boyle in March 1929. The Abbey Theatre Company presented Lennox Robinson's *The White-Haired Boy* from the Belfast studio on 17 February 1930, and it proved to be the first of many performances by the company for the BBC. Thus 1931 began with productions of Synge's *The Shadow of the Glen* and Lady Gregory's *Spreading the News*, followed by Lennox Robinson's *The Far-Off Hills* and T. C. Murray's *Spring*. It is worthy of note that the first performance by the Abbey Theatre Company from the Dublin studio of the Irish broadcasting service was not to be until 23 August 1935, more than five years after the first from Belfast.

To judge by the voluminous correspondence in Belfast newspapers these drama productions provoked a mixed reception. There were those who were incensed that the BBC should give air time to such southern productions.

> Permit me to protest against the practice of continually inviting actors from Dublin to broadcast plays from the Belfast studio. The type of play performed always depicts a society whose ideals, religious, temperamental, and racial, differ radically from those of the majority of the people of Ulster. The extreme looseness with which these actors handle the name of the Deity is offensive to many listeners. These broadcasts from the Belfast station encourage the belief, very prevalent in England and Scotland, that all Ireland is inhabited by brothers and sisters of the proverbial stage-Irishman. Personally I am proud of Ulster folk, and I hope that they will be represented more frequently on our programmes . . . [15]

The plays from the South, however, had their defenders:

> As one of several who thoroughly enjoyed the recent broadcast plays by the members of the Abbey Theatre Company, I was thoroughly disgusted by the letters of bigoted, narrow-minded people who thought it necessary to rush into print at once condemning the plays, evidentally under the impression that nothing good could possibly come out of the Free State . . . [16]

While the BBC did produce a steady stream of Ulster plays, their provenance did not protect them from severe criticism. Again the Belfast newspapers opened their columns and there were many letters:

> I have been distressed by the number of friends who have asked me from time to time to write to you regarding the quality of plays broadcast by the

BBC, whose repeated references to the misrepresentations of Ulster folk life from the local station are, I regret to say, more than justified.[17]

This letter provoked a playwright, who did not sign his name but was probably Richard Hayward, to reply:

I have contributed many sketches of Ulster life and always with a warm love for my fellow Ulstermen in my heart. I have tried to portray their loveable nature, their keen sense of humour, and their undoubted ability to laugh at themselves and their idiosyncracies . . . A writer of playlets is accustomed to find he cannot please everybody all the time, and I shall say no more on that head. But 'Pro Bono' proceeds to speak of the 'absurd and ignorant' dialects used. It is not quite clear if he means to impute the concoction of bogus dialects to us who write the sketches. If not, then, alternatively, he must mean that the dialects are absurd and ignorant in themselves.[18]

The writer then affirms the authenticity of the dialects and the dialect words he uses and proceeds to defend dialects. Later, in the 1930s, dialect was to be the topic of much correspondence in the newspapers as the BBC's Ulster plays came in for further bouts of criticism.

Another author who was provoked to respond to critics was County Antrim writer, George Shiels. A number of his plays were produced by the Belfast Station and indeed a couple were specially written for radio production. Shiels did not challenge the right of critics to have their say, but he appealed to them to give intelligent expression to their criticisms and to recognise that these were not necessarily shared by all. He went on:

Recently two plays of mine were broadcast from the Belfast Studio, and, while a number of friendly people expressed their unqualified pleasure, one candid fellow shook his head and said 'Putrid!' And probably he was not the only one. So it all boils down to this: What I think is entertaining, is entertaining, I think, and vice versa . . . One other word. I should like here to pay my humble tribute to the players and producer of my *Insurance Money* . . . In my opinion their work was better than the little play deserved. Other performances from the Belfast studio which linger pleasantly in the mind are *Apollo in Mourne*, *Crabbed Youth and Age*, and *The Drone* . . . [19]

Thus Shiels singles out two Ulster plays and one from the south for praise. For St Patrick's Day 1930, 2BE offered a play from each source. W. B. Yeats' *Cathleen ni Houlihan* was relayed directly from the stage of the Abbey Theatre, Dublin, and *The Unlucky Baste* by C. K. Ayre was produced in the Belfast studio. In the interlude between the plays, folksongs and traditional ballads were sung, the uilleann pipes were played and Mat Mulcaghey told a tale in dialect. The whole programme was carried throughout the United Kingdom on the National Programme. The particular mixture of items chosen for the occasion provoked little reaction.

Not so in 1931. In that year the special programme for St Patrick's Day stimulated a correspondence in the Belfast *News Letter* and the *Northern Whig* which went on for weeks. The sharpness of the controversy owed much to the awareness that an image was being projected to Great Britain. The programme, based entirely in Northern Ireland, consisted of Irish airs played by the Belfast City and Cathedral organist, Charles J. Brennan; his performance was followed by an Ulster sketch entitled, 'The Things that Happen', written by A. McClure Warnock, which involved a conversation between a practical Belfast woman and an impractical poetic countrywoman; the Derry Orpheus Male Voice Choir sang folksongs by Irish composers; Mat Mulcaghey recounted one of his tales of County Tyrone; the Irish pipers of the Royal Inniskilling Fusiliers and the Belfast Wireless Orchestra gave a selection of jigs and traditional airs; the seventy-minute programme concluded with the carillon from St Patrick's Cathedral, Armagh.

The programme received favourable reviews in a number of British national papers including the *Manchester Guardian* and the *Observer*.

In the popular imagination St Patrick (together with shamrock, shillelaghs, eternal twilights, keenings and the Abbey Theatre Players) is more closely associated with Southern Ireland than the North. But last night's broadcast of the St Patrick's Day programme from Belfast gave us quite a new set of associations to link with the Saint's name . . . [20]

The *Guardian,* however, went on to suggest that, 'It would have been a more complete experience, though, if one could have heard part of Dublin's station's broadcast last night. We should then have had a more composite picture of Ireland, North and South, the green and the orange blending to make a harmonious whole'.

By contrast, a correspondent in the Belfast *News Letter* had no praise and no reservations: 'For sheer banality I commend the St Patrick's night broadcast for your readers' condemnation . . . How can anyone say this was Ulster (much less Ireland) is beyond me'.[21] He was supported by another who bemoaned the fact that it was one of the few Belfast broadcasts relayed during the year throughout the United Kingdom: 'I would suggest that for the future when an Irish or Ulster night is being given, the programme should not be solely made up by Englishmen, who in the nature of things cannot have much Irish feeling and that pure "classical" musicians be asked to take a back seat.'[22]

A dozen or more correspondents took up the refrain in both the Belfast *News Letter* and the *Northern Whig*. The general tone was expressed by one who wrote, '. . . the organisation of this unfortunate 'concert' was another glaring injustice to my native land'. Correspondents began to exempt Mat Mulcaghey's performance from the general criticism. A couple quoted the enthusiastic reception accorded the programme by the critic of the *Observer* in its defence. Constructive suggestions were made by many indicating possible contents of future programmes but there was a return to the proposal that 'if the BBC staff have no appreciation of Irish sentiment, why not be modest enough to ask a small committee of Irish authors, playwrights, and composers to arrange, or suggest, a St Patrick's night programme'.[23]

The programme as transmitted had one determined defender who signed himself 'No Surrender':

. . . With no part of Ireland has St Patrick been as closely associated as Ulster. Slemish, Armagh, Downpatrick. It is fitting, therefore, that Ulster's capital should have the honour of sending out to the balance of these islands the annual programme. By implication, some of your correspondents would have us believe that Ulster is bankrupt in culture, and would have us borrow the culture of our neighbours on a night like St Patrick's.[24]

'No Surrender' took each item and made an ironic gloss on it. He defended the two ladies who spoke the parts in the playlet, 'Miss Warnock and Miss Erskine are cultured Ulsterwomen. Both have been teaching that cultured speech mentioned most of their lives. Both are as much at home in the dead languages of Greece and Rome as in the vernacular of Ulster. One is a graduate of Cambridge. Both love the old Ulster speech, but what good thing can come out of Ulster? The fact that the little play took a high place at a recent competition just shows how little adjudicators know.' Miss Warnock, the author of the piece, felt impelled to answer '. . . that the possession of all the degrees in the world is of little account when it comes to writing or interpreting Ulster sketches' but added that 'it is hard to please everyone'.[25] 'No Surrender''s comment on Mr A. J. Cunningham and his Orpheus Male Voice Choir was that they 'were household words in Ulster, but we understand those old things they sang. How much better it would have been if they had sung in Gaelic. It would have so charmed the English listener, but it would not have conveyed Ulster to half Europe . . .' 'No Surrender' turned on one protagonist with a parting shot: 'Mr Pitney suggests borrowing someone to do the announcing. I would go further and suggest we get the real Irish atmosphere into the BBC Orchestra by borrowing the musical director of the Free State Army. He is a German, but so long as he is not an Ulsterman we will say nice things about him.'

The editors of the two morning papers eventually closed their columns to this particular spate of correspondence. In doing so they were only temporarily damming the flow which had begun earlier with the reactions to the performances of the Abbey Theatre players on 2BE. Thereafter programmes with an Irish dimension could usually be counted on to provoke listeners to write to the papers. The phenomenon suggests that a decade after partition people in Northern Ireland, especially in the Protestant community, were awaking to its cultural consequences. When Beadle arrived in 1926 there would appear to have been little sensitivity to the situation. His first essays in Irish programming had elicited no recorded reaction, and he had found that by avoiding the overtly controversial he could avoid controversy. Now he discovered that the cultural assumptions inherent in a programme could at one and the same time enthuse some listeners and enrage others. The divided communities were adopting their preferred cultural positions. Broadcasting was undoubtedly a catalyst in the process of cultural differentiation.

The correspondence columns of the newspapers are a source from which some generalisations may be made. It is noteworthy that the two unionist morning papers the *Northern Whig* and the Belfast *News Letter* gave generous space to many hundreds of letters in the 1920s and 1930s which commented on all aspects of the BBC's performance. The Catholic and nationalist *Irish News* had fewer letters by far, but whether this was due to editorial policy on correspondence or to a lack of interested response to the BBC among their readers is difficult to say. On the other hand, the *Irish News* did maintain a friendly attitude to the Belfast Station and to broadcasting generally, publishing all possible matters of interest. The *Belfast Evening Telegraph*, which had much the largest circulation among the newspapers, was hostile to the BBC, taking the view that broadcasting was harmful to the press. This hostility was carried to the point of calling the Belfast Wireless Orchestra 'The Belfast Orchestra' to avoid reference to broadcasting. Gerald Beadle was of the opinion that the *Northern Whig* and the *News Letter* were in fact no less antagonistic to the local BBC, but that they revealed their attitude by throwing open their correspondence columns to the many critics of the broadcasters.[26]

From the correspondence it is clear that the Protestant community had problems in deciding on its cultural alignment. Some Protestants protested their Irishness by assertion or implication. Others affirmed their distinctive Ulsterness. Those who took the view that they were first and foremost British would in many cases have been quite happy simply to have had programmes relayed from Great Britain and to have done without locally produced programmes. The rejection of regional accents, of Ulster dialects and of portraits of rural life revealed in local drama indicated a disposition to deny an Ulster identity and a wish to be aligned with the cultural attitudes and values of the south east of England. 'Malone Road', as correspondents designated the more pretentious middle class, wished to be seen to be metropolitan, not provincial. The BBC in Linenhall Street could scarcely share this particular outlook, charged as it was with the production of local programmes. Nevertheless, reflecting the BBC's own middle-class stance at the time, the local BBC endeavoured to prevent most manifestations of Ulster Protestant working-class culture from appearing before the microphone. Orangeism in any form was denied access; pipe and flute bands appeared only rarely.

So long as there was local production, however, the BBC policy of staffing the station with English and Scottish personnel was bound to provoke criticism. 'Why should the Belfast Station announcers not be local people with Northern Ireland accents, and thus be characteristic of the people whom the station serves?'[27] '. . . the time has fully come when a representative committee ought to make suggestions to the Ulster Station – putting before them the local point of view . . .'[28]

But press controversy about the BBC was by no means confined to issues involving distinctive local cultural sensitivities. Belfast made its contribution to the barrage of criticism of BBC programme policies which came from every part of the United Kingdom. A special correspondent in the *Northern Whig* reported on these wider complaints: 'The growlers want to be entertained through the medium of their wireless sets, and the BBC (so they say) will insist upon firing at them through the ether in the interests of culture . . . matter that neither entertains nor instructs them.'[29] 'It is good to see that Belfast listeners are awakening to the fact that they are being slowly but surely chloroformed by heavy doses of the Belfast Wireless Orchestra.'[30] Suggestions flowed as to how the programmes might be made more popular: 'Cut out 75 per cent of the talks and substitute gramophone records (not of the pianoforte variety). Have more brass bands, light orchestral music and groups of songs (confined to two songs). Give vaudeville in plenty. If we must have a symphony concert let us have it on Sunday afternoons, 3.30 p.m. to 6.00 p.m. . . .'[31]

In the autumn of 1931, the attack reached a crescendo – the *Northern Whig* referred to 'the enormous number of letters in our columns' – and the 'lowbrows' fought the 'highbrows' through hundreds of column inches. The Belfast Station Director, Gerald Beadle, found it necessary to defend BBC policy. 'I always welcome criticism from our listeners, because that is the best means by which we can estimate the public tastes, but listeners must remember that we have to cater for a large variety of tastes, and it is quite impossible to please everyone all the time. All tastes are catered for as far as is possible, and it is up to the listener to choose those programmes which he likes and to avoid those which he does not like.' Asked, 'Is there any foundation for the criticism made by some correspondents that there is too much orchestral music?', Beadle replied, 'That is an impossible question to answer because what is too much for one listener may not be enough for another.' 'On the subject of "highbrow" music, Mr Beadle said that the term "highbrow" was a very unfortunate one. It meant different things to different people. What was highbrow to one man was lowbrow to another.' On being asked how he gauged public taste, Beadle replied, 'By experience' and added, 'The secret is to acquire the art of suppressing one's own likes and dislikes. The critical listener can seldom do this. He nearly always falls into the trap of imagining that the majority share his own tastes.' Beadle concluded by saying that 'he would like to be able to give his listeners more humour and more Ulster dialect plays, because he knew there was a very big demand for both. Unfortunately good humourists were very rare indeed; there were not nearly enough of them. As to plays, a few of the good playwrights had shown signs of writing for the microphone, and he hoped many more would do so in the future.'[32]

A solution, at least in part, to these problems was being developed which, among other things, would save Beadle prevaricating. The provision of two contrasting programme schedules on different wavelengths throughout the United Kingdom would ensure that all listeners had a choice and therefore a greater chance of being satisfied. In 1926, before Beadle returned from South Africa, it had become apparent that technological advances had made this possible. The change was only one facet of a major transformation proposed for the BBC system. Much more powerful transmitters could now be built and the existing network of main and relay stations replaced. Fewer transmitters were necessary and these were to be sited at strategic points throughout the United Kingdom, away from the centres of population which had had to be favoured in the first instance; the signals would become much more readily available to country dwellers. This was the BBC's 'regional scheme'. Initially, the planners thought that both schedules should be produced in London with programme production centralised and, as a consequence, standards raised. Subsequently it was decided that one schedule would be left to be filled by a reduced number of provincial production centres.

The first transmitter in the new 'regional scheme' was built at Daventry. It came on air in August 1927 and was soon offering trial alternative programmes on two wavelengths. The 'regional scheme' had to proceed very slowly, however, because of the disruption caused among the listening public, many of whom found that their receiving apparatus needed major adjustment or replacement. The immediate effect of Daventry on Belfast's 2BE was to provide another means by which simultaneous broadcasts could reach it. Instead of using land lines and the submarine cable it was now possible to take programmes off air and relay them. For some time this occurred mainly during the daytime; interference prevented its effective use at night.

The number of simultaneous broadcasts taken by 2BE by lines from London and from other stations had begun to rise some six months after the opening night in 1924 and, in consequence as time passed the proportion of locally produced programmes dropped. The demands on the Station Orchestra in particular were reduced and it became possible for it to give more public performances. Before that happened, however, it had to be improved. In December 1926 J. C. Stobart inspected the Belfast Station for Head Office and reported that he was 'not entirely satisfied' with the Orchestra, and that he thought it sounded thin and unpleasing. Much effort had been made to avoid roughness and blasting but it was still unsatisfactory and the acoustics of the studio did not suit it. The Director of Music, Godfrey Brown, thought that an increase in the number of players would help. It was noticeable that when the Orchestra was augmented once a week to become the Symphony Orchestra, its quality was distinctly improved. Stobart remarked, 'It might be claimed that for a provincial city, our music is of as high a standard as can be expected, and that one must not be too critical under the circumstances. Personally, I cannot accept this attitude for two reasons: (1) That the BBC has a reputation for giving the best money can buy, (2) That the public's ability to discriminate between first rate and second rate music has been enormously stimulated by the concerts S.B. from London and by the gramophone.'[33] The Orchestra got an additional two violins and a second trumpet as a consequence and within three years its complement rose from twenty-one to thirty musicians.

The Orchestra was not threatened by the 'regional scheme', as elsewhere other station orchestras were, sometimes being reduced to octets or nonets. The unreliable lines from Great Britain helped Beadle to argue that the Orchestra remained as an essential provider of programmes. Nonetheless the drive which Head Office was making at the time to raise programme standards by concentrating production increasingly in London did affect the Orchestra. Local station directors were required to 'take from London what you cannot do better yourself, and do yourself what London cannot give you'.[34] When Godfrey Brown began planning a production of the opera *Samson and Delilah*, he was stopped by the Music Director in London: 'Our policy is definitely to concentrate large musical works on London, where conditions are more favourable.' Beadle accepted London's diktat but remarked:

> I am afraid I have always acted on the assumption that Belfast was outside this policy, and that so far as possible we were expected to run our own programmes . . . We are expected to do 4½ nights a week of local work, a difficult task if a high standard is to be maintained. During the last

49

eighteen months we have done many large musical works in order to make up for those things we do not take from London. Of course, we take all the libretto operas from London and, therefore, a ban on opera pure and simple would not handicap us so badly, though it will mean that Belfast listeners will seldom hear an opera decently transmitted. A ban on all large musical works is a different matter and, I am afraid, will involve a considerable curtailment of local activities and a corresponding increase in S.B. work with its accompanying technical imperfections.[35]

Beadle asked for guidance on what programme policy was meant to be for Belfast. He was told he could go ahead safely on the following basis:

Music: Everything except opera and very ambitious symphonic work. Productions: *Plays*. Only limited by studio and technical equipment necessary to give an adequate performance. *Vaudeville* entirely according to your own judgement, bearing in mind the quality of S.B. programmes as received by line, and the expense of local productions.[36]

Beadle had always regarded drama as the most rewarding field to promote. On arrival in 1926 he had endeavoured, without success, to persuade Tyrone Guthrie to return from Scotland to be his drama assistant. He was, however, lucky enough to get John Watt instead, for here was a talented man who was quickly to rise to be the BBC's Head of Variety Programmes. Watt stayed in Belfast from 1927 to 1930. On his departure a correspondent in the *Irish News* wrote to say how sorry he was to see him go.

I once saw him do an extraordinary thing: I saw him conducting a play, just as a conductor directs the orchestra and the singers in an opera. Wireless technique in plays is a comparatively new thing. When a play is being produced the actors sit round, scripts in hand. The producer gives the sign and conducts the small orchestra for the preliminary effects. Then, at the right moment, he points to the beginners to get ready, just as the conductor of an orchestra warns his violins. Then he points to the microphone, and off the play goes . . . Then the producer scans his script, gets the next players ready, points to them at the critical time, and gets them speaking. It was an extraordinary sight to see a play being produced like this . . . I am not surprised to see Mr Watt has gone to London.[37]

Beadle had, in fact, two drama assistants for a while. The second came in 1928 but stayed on after Watt had left. Lieutenant Commander H. C. Pearson had recently retired from the Navy and had been sent by Vice Admiral C. D. Carpendale, Controller of the

BBC, as Assistant Station Director to Belfast. Pearson also took responsibility for 2BE's efforts at vaudeville programmes, which usually consisted of light musical items strung together with amusing banter. Artistes were sent on tour around the main stations in order to make the genre possible. There were attempts made to provide a home-grown version of variety in the Belfast Station; Mungo Dewar, an assistant sent from Glasgow, devised and wrote *Eight Bells*, a revue set on a ship's quarterdeck, which ran for a few years as a series.

Beadle had in the Station Orchestra the only permanent full-time orchestra in Northern Ireland. In the beginning it co-operated closely with the Belfast Philharmonic Orchestra. Once every week instrumentalists from the Philharmonic joined the Station Orchestra in the studio to provide a symphony concert and in return BBC players augmented the Belfast Philharmonic Orchestra for public concerts. In 1927, however, the BBC Wireless Orchestra began to give public concerts in Belfast on its own account. The number increased in 1928 and 1929 and the Orchestra travelled to Ballymena and Londonderry. Then for the autumn of 1930 the BBC made an arrangement with the Belfast YMCA whereby the YMCA's Wellington Hall was hired for a series of twelve weekly concerts on Saturdays. There were 1,500 seats in the Hall and 1,000 of these were made available at 6d each unreserved. The scheme was a great success and the Orchestra played to packed houses. The experiment was repeated in the spring of 1931 and the Belfast Corporation was so impressed that it persuaded the BBC to carry on the Saturday evening concerts into the summer in the Corporation's Ulster Hall. Sir Henry Wood travelled across to Belfast on many occasions in these and later years to act as guest conductor, and a number of soloists of international reputation were attracted to perform at the concerts. The contribution of the Wireless Orchestra to musical life in Belfast and its environs as a consequence became immense. The Orchestra placed Belfast citizens further in its debt by offering free concerts every Wednesday afternoon in the Museum and Art Gallery. Its efforts to promote music were extended to school-children, for whom special concerts were provided in association with the Northern Ireland Ministry of Education. An incidental but significant facet of the Orchestra's activities was the manner in which it made Ulster audiences familiar with the works of Ulster-born Sir Hamilton Harty and enabled Norman Hay, the other Ulster composer of note, to have his compositions performed.

Most of the public performances were relayed by 2BE; indeed, they formed the major ingredient of the Belfast Station's outside broadcasts, with special telephone lines being laid to the Ulster Hall and to the Wellington Hall for the purpose. Such lines were increasingly provided for other outside broadcasts. Cinemas, hotels and dance halls were linked to Linenhall Street, and their organs, orchestras and dance bands were a source of lighter music for listeners. On 13 December 1927, the revue *Hip, hip, hooradio* was relayed from the stage of the Empire Theatre, Belfast, the first performance from an Irish theatre to be broadcast. There were to be many others from the Empire and in 1931 acts were taken for the first time from the Hippodrome, Belfast. In the words of the *Radio Times* such broadcasts from theatre stages 'breathe romance into a wireless vaudeville programme'.[38]

Until the BBC became a corporation it was not allowed to cover public events and sporting occasions with outside broadcasts. The press had been determined to prevent any encroachment on what it regarded as its preserve. From January 1927, however, running commentaries and eyewitness accounts became possible. As a consequence, that summer the Ulster Grand Prix motorcycle races were relayed for the first time and in the following year, the International Tourist Trophy race on the Ards Circuit was covered. The first of many launchings of Belfast-built ships was described on 2BE in 1927: 'The cracking of timber and the rush of water as the ship took to her natural element were conveyed in a most realistic manner to those who were unable to witness the launch.'[39] Important rugby matches were relayed from Ravenhill Road and then from Lansdowne Road, Dublin. The Association Football authorities were not nearly so co-operative because they were convinced that broadcast commentaries affected 'the gates'. 2BE crossed the border for other commentaries besides those on the rugby internationals: the Irish Derby from the Curragh and similar events in the racing calendar were covered and relayed to Britain.

The activities of the devolved government and of the local houses of parliament provided the occasion for a variety of outside broadcasts. On 19 May 1928, for example, the laying of the foundation stone for the government buildings at Stormont took place and the microphone was there.

In the beginning special telephone lines were laid to St James's Parish Church and to Fisherwick Church in Belfast so that Church of

Ireland and Presbyterian services could be relayed from one or the other once a month on Sundays. To these were soon added lines to Belfast Cathedral, Carlisle Memorial Methodist Church, and the Church of Ireland Cathedrals in Derry and Armagh. No lines were laid to Catholic churches because no co-operation was forthcoming from the Catholic bishops . . . at least until 1932, when Cardinal MacRory let it be known that he would welcome coverage of the Eucharistic Congress which was called to celebrate the 1,500th anniversary of St Patrick's landing in Ireland. Such was the national and international interest in the Congress that the Catholic hierarchy was keen to involve the broadcasters, north and south. In the Irish Free State pressure was put on the authorities to bring the powerful new transmitter at Athlone hurriedly into commission for the period of the Congress. The Belfast Station Director, Gerald Beadle, travelled to Armagh to discuss the arrangements in the north. He hoped he could persuade the Cardinal to co-operate with the BBC in return. Years later Beadle recalled their extraordinary conversation. 'I remember the Cardinal saying one thing to me that shocked me. "I wish you would yourself appear before the microphone," I said. He replied, "You wouldn't let me, you'd censor me." "We would not but we would have to restrain you from being rude about Protestants." He said, "What do you think I'm here for? What do you think I'm employed for?"'[40] The Cardinal clearly shared with other Catholic churchmen a dislike of the 'common Christian platform' which the BBC required the churches to take. In fact, the fear that the Congress was intended to be 'a militant and controversial occasion' had caused the BBC to hesitate in offering its co-operation. In the event, a commemorative service of pontifical High Mass was relayed from St Patrick's Cathedral, Armagh.

The other outside institutions with which the BBC endeavoured to establish a sound relationship were the schools. The Educational Advisory Committee which Beadle had inherited was very keen for him to organise, in contrast to previous experience, a successful demonstration of schools' broadcasting for teachers. This he did in the Ulster Minor Hall on 14 December 1926. There was a good attendance including some leading figures from Northern Ireland's educational world. The Minister of Education, Lord Charlemont, was one of those who addressed the meeting. 'Wireless,' he said, 'had done an enormous amount of good to heighten the cultural standards of the community' but as far as schools were concerned, while recognising the potential of broadcasting for them, he had to be conscious of the expense involved. '£50 is needed for a set and most regional committees would prefer to spend this amount on improving sanitary arrangements or accommodation.' The Minister praised the programmes he had heard, for he had taken the trouble to attend a conference and demonstration before this in Glasgow. He still ended on a warning note: 'When all is said and done, wireless could never be more than a supplementary aid in schools, and could not attempt to replace the teacher. Children must be coaxed and led in the direction of knowledge, and a teacher would teach more in an hour's personal teaching than could be done on wireless in the course of a year.'[41] Lord Charlemont was no help to the BBC in its educational mission. The reception of the London programmes for the demonstration had, in fact, been very good and the audience had been made fully aware of what was on offer.

Beadle was conscious of a challenge and was keen to press forward persuasively. So, in one of his quarterly broadcasts to listeners shortly after the demonstration, he devoted some time to the objections raised by teachers. The first was 'the loudspeaker is a dead thing and though it may be very wonderful, it cannot hold the attention in the same way as the presence of a living teacher'. Beadle quoted scientific experiments in a classroom in Scotland to show that this was not true. He turned to a second objection: 'What is the use of wireless, when we are here to teach the children? Wireless must be either superfluous or else we are superfluous.' Beadle said that 'wireless can no more take the place of the school teacher than books can'. He went on to quote teachers who came from the Ulster countryside and had spoken with him. 'They all tell me the same thing – that books are difficult to get; that sometimes it is difficult to keep in touch with the latest cultural developments, and that if wireless can do this for them, it will be bestowing an inestimable benefit upon them. I am sure that it can.' Beadle offered to provide individual schools with demonstrations.[42]

His efforts did not prove particularly fruitful and he was forced to declare that 'the BBC has gone as far as it can until some Authority takes it up seriously'.[43] He was about to lose the support of his Educational Advisory Committee too. It had been established to advise the Company on local production but when the BBC became a corporation in 1927 it was resolved to concentrate schools' production in London and to have a central advisory body, the Central

Council for Schools' Broadcasting, which would meet there. This arrangement took a year or so to implement. The Advisory Committee in Belfast was wound up and local production of schools' programmes came to an end. Such production was not to be renewed for more than thirty years; in the meantime Northern Ireland was represented on the Central Council, at first by a lone inspector from the Ministry of Education.

The Belfast BBC's other provision for children, originally called *Children's Corner* and then *Children's Hour*, was very much more successful. The programme occupied a 45-minute slot which varied over the early years in its placing between 5 p.m. and 6.30 p.m. The tangible sign of its success was the membership figures in the Radio League, a charitable organisation run by the programme. After a little more than a year, in December 1925, over 3,000 children in the Belfast area were members. Again, the numbers of letters which arrived from the young listeners permitted the launching of a regular short programme, before the main programme, devoted to readings from them.

Children's Corner seems to have provided an opportunity for members of the programme staff to let their hair down. They were all referred to as 'aunts' and 'uncles', and sang, played instruments, told stories and read poems. They were very careful to avoid a didactic approach; the intention was to provide pure entertainment. Evva Kerr, a music teacher, was the first organiser. She taught during the day and then ran the programme in the early evening, and impressed Stobart on his visits of inspection from London. 'She reads well and sings pleasantly. They take little or nothing from London for the *Children's Hour*. What I heard was distinctly good.' Outside part-timers were often invited in as 'aunts' and 'uncles', and there was a serious effort made to provide an Irish dimension to the programmes. One correspondent in the *Northern Whig* who asked of 2BE, 'Why do they broadcast so little Irish national music?' exempted *Children's Corner* from the charge and gave his 'grateful thanks to the "Uncle" who often sings our beautiful old songs'.[44] He was referring to Richard Hayward who, among other things, was a well known singer of Irish folksongs. Evva Kerr eventually became a full-time member of staff but later moved on to the Edinburgh Station. The programme formula changed little throughout Beadle's time as Station Director, but there were some minor reforms. The titles 'aunts' and 'uncles' were mostly dropped. Cross-talk between the performers, which was often pointless, was barred. The stories told were required to be of some literary merit, and the number of informative talks was increased. Competitions were introduced and brought a fair response. An atmosphere of friendliness and informality was, however, carefully maintained.[45]

All of the station's programme activity, rehearsals as well as productions, was for long confined to one studio, the one so vividly recalled by Tyrone Guthrie. When Beadle arrived he realised that this cramping of a heavy work schedule into such a limited space had a serious effect on standards of production. He was able to persuade London Head Office to expand BBC premises substantially in Linenhall Street and to reconstruct them along the latest lines. Two new studios were built to replace the old. 'No. 1' was a 'spacious, luxuriously carpeted hall, 29 by 53 feet ... decorated in the modernised Greek style, its slender grey pilasters rising to a height of 19 feet. Gone are the old days when the ambition of the BBC engineers was to damp out every trace of echo or resonance; the walls are innocent of draping and the panels between the woodwork are covered with wallpaper of a tasteful design, over a layer of specially prepared felt. This studio is used principally for Orchestral and Band Concerts, and there is no difficulty in accommodating a full orchestra, chorus and principals for operatic productions ... No. 2 studio is a very much smaller affair and resembles more a comfortable music lounge. The decorations are in dark oak with panelling of Japanese design in buff and gold. Here are performed plays and chamber music, and the studio is also used for talks and what is probably one of the most popular of all transmissions – the Children's Hour.'[46] The new extension also provided, for the first time, an effects room, an echo room and a control room.

On 20 March 1928, 'No. 1' was used for a major inaugural programme, a production of *Peer Gynt* given to mark the centenary of the birth of Ibsen. The lead parts were played by Irene Rooke, better known at the time as a film actress, and by the young Robert Speaight. It was a memorable occasion.[47]

In 1932 Beadle had the satisfaction of presiding over the opening of a third studio and a dramatic control room. In the course of his last two years he also added to his staff. Until 1930, outside broadcasts were handled chiefly by the Station Director himself. As Beadle wrote: 'Whenever possible I myself have attended any OBs of a specially important or difficult nature, and acted as the BBC

56

representative. However, owing to other calls on my time, I have had to miss many such OBs and in practice the senior engineer present has had to carry out functions which are not normally his. Furthermore, I am often invited as a guest to functions which we are broadcasting, and it is difficult for me under these circumstances to attend to the OB.' Beadle added 'the amount of OB work is on the increase, partly because the province is going ahead rapidly and there are a larger number of broadcastable events than there used to be. Lately, moreover, we have done a few OBs from the Irish Free State and we now find that there are a number of valuable OB sources in the Irish Free State which we could with advantage make use of. But it will be difficult to extend activities in this field without more staff.'[48]

Beadle was also concerned about the nature of the local news bulletins. These were still supplied as ready-made bulletins by a local journalist from the *Belfast Telegraph*, nominated by the Central News Agency. Beadle thought that he was 'not fully conversant with the subtleties of the BBC's news policy. I doubt whether he could ever be made to appreciate the finer points, and, also, his literary style is poor'. Beadle reported that London news department itself had complained about the local news and he was of the opinion that the situation would only improve if they had a satisfactory news editor on the staff. 'At one time,' he continued, 'I thought we might be able to improve things by changing our news representative and getting a man on the staff of one of the two morning papers*, but I now find that the morning papers are rather annoyed with our news representative because he gives too much news. They say he frequently gives us items which are too late for inclusion in the evening paper and, therefore, ought to be held over for first publication in the morning papers.' Beadle thought a news editor on the BBC staff would be able to 'vet' and rewrite the bulletins which arrived from the *Belfast Telegraph*.[49] The outcome of Beadle's representations was that C. A. Roberts was appointed in December 1930 to be news editor, publicity man and to have responsibility for OB work. Roberts was joined by Henry McMullan at the beginning of 1931. Roberts resigned in June 1931, and his role was taken over by McMullan, who was to remain with the BBC Belfast for the next forty years.

* A significant remark. There were three morning newspapers, the third being the Catholic *Irish News*. Beadle clearly did not contemplate employing a member of its staff.

Henry McMullan had been a journalist on the staff of the *News Letter* and in that capacity had discovered in London, on inquiry at the BBC's Head Office, what the fate of the Belfast Station under 'the regional scheme' was to be. It had been decided that a new high-powered transmitter would be established outside Belfast and that as a consequence the whole of Northern Ireland would be served for the first time. Beadle had subsequently confirmed that this was the proposed arrangement. At the time he denied the rumour that the new transmitter would simply be a relay station and that local production would stop in Belfast as a consequence.[50] The *News Letter* kept this rumour alive and three years later was suggesting that the Belfast Station would be closed down altogether because of the comparatively small number of licences taken out in Northern Ireland.[51] The BBC, however, not only accepted its obligation under the Charter to provide broadcasting services for Northern Ireland but also recognised that local programme production was necessary because 'of the bad SB lines, which tended to exclude Belfast from SB schemes in general and to make it an isolated unit, and the fact of its being a separate Governmental Centre'.[52]

In 1963, Sir Gerald Beadle recalled his time in Northern Ireland and the efforts to protect Belfast and other regional stations from centralisation.

My six years there turned out to be a period of difficult relations between the BBC's regions and the Headquarters at Savoy Hill, because the new Director of Programmes in London, Roger Eckersley, had realized that the newly-perfected network made it possible to concentrate programme production on London and feed the rest of the country from there. This in turn would enable the BBC to concentrate more money and talent at the centre and thus raise programme standards for the whole country. The regional controllers opposed this form of centralization as damaging to the proper reflection of local life and talent, which was their special concern . . . It was largely due to the inevitable clash of interests that regional controllers were encouraged to spend a lot of their time in London. I calculate that I crossed the Irish Sea, generally by night, about a hundred and fifty times in the six years between 1926 and 1932 – and that was long before the journey could be done by air. In a further attempt to maintain regional harmony Reith appointed a travelling liaison officer . . .[53]

Modesty prevented Sir Gerald Beadle from stating that the appointment of this Director for Regional Relations had been suggested by him and that it had been the outcome of a crucial struggle in which the power of those station directors who survived as regional directors had been preserved from the pressures for programme centralisation. The intention had been to place whatever programme production continued in the new regional centres directly under the control of the heads of programme production departments in London and thus leave regional directors as mere BBC ambassadors in their regions. Beadle's resistance preserved the directors' power in the regions and ensured that the regions could preserve and develop their own distinctive regionalisms.[54]

Beadle's success in this respect was a fitting culmination to his work in Belfast. He had accomplished much in his six years. 2BE had been consolidated into a significant institution. His achievement had been recognised by his senior colleagues in London and elsewhere.[55] Above all he had been responsible for some notable programme productions. The Abbey Theatre Company of Dublin had made its first radio broadcast from Belfast and had gone on to give two distinguished seasons of plays from the Station. W. B. Yeats had also been enticed to the microphone for the first time.[56] George Shiels had been persuaded to write for radio and Ulster drama had made its own distinctive contribution over the air. The Wireless Orchestra had given many public performances and, to judge by its popularity at concerts, was revitalising musical life in Belfast.

3

Towards a Regional Service

During the 1930s a regional service for Northern Ireland was planned and launched by the BBC. Its inauguration occurred in 1936 at a time when the population had begun to grow accustomed to living within the confines of the political entity created in 1920. In other circumstances broadcasting might have contributed to the formation of a regional consciousness and pride. Inevitably the divisions in Northern Ireland inhibited this process and as they sharpened in the 1930s the BBC endeavoured to distance itself from the friction and the conflicts. This was not difficult given the broadcasting style of the time.

The period from 1926 to 1932 when Gerald Beadle had been in charge of the BBC in Belfast had been a relatively quiet one. The social, economic and cultural implications of partition only slowly impinged on people. The fact that there was a not unfriendly government in Dublin meant that the issues were not sharpened. From 1932 onwards however this changed. A violent railway strike in Northern Ireland, spilling over into the Free State, proved socially disruptive and had political undertones. The government in the Free State fell and was replaced by a republican regime with a determined, antipathetic policy towards Northern Ireland. Sectarian politics in Northern Ireland were stirred up and in 1935 serious communal strife broke out in Belfast arising from riots following the usual Orange coat-trailing exercise on the Twelfth of July.

The 1930s were a time when people in Northern Ireland gained a renewed awareness of what divided them. The BBC, steering what it regarded as an impartial course between the divisions – more accurately *above* the divisions – was bound to be buffeted by them. Its general stance, of course, was to be favourably disposed towards the unionist regime which provided its *raison d'être* in Ireland. Nevertheless it tried to avoid overt cultural manifestations of unionism, as well as of nationalism. Politics had no part in its programmes.

As the promotion of regional consciousness became BBC policy, there were those in the Corporation who maintained that there was nothing new in the policy. In the report on Northern Ireland which appeared in the BBC *Year Book* for 1934 the claim was made that, 'The reflection of regional activities by a region's own particular station has always been recognised as one of the aims of broadcasting in the British Isles.'[1] The author exaggerated. There is no evidence of such a purpose in the policy statements of the original British Broadcasting Company. John Reith's *Broadcasting over Britain*, a comprehensive policy survey published in 1924, provides no hint of it. Main stations, like that in Belfast, sought whatever suitable programme material was to hand and made use of it. The process was ad hoc, although of course there was a realisation that local audiences contained many people who wished to hear local artistes and to hear about local affairs, cultural and otherwise. It has been well said that 'the sole purpose of the early local stations was to extend coverage, not . . . to develop local broadcasting resources'.[2] It was only in the course of the first decade that people in the regions, including the broadcasters themselves, began to see in broadcasting 'the physical means of giving expression to old loyalties and affinities, and of perpetuating and developing their own unique contributions to the national culture'.[3] The 1934 report came much nearer the truth when it said of Northern Ireland: 'Its character, from the cultural point of view, is still in the process of formation, and broadcasting has been called upon to play its part.'[4]

The limited service area of 2BE imposed severe constraints on any policy of promoting regionalism and was criticised for that reason. The signal was only effective within a thirty-mile radius of Belfast. As a *Northern Whig* correspondent wrote in 1929, 'Not a single complete county of the six comes inside it. One-third of the area is taken up with the Irish Sea on the one side, while Lough Neagh, with its 153 square miles, comes in on the other side. Fermanagh is shut out completely. The only towns in Derry served are Moneymore, Castledawson and Magherafelt. A very small corner of Tyrone comes inside, including only the towns of Dungannon, Coalisland and Stewartstown. Portadown and Armagh City are just on the border line, while Ballymoney with all of Antrim north of there is out in the cold . . . Here are just a few of the important centres outside the range of Belfast – Derry City, Coleraine, Portrush, Strabane, Omagh and Enniskillen.'[5] The correspondent was concerned about the excluded parts of Northern Ireland and suggested that Daventry, with its more powerful signal, should from time to time radiate special programmes for them. 'Only by the adoption of this plan can 75 per cent of the Ulster listeners ever get a programme with any Ulster colour to it.' He greatly exaggerated the proportion of people outside the area served by the Belfast Station, but he voiced a commonly expressed grievance.

People in Derry were particularly prone to complain. In 1930, for example, a petition was presented to the BBC signed by many of its prominent citizens. Sir John Reith replied: 'We are anxious to provide satisfactory reception conditions in Northern Ireland' but he went on to blame the scarcity of wavelengths for the failure to serve Derry.[6] He did not advert to the 'regional scheme' or to the proposed new powerful transmitter for Northern Ireland.

When George Marshall arrived in Belfast to take over the station directorship from Gerald Beadle on 19 September 1932, arrangements for Belfast to join the 'regional scheme' were well advanced. Marshall was able to say so in his first press interview: 'We are now engaged in the complicated task of selecting a site (for the new transmitter) . . . It will give much better service all over Northern Ireland . . .'[7]

Marshall was, like Reith, a Scot and they had, in fact, known one another since childhood. He joined the BBC in its earliest days and was sent first to Glasgow and then to Edinburgh as Station Director. Later he had been transferred to the directorship of Newcastle upon Tyne. Of men like Marshall, the earliest station directors, Reith wrote, 'An exceptional range of qualifications is demanded of them; diversity of gifts, but the same spirit. They must be capable of negotiating with many different kinds of men and women; social, business and educational standards are required in them. They must carry on, as those in headquarters do, the everlasting struggle for acceptability and balance in programmes. Abounding energy, initiative, tact, human understanding, imagination – these are essentials to success . . . Not infrequently, some musical knowledge is also required . . .' Marshall was a very competent pianist, a skilled interpreter of Chopin, and he claimed some knowledge of bagpipe playing. Of his personal qualities at that time, the man who was eventually to succeed him recalled, 'He was competent, loved music, had a feeling for the arts, could make a decision – yes, he was well qualified then'. When he had been in Belfast for sixteen years, no one was so sure.[8]

Soon after arriving in Belfast, Marshall said, 'We hear a great deal about the BBC in connection with music and drama in their various forms, but the educational aspect is not so widely realised. True, primarily we are entertainers, but it would be a perversion of so great an organisation to employ it for purposes of entertainment alone.' He was a strong advocate of wireless education in schools and wished to introduce to Ulster the listeners' 'discussion group' which was proving so successful a factor in adult education in England.[9] Like his predecessor, Marshall began his rule in Northern Ireland with an appeal on behalf of the most worthy side of broadcasting. He was to find, like Beadle, that its promotion in the Belfast area was a very taxing and unrewarding task.

Within a year to two he discovered that Northern Ireland was very different in other respects from the areas in which he had previously served. His baptism of fire came with his first St Patrick's Day programme in 1933, *Turf Smoke*, relayed to Great Britain and parts of the Empire. Its main idea was to recall 'to the exiles those things in Ireland which have universal appeal'.[10] There was a Prologue spoken by a number of voices and an Epilogue which referred particularly to Belfast. In between there was music, poetry and songs. All the performers were anonymous.

The reaction of the listeners who wrote to the newspapers was mostly unfavourable:

I would like to register my keen disappointment with the programme. In the first place the songs and music were of a poor standard, considering the field of selection at the disposal of those responsible for the entertainment. Secondly, it is a pity that the night was taken advantage of to eulogise Belfast industries, and I feel sure that many listeners outside Ireland expected to hear, as I did, a programme of good old Irish songs and music throughout the entertainment, and not partly an advertising stunt which I always understood the BBC would not stand for . . .[11]

I thought that the programme, with the exception of the song 'Father O'Flynn' – very well done – was mournful, depressing and 'stagey'. The whole atmosphere of it was redolent of despair, tears, and nationalist propaganda of the pre-war period. If the BBC cannot do better than this it ought not to attempt such programmes at all.[12]

All the 'Irish' programmes from Belfast are equally poor, and the worst result comes when someone with an uneducated English accent tries to assume an Irish brogue! . . . If Linenhall Street would understand that we want – and pay for – trained and decently educated voices, such as we get from the London permanent staff, and such as we got last week from a reader of some Scottish tales – perhaps it would relieve us of some of these other failures which have been inflicted upon us.[13]

They kept away from all the sickly and sentimental Irish airs and gave us the true music and spirit of Ireland. The dialogue was clever – one could almost see the hills and valleys and the little thatched cottages through the mist, and hear the sea-gulls screaming on the shores. The readings were well chosen and I thought the whole thing was splendidly done, the background of the harp being most effective.[14]

The music was not only real Irish, but the most charming Irish music, both vocal and instrumental, I have heard for years . . . What better music than 'The Lark in the Clear Air' or Harty's 'Irish Symphony' or songs more sweet, artistic and humorous than 'Open the Door Softly', 'The Bard of Armagh' and 'Father O'Flynn' or a better Irish baritone than James McCafferty?[15]

It is sad to see such an opportunity for showing the world some of the real Ireland frittered away in an hour of aimless talking, interspersed with a modicum of music.[16]

The tone of the many critical letters was more one of regret than of acrimony. At the same time a row was raging in the press about the BBC's treatment of St Patrick. It concluded with the remark of the writer who had initiated the correspondence: 'The officials of the BBC in Northern Ireland are almost exclusively English or Scottish, and cannot be expected to understand Irish feelings or Irish archaeology.'[17] Again this was merely dismissive. It was the contribution of the Belfast Station to the major Christmas Day programme for the United Kingdom and the Empire which brought forth real ire.

The item lasted less than four minutes. It was called 'Absent Friends' and was intended to be 'an impression of how a distinctively Ulster household might be spending part of Christmas. From the point of view of the programme arranger, it was essential that the contribution should be distinctive, and that it should be done in such an accent or dialect that "absent" friends would recognise at once that its place of origin must be Northern Ireland.'[18] 'The programme was written by an Ulsterman and performed by men and women of Ulster birth and heritage.'[19] 'Absent Friends' featured among a variety of short pieces from different part of the British Isles, including Dublin, which preceded the King's Christmas address.

Immediately after the broadcast W. E. Trimble, known as 'Bertie', who was one day to become editor of the *Impartial Reporter* of Enniskillen, sat down and wrote letters to the *Northern Whig* and the *News Letter*. He enthused about the contributions to the programme from the English stations.

It remained for our own station to ignore Ulster. The broadcast from here was more like what one would hear from Cork with a spurious Ulster accent. Have we no ballads worthy of reproduction instead of going off to Dublin for 'Father O'Flynn' and 'Come back to Erin'? Even 'Kitty of Coleraine' and 'The Ould County Down' would have been much more preferable.'[20]

Trimble's letter was followed by seventy-two others within a fortnight, two-thirds of them critical, often highly critical.

The feelings of thousands of Ulster people must have been outraged when listening to this 'ballyhoo' performance, coming as it did in the middle of an impressive Christmas message. One listened first to the carefully-chosen words of the London announcer and to Mr Howard Marshall, delivered in their delightfully cultured voices, then to the nice, simple messages from hospital children, lighthousemen, miners, crofters, etc, in their natural dialects, musical and unexaggereated in every case. But what a shock, when Ulster was called, to hear what was evidently considered an amusing example of Ulster dialect, but what in reality was a mere parody. What must the world at large think of Ulster when that is the only form of Christmas message we could send on the ether?[21]

It was not Ulster dialect at all, it was an imitation of the dialect of the Free State.[22]

. . . Surely it behoves the BBC to see to it that Ulster shall not again be maligned and misrepresented by travesties of the real language of the Ulsterman.[23]

. . . a piece of crudity to contribute towards an otherwise beautiful item of loyalty and seasonable sentiment . . . Might I suggest that a few words from our Lord Mayor or our Prime Minister would be more opportune . . . Christmas Day was a lost opportunity of offering our expressions of loyalty to His Majesty.[24]

I think that no person would have objected to the broadcast being done in the Ulster dialect. The point that arises is that many of us would quarrel with the Ulster accent as broadcast by the Belfast Radio Players, on the ground that it is a far too exaggerated representation of our Ulster tongue.[25]

We are cut off from the rest of Ireland by the Border. We have not anything to do with it, and we never will have. Erin is Ireland. Ireland is on the other side of the Border: yet we hear the voice of Ulster proclaiming in song, 'Come back to Erin'. Ye Gods! Think of it. Who arranged this programme which was of world-wide importance to our province? . . . Who selected 'Father O'Flynn' as a typical Ulster song? Many people have thought for a long time that there is too much of the Irish pipe, the Irish jig, and the Irish atmosphere in the BBC programmes from Belfast.[26]

We heard four lines only of 'Father O'Flynn' and less than two lines of 'Come Back to Erin' sung happily and naturally by a talented chorus. The short message to 'Absent Friends' was Ulster at its best, and the music Irish to the backbone. We in Ulster are Irish and we will remain Irish.[27]

I defy anyone to produce one Ulster family who on Christmas afternoon gathered together to indulge in the buffoonery and uproar that we and (awful thought) perhaps the King had to listen to.[28]

. . . the disgusting Christmas Day effort of which we are so much ashamed, was, in my view, not attributable to any perfunctoriness, or indifference, at the local station, but to a quite different cause – which I am surprised has not suggested itself to others of your correspondents, viz. to the fact that the local station is run by Englishmen.[29]

I do not know who the Station Director is, but I suggest that he should seek the help and advice of representative Ulstermen and women before he again assumes the responsibility for broadcasting from the Imperial province on a similar occasion.[30]

Marshall ignored this suggestion but he paid attention to the abuse and resolved not to incur it again. So, on the next Christmas Day, i.e. 1934, there was no Belfast contribution to the expressions of seasonal goodwill which preceded King George V's Christmas message. There was, however, an item from the Aran Islands arranged with the help of Radio Athlone. This caused a different kind of anger in Northern Ireland.

In the course of 1934 there occurred a controversy which fused the sectarian and political strands in the Ulster Protestant reaction. It arose from the decision of the BBC authorities in Belfast to include sports results in the Sunday news bulletins. Correspondents to the Protestant newspapers were strongly provoked: . . .

It is clear that the majority of the citizens of our province do not want this class of news in the Sunday programmes. I fully appreciate the difficulty of the BBC in the matter of broadcast news, but I would point out that the Irish Football Association have notified clearly that they do not want

Sunday football . . . I would suggest that from the various Presbyteries next week a resolution to this effect be sent to those concerned pointing out the mind of the people of Ulster that this must be discontinued at once.[31]

Another correspondent was much more explicit:

It has become the custom of the Belfast Station of the BBC to broadcast on Sunday evening, as an item of news, the results of the local Gaelic football matches of the day. I am, I think, representative of the majority of the citizens of our loyal province – a respecter of the Sabbath observance as a day of rest. We do not want to hear of exploits in the realms of a sport which holds no interest for most of us – loyal citizens of a mighty empire to whom the Gaelic mind, speech and pastimes mean nothing.[32]

The Loyalty League weighed in:

. . . the members . . . strongly resent the action of the BBC in consenting to broadcast from Belfast the results of Gaelic games or others played on Sunday as degrading to our city or province and an offence to the great bulk of the licence-holders in the district . . . We earnestly urge that all catering to the secular side on the Lord's Day may cease definitely . . .

The Loyalty League called for:

definite action to compel the BBC to have regard to the sentiments of the bulk of their supporters, who are British and Protestant, and who most strongly resent anything that tends to dishonour God . . . Those in authority in the BBC are the servants of the people and should realise the need for steering a course in harmony with Reformation principles.[33]

Years later, in 1946, Marshall summarised what happened in 1934:

. . . numerous complaints were received, to such an extent that the then Prime Minister, the late Lord Craigavon, intervened and, after a certain amount of discussion and consultation with the Director General at Head Office, it was decided to give up broadcasting such results on the grounds that they were hurting the feelings of the large majority of people in Northern Ireland.[34]

The issue of dialect and accent did not long stay dormant. In October 1935 the head of programmes, then called the Programme Director for Northern Ireland, John Sutthery, stirred the hornets' nest. An Englishman who had had extensive production experience, he was sent to Belfast and, before he became really well-established there, had an informal chat with a journalist who wrote as 'Aerial', the radio correspondent of the *Northern Whig*.[35] She seems to have taken some liberties in that she reconstructed the conversation without benefit of notes. She reported Sutthery as saying that 'ever since I came to Belfast I have been looking for someone with the London announcer type of voice to read poetry . . . I want a casual voice that will let the poem tell the story. I don't want any intrusion of personality.' He is then supposed to have added, 'there is practically no one in the Northern Ireland studio who has not . . . an "Ulster idiosyncracy".' Sutthery concluded from this that such voices should be used only in local scripts and not in scripts which came from England. 'I could not endure to listen to a typically English play such as any of Somerset Maugham's broadcast by Northern Ireland actors. They are none of them accentless, to my ear, though perhaps they seem to speak standard English to any local audience.'

Sutthery, if 'Aerial' is to be believed, was not content to stop at that. He said he did not favour the typical Ulster kitchen comedy as a medium for the expression of Ulster accents.

When I first came to Belfast and read the so-called radio plays, which were submitted to this station, I was amazed. I wondered if such characters really existed and thought how unpleasant a province this must be, since they appeared in every play. Now I have come to realise that these types are simply a convention, though why on earth such a convention ever obtained is more than I can understand. I do wish that playwrights would get out of the rut. At first I wondered if they ever would, it was so difficult to teach them anything of the requirements of radio drama. Now I am becoming a little more hopeful. Recently, I came across two plays which have really been written with the microphone in mind. And with a few slight alterations I hope that these plays will be broadcast in the near future . . .[36]

The reconstructed conversation did not immediately spark off a response. 'Aerial' in her next piece took up the issues raised by Sutthery. She began, 'Northern Ireland has always been somewhat doubtful about the "London announcer" type of voice extolled in my interview last week . . . Ulster folk are not quite certain if there is not some personal slight in such a recommendation, and the new, monotonous reading that comes from London is not very popular here.' 'Aerial' went on to agree that no one wanted the 'old pyrotechnic style' but that in poetry reading, for example, there was a need for 'an impression of genuine thoughtfulness and feeling. The present trend is all for flatness.' She accepted that this was all right for news reading but was very concerned lest it might be applied in other programme areas. She felt that 'several Northern Ireland programme features have been striking a bright note, which is in distinct contrast to this other rather depressing levelling of individuality . . .' and she approved of this 'personal element in broadcasting'.[37]

A considerable controversy was then begun. The contributors were all familiar with 'Aerial's' two articles. A correspondent from Coleraine was incensed on several counts '. . . our poetry is to be recited in the voice of a London announcer. Parrots should be at a premium if human beings are to be at a discount . . . We want by the intonation of voice, the full import and beauty of the poem to be conveyed to us . . . The sweeping assertion of the lack of talent in Ulster is as unreasonable in its inclusiveness as that of David that "all men are liars." It is not the function of the BBC to impinge its cultural eccentricities on the people of Ulster, but it is their duty to find out what the people want and supply that which will cater for every laudable desire in the cultural world.'[38]

A Lisburn correspondent joined in support saying that the efforts to produce plays in which the actors were required to speak with flat, inexpressive voices 'were "not to the pleasement" of the Ulster people, whose own speech is naturally vigorous. They will expect the BBC to continue to give them plenty of Irish plays that touch the lives of our people at every angle. Local drama, and plenty of it, has been admirably presented from the Belfast Station in recent years. Mr Marshall, the Director, was right in expressing the hope, in his recent talk, that there should be a wider range of theme; but if city listeners think we have too many "kitchen" plays, let them remember that these are the chief joys of country listeners . . .'[39]

Several correspondents took up the theme of 'we can have enough "standard" English in other programmes without imposing it on Northern Ireland . . .' 'With the opening of the new transmitter Ulster will be for the first time equal in importance to any of the regionals, but if it is the intention of the BBC to sink Ulster individuality and culture, and make the programmes an imitation of English stations, why have an Ulster station at all? I suggest that one or two Ulstermen at least should have some say in the selection of the Northern Ireland programmes.'[40] 'We are forced to listen to entertainment conceived and directed by Englishmen and delivered with this "English voice" from the other stations of the BBC, so why must this policy be duplicated in the Northern Ireland station?'[41] 'I trust that the Director will handle Ulster susceptibilities with caution. He should realise that he is among a people with great traditions, and I am sure he will appreciate the tenderness they feel towards their cherished Ulster tongue.'[42]

Marshall felt that John Sutthery must reply to the correspondence. Sutthery made the point that 'Our talks series *Ulster Speaks* and many other sides of our work surely disprove the assumption that we are opposed to accent and dialect – in their proper places. We differentiate, however, between the reading of Ulster and of English authors.'[43] *Ulster Speaks* was a series of talks given by the Reverend W. F. Marshall on Ulster dialects. A very popular performer on radio, he had made a lifelong study of the language of his fellow Ulster people. His talks aroused such interest that a demand arose that they should be published; thousands of copies of the resulting booklet were sold.

In the course of the controversy one letter writer had remarked, 'I do hope that when Mr Sutthery finds the type of voice he wants he will not allow that voice to speak Shakespeare.'[44] Elizabethan English was not 'standard English' according to Marshall. The nearest existing analogue to it was to be found in the speech of Tyrone men. Perhaps the real Ulster answer to Sutthery was the performance of selections from *A Midsummer Night's Dream* spoken in the accent of Tyrone and transmitted from the Belfast studios in June 1936.

George Marshall's first impressions of the Belfast Station had been good. 'All the arrangements are very satisfactory,' he had said.[45] He was after all taking over a production set-up which was quite up-to-date: two studios had been wholly built and equipped only five years earlier and the third had been opened eight months before his arrival. He was as soon to become as aware, however, of the limitations of the premises as he was of the idiosyncracies of the audience the station served. Those limitations, along with other features, struck the new Director of Regional Relations who arrived from Head Office at the end of March 1933. He presented the following report to London:

I reached our Belfast Station on March 17th, despite a railway strike and posses of policemen carrying rifles and revolvers, in the station and the streets. I have never been anywhere that seemed to me more like Bedlam. I can now fully credit Marshall's claim that Belfast has to be visited to be believed. The conditions are quite abnormal, and I think it a pity that Head Office staff have visited the station so little. My presence seemed to create quite a hubbub . . . and all of them really seemed to me to have something of the desert island mentality.

I was not impressed with the premises, either externally or internally. Marshall's office, nice enough in itself, was a perfect babel during rehearsals and transmissions of the orchestra. I attended a rehearsal of the orchestra, under Godfrey Brown, and noticed that the ventilation of the studio, as of others in the building, was very inadequate. I gather that in summer the heat is quite appalling. The accommodation for the orchestra, in terms of a band room, is also far short of normal requirements.

During my visit, I lunched with the Vice-Chancellor*, who is well acquainted with our work, and is a useful outpost of intelligence, and with Mr Redwood, Editor of the *Irish News,* with whom Marshall and I discussed the difficulty of a fair representation of the Catholic minority interest in Northern Ireland in the Regional News Bulletins. I have spoken to you about this, and I am shortly seeing Murray of Reuters in case any adjustment is possible . . .

. . . Here, as in Scotland, I was impressed with the variety of duties carried by individuals, and by the general goodwill and readiness on all sides to carry burdens and to contribute in person, as well as in invention, to local programmes.[46]

The outcome of this report was that additional buildings in Linenhall Street were taken over and an office and another studio were built. It was all in preparation for the proposed regional role.

On 9 May 1934 'the Northern Ireland Region' officially replaced 'the Belfast Station' and George Marshall became 'Northern Ireland Regional Director'. The new titles preceded the substance by some months. It was not until 1 October of the same year that Northern Ireland became a full member of the regional scheme. This meant that 'a *Regional* programme would be radiated from the Belfast transmitter – that was, a programme of local items, music, plays, talks, etc. reflecting the life of the province together with certain items selected from other Regional programmes.'[47] Belfast would now contribute twenty hours of production weekly to the regional pool compared with twenty-five from each of the other regions. The new arrangement caused a reduction in Belfast's production and there were some casualties as a result. For example, the Wednesday

* F. W. Ogilvie, Vice-Chancellor of the Queen's University, who was to succeed Sir John Reith as Director-General of the BBC in 1938.

afternoon concerts given by the Wireless Orchestra in the Belfast Museum and Art Gallery ceased as there was no longer a slot in the schedule available for the relays. A complete alternative to the Regional programme was available from Droitwich. It broadcast the National programme. It was thus intended that listeners in Northern Ireland would have a choice – the National or the Regional.

Belfast was the last remaining station to come into the regional scheme. It had for some time previously been transmitting a mixture of Regional, National and locally originated programmes. Now anyone who wanted National programmes had to tune into Droitwich. Droitwich came on air on 7 October 1934, but from the beginning, in spite of its strength at point of origin, the signal was poorly received off air in Northern Ireland. There were many angry reactions in the newspapers. Owners of crystal sets were, of course, now denied all National programmes but owners of anything less than a three-valve set found reception of the National programmes was marred by constant fading. Many felt that the National programmes were superior to the Regional and protested they were being fobbed off with the inferior alternative. The BBC was obliged to recognise the uproar and to admit the Droitwich signal was subject to fading but to imply that as time passed it would improve. It made no apology for the fact that crystal sets would only take the signal if they were attached to high aerials which would cost more than new valve sets. The *Irish News* came to the BBC's defence as regards the loss of the National programme: '. . . it is strange that the National programme, which, according to listeners' letters last season, was by no means satisfactory, has apparently now become the ideal programme. The BBC have an unenviable and quite impossible task of trying to please everybody.'[48]

If the National programme had a troubled start in Northern Ireland, the Regional had its problems too. There was still to be a lapse of nearly a year and a half before the new transmitter which was being built at Blaris, near Lisburn, came on air. So for the time being the Regional programme continued to reach only listeners in the Belfast area. Nevertheless the programme makers began to prepare for the emergence of true regional coverage. A series was started called *Provincial Journey*, with each programme dealing with a different town in Northern Ireland.[49] The first was on Portadown and 'although not of great programme value, this production brought forth a considerable volume of appreciative letters and was a clear indication of its value from the point of view of licences.'[50] *Provincial Journey* continued dealing with town after town, but carefully avoided those which did not receive the Belfast signal until Blaris came on the air.

> To have dealt . . . with such places as Enniskillen, Omagh and Coleraine [before then] would merely have been a source of irritation to the inhabitants concerned. There are few things more irritating than for the people of the district to know that their countrymen are broadcasting, and to be unable to hear them. So you will see a steady reaching out in this direction, and the same policy will be pursued in talks and in feature programmes . . . Both these will definitely focus on the province as a whole . . . A diligent search for talent will be made in those districts in the West which have had so little representation up to the present, and we shall try to present to you the lore and the remote existence of those in the Province who live in such places as the Sperrin Mountains and Rathlin Island, which have remained so little affected by the march of industrialism . . .[51]

Two series which anticipated the idea of looking at the region as a whole were *Ulster Writes*, which consisted of readings of selected passages from the works of a number of the most notable Ulster writers of the time; some were read by the authors themselves. The other was *Six Men went forth;* this dealt with six famous Ulstermen who went out of their native land to achieve fame elsewhere – Lord Dufferin, John Dunlop, Colonel Ross, Lord Kelvin, Lord Lawrence and Lord Castlereagh.

The announcement that the Blaris transmitter would be opened on 20 March 1936, led the *Northern Whig* to comment, 'The new development will give the Northern Ireland area a new dignity and importance among the regional stations of the United Kingdom. With the increase of power the station will be heard across the water by many who at present find it unobtainable.'[52] The *Northern Whig* further commented on the plan for the *Ulster Writes* and *Six Men went forth* series that it was 'an admirable idea, and gives promise of still further advance in making broadcasting a powerful cultural force as well as a source of entertainment'.[53]

As the programme makers prepared to meet the challenge of providing a true Regional service, it became apparent that Radio Athlone might supply some programmes. John Sutthery, Programme Director for Northern Ireland, realised this on his first visit to Dublin to meet the Director of Broadcasting in the Irish Free State. Dr T. J.

Kiernan. Sutthery was enthusiastic about the possibilities for co-operation. His enthusiasm was reflected by London: 'It does seem that it would be an excellent thing which might achieve valuable results.'[54] Sutthery was encouraged to develop 'as much co-operation as Kiernan is ready to accept.'[55]

Dr Kiernan had been appointed Director in Dublin by the republican Fianna Fáil Government which came into power in 1932. The new Government made its dissatisfaction with Seamus Clandillon, the first Director (and appointee of the previous Govern-ment) very public, and looked to Dr Kiernan to institute many reforms in Radio Athlone's programming. A strong nationalistic line was to be taken. This did not, however, affect relations with the BBC Head Office. London reported, 'we have had very friendly relations with Dr Kiernan since his appointment'.[56]

BBC London wrote to Kiernan: 'It seems to us, if you agree, that it would be a satisfactory plan for the detailed arrangements for specific interchange of programmes between Dublin and Belfast to be negotiated direct between our Northern Ireland offices and your own in Dublin'.[57] London hoped for programmes suitable for both the National and Regional services. Several members of the Belfast programme staff journeyed to Dublin to explore the possibilities, particularly in the drama field. News of the negotiations was leaked to the press in Britain and in the Free State, and was eventually picked up by the Belfast papers. The *Daily Mail* headline was PROMISE OF RADIO POOL, INTERCHANGE OF PROGRAMMES, PLANNING RELAYS FROM ULSTER AND FREE STATE, BBC'S FRIENDLY TALKS.[58] The *Evening Standard* developed the same theme, BROADCASTS FOR ENGLISH LISTENERS FROM AN ALL-IRELAND POOL and reported, 'The new arrangement will come fully into force when the new BBC high-powered station at Blaris, near Lisburn, is opened. In the meantime the two Irish stations will work harmoniously together . . . There is no political significance to this, except that radio recognises no artificial frontiers.'[59]

In the eyes of John Sutthery this press coverage 'complicated any scheme of programme interchange that might be desirable'. He went on:

Kiernan struck me as an extremely live wire, moderate in outlook, and progressive in policy, but I got the impression that he is hampered by financial and high policy considerations to such an extent – to say nothing of shortage of staff – that I very much doubt whether there is much programme material emanating from Dublin, or the South generally, which is of value to us.

On top of that, there is the difficulty that there is a section of the public on both sides of the Border, which will make all the trouble it can at the first sign of programme interchange and friendly relations generally between the two broadcasting systems. It is my personal belief – not official – that this is more likely to be very much stronger in Northern Ireland than in the Free State.

As matters stand, I see no likelihood of frequent interchanges of programmes. Moreover, I think it would be undesirable. At the same time, a regular exchange of projected arrangements between the two systems would lead to the occasional taking of some non-provocative programme from one side by the other, and done with discretion, this should be to the common good. At the same time, an undesirable type of press publicity might well have the effect of turning such interchanges from good to harm.

There is no doubt that there is a great deal of good programme material in Dublin, but I don't think that the present scope of the Free State broadcasting service is sufficiently developed to handle it in a way which would be satisfactory to us.[60]

The newspaper reports produced considerable flak in the North and the issues involved became entangled in a demand, for other reasons, that the Unionist Government should take over the BBC in Belfast. This proposal was made by Captain T. H. Mayes at a Unionist Party meeting in protest against the very brief news coverage by the Belfast Station of the serious sectarian riots in Belfast following the Orange parade on the Twelfth of July 1935. However, on being pressed subsequently, Mayes said that he only demanded 'that the Northern Government should have the power, which apparently they do not possess at the moment, to take over the local broadcasting station in case of emergency. I do not suggest for a moment that the Government should interfere with the general running of the station programmes, which apparently satisfy the great majority of listeners.'[61]

The suggestion of co-operation with Radio Athlone was not likely to meet with a favourable reaction among unionists in Northern Ireland because, among other things, Athlone had broadcast full bulletins covering the Belfast riots and had presented a nationalist interpretation of the events. The BBC in Belfast felt obliged to declare publicly that no intention existed to create an Irish pool of programmes, but that 'programmes emanate both from Northern Ireland and the Irish Free State, whose appeal is not limited by territorial boundaries, and listeners in both areas might benefit by an occasional exchange of this type of programme. Nothing, however, involving the slightest deviation from the BBC's established policy would be considered.'[62]

John Sutthery reflected, 'I cannot say where the undesirable publicity originated, but it was almost certainly from the Dublin end, as we took no steps to ask Kiernan to regard our discussions as secret. At the same time, I think I should make it clear that the publicity from the Southern end was favourable, and friendly, and encouraging to the interchange of programmes. The general trend was "that this would be for the making of better relations between the two sides of the border". The real trouble arose when these articles were read by the more rabid type of Ulstermen, who have no desire whatever for better relations. Reading between the lines, you will see that the more contact there is between Dublin and Belfast, can be read by the nationalist as a step nearer the co-ordination of the whole of Ireland on a Free State basis, and that anything which might tend in this direction is as the proverbial rag to a bull, from the Ulster point of view.'[63]

The contribution to the new regional service from south of the border, then, was going to be modest. The radio correspondent of the *News Letter,* 'Blaris', had been well informed and predicted that this would be so. He was, however, concerned about other aspects of the Belfast operation:

... it is a policy of local programme planning (with which I entirely disagree) to feel that certain subjects should be dealt with from [London]. There have never, for instance, been discussions from Belfast on art in Ulster, there are no reviews of local books, and no attention paid to Ulster architecture, because such subjects as art, literature and architecture are considered the prerogative of London. My attitude to this policy is that although it is neither wise nor desirable to attempt to localise any art, some allowance should be made for the fact that Belfast in this respect is not so close to London as English cities are. Northern Ireland has an art of its own and it should at least be given the same rights as Scotland which, alone among the regions, appears to have a broadcasting service completely representative of the life and culture of the country ... I do wish that whatever our political associations with the rest of Great Britain may be, the BBC would try to think of Northern Ireland culturally, not as a kind of smaller and more backward England, but as a country, like Scotland, with some articulation of its own.[64]

'Blaris' hoped that this would be realised in the new era which commenced on 20 March 1936, when the Blaris transmitter was officially opened. The ceremony was performed by the Duke of Abercorn, the Governor of Northern Ireland, who had played the same role at the official opening of the Belfast Station in 1924. It had been decided shortly before the event that the transmitter would be named Lisnagarvey and not Blaris; the recording made of the event in 1936, which survives, shows that Abercorn had some difficulty in pronouncing the name of the new transmitter. Dignitaries from the Northern Ireland Government and from the BBC in London were present. There followed a week of special programmes designed to show how it was now intended to reflect the whole region. In addition, the Prime Minister, Lord Craigavon, gave a talk on the significance of broadcasting for Northern Ireland and a programme of reminiscences of 2BE was transmitted. In succeeding months *Provincial Journey* went to Portrush, Strabane, Newry, Cushendall and other towns previously outside the range of the Belfast signal. Another programme series, *Village Opinion*, was launched. Accounts of their lives and times by the inhabitants of Fintona, Feeny and other small settlements were relayed.

In May 1936 the BBC took a decision which had been in the offing for some time. A completely new Broadcasting House, modelled on that in London, was to be built, which would replace the Linenhall Street offices and studios and be sited on the same block alongside them. It had for some time been clear that the existing adapted premises were inadequate. The new site was occupied by a linen factory and warehouse; these had been acquired and their demolition duly began later in the year.

The Catholic and nationalist morning paper, the *Irish News*, greeted the news and remarked that it meant 'the wireless authorities are now alive to the importance of regional stations, and intend to develop them'. It continued:

. . . whether wireless can, in the long run, avoid being a standardising influence is not yet easy to say. Local or regional characteristics will persist. Speech, for instance, will have its local idiosyncracies, and we must hope that the various parts of the country which have so vigorous an individuality will retain their distinction, which contributes so much to the richness and interest of the national life. It must be recognised, however, that wireless is not the only factor which tends to create uniformity, and may, indeed, have to combat these other influences. Lately the Northern Ireland Station has been inclined to emphasise its individual nature but it is still a long way from being an ideal Irish station.

Perhaps the acquisition of a new and palatial home will encourage it to progress further in that direction.[65]

Six months later the *Irish News* returned to the topic and devoted another leader to it.

Programmes from Belfast have improved considerably during the past year or so, but they still leave a lot to be desired. Listeners, for instance, still get an overdose of heavy music, and there is a general stiffness and lack of imagination about the programmes. Moreover, the Belfast Station seems to be inclined to depend on the regional 'pool' arrangement, inaugurated about a year ago, with the result that relays from English stations are far too frequent. In some weeks the total contribution of Northern Ireland is surprisingly small.

But the main drawback about the Northern Ireland Station is that it remains un-Irish in character. The Northern, Western and Scottish regional stations in Britain are definitely in the character of the area they serve, and the Dublin Station is unmistakably Irish; but anyone tuning into Belfast might take it for just another English station. Save for some talks of special Ulster interest, a few outside local broadcasts, and several dialect plays, there is little to give the local station the authentic atmosphere of its setting.[66]

The *Irish News* noted that Charles Siepmann, the BBC's Director of Regional Relations, had been making an intensive study of the regions with the purpose of stopping 'the drift to London'. The BBC, he was reported as saying, intended to 'foster local loyalties' and to spend more on provincial programmes; the *Irish News* welcomed the intention.

Siepmann's investigation of the Belfast operations of the BBC is probably the most thorough that has ever been undertaken. He came over for the opening of the Lisnagarvey transmitter and carried on from there. His report began with a critical and unflattering description of Northern Ireland – quoted in the Introduction above – which he summarised as follows:

Such then are the circumstances in Northern Ireland, a small area, a small population, awkwardly divided between town and country, slender cultural resources, cross-currents of bitter religious antagonism and a lamentable dearth of talent both among authors and artistes. So great is the dearth of talent that I found the head of one department limited to periods of rehearsal prior to 7.30 p.m. because of the frequent use of the same artistes by other departments in evening programmes. Our programme staff valiantly attempt the hopeless task of making bricks without straw.

Siepmann undertook a detailed analysis of the resources available to each of the major programme areas with a view to the assessment of future possibilities. His feeling was that the details confirm his depressing general diagnosis.

DRAMA There has been a considerable output in the past but the standard has been poor and a small coterie of artistes has been run to death. There is not much distinctive local material to exploit. A certain amount of kitchen comedy is available and popular but there are limits to its use. There is no repertory company equivalent to those working in the North and in the Midlands. The Ulster Players were once good but are no longer so. There are a good many amateur societies but their performances are at such a crude level of efficiency as to be of little value to us. This, despite the fact that I find our programme people inevitably more accommodating than they are or should be in other regions. While ninety-two players were in fact used last year, it was freely admitted that not ten of these even approximated to the standard of London expectations. There are a few playwrights, very few. The most promising of these, as I understand, has recently thrown his hand in, not finding the inducements of our fees alluring.

LIGHT ENTERTAINMENT Use is made exclusively of amateur artistes. Auditions have hitherto revealed a low standard among applicants. Within the Province, there are two or three reasonably good syncopated turns, a single syncopated pianist – a half-dozen turns shall we say in all and then a lapse to gloomy depths. There is but a single good author of light Belfast material. On average one real show is put on a fortnight. There are a number of minor sketches. The overall output within a year amounts to about 120 shows. Very few indeed are fit for export.

OUTSIDE BROADCASTS Here, variety apart, the resources are more plentiful. There is only one theatre that we can tap and that a poor one. One church organ, one cinema, two light orchestras and two dance bands – one very indifferent – are wired up for repeated use but that is all. Light material is more or less on a subsidy basis. Two hotels and one road house have been induced by Sutthery to secure artistes of a standard passable for broadcasting. Something may be achieved on co-operative lines though it is difficult to see how it could be extended. The general standard in the entertainment is so low that our OB people have practically to put on the shows themselves. Things may improve but they can never be satisfactory. This apart, there are, of course, the TT Races, the Co Down Trophy, the Grand Prix and the Ulster Derby, as a regular standby. *Provincial Journey*, a series of OB feature programmes, has hitherto been of doubtful standard but it has provoked local enthusiasm and is good propaganda. When the recording vans become available this side of the work should and will be considerably extended.

MUSIC Here again our Orchestra and our endeavours provide the only prop to the languishing musical culture of Ulster. Our Orchestra gives eight concerts a year which are now reasonably well attended. A second tentative effort to spread interest by a visit to Londonderry proved disappointing. A military band and a brass band* supplement our activites and provide useful programme material but there seems little musical consciousness in the province at all and we can only keep our gaze on the future.

TALKS Here there are possibilities despite the ban on controversy necessitated over a wide field by the political-religious issue. Sutthery is very sensible of the possibilities of talks development. The talks to farmers are already popular and a genuine public service. The recent series on dialect provoked extraordinary interest and there is in my view scope for a great deal of constructive social work by the discovery on a strict factual basis of the conditions of Ulster in the sphere of health, education, etc, to the people themselves.

FEATURE PROGRAMMES Here there is great scope both for programmes from the studio and extensive OB work. This indeed is the most promising field for programme development and the resources of the region are not at the moment being exploited to the full, partly through what seems to me a maladjustment of the staff, partly pending the arrival of the recording vans. Even here, however, it is likely that we shall have to draw on our own resources for the drafting of scripts. There is a serious shortage of writers and as in other departments a depressing shortage of people who are suitable as narrators or for intelligent reading.

RELIGION Northern Ireland is the only region in which religious services are broadcast during church hours with the express approval of the Advisory Committee. This is rather remarkable. The only difficulty is that the Roman Catholics will not come into line and despite repeated efforts it has not yet proved possible to secure a Roman Catholic member for the Religious Advisory Committee. This, of course, is simply a reflection of the political situation. The relations of the Northern Ireland regional staff with the Roman Catholic Church being entirely cordial.[67]

The conclusions which Siepmann as Director of Regional Relations reached on the basis of his survey of Northern Ireland's programme resources were drastic. He recommended that all studio-based variety and all drama production should cease. Drama had been a mainstay of Linenhall Street's offerings since 1924 and so this suggestion proved a shock to the Belfast staff. Siepmann, however, held that 'the standards of performance and the quality of the plays

* These bands were made up of members of the Orchestra, slightly augmented.

hardly seems justified as an indispensable contribution to regional culture'. Siepmann was convinced that a great future lay in the production of features and topical talks. There was a condition attached to this: 'I would further recommend that in any new appointments that are made special consideration should be given to the claims of Ulstermen. I am much impressed by the need for a true native understanding of the conditions and outlook for the people of Ulster. An Englishman can bring sympathy to the problem but I doubt very much, particularly where field work is concerned, whether he can win the confidence of Ulster people to the extent that is necessary if we are to secure good progress.' Siepmann favoured the two Ulstermen on the staff. He felt that Henry McMullan, who at the time was in charge of feature programmes, should, in due course, succeed John Sutthery as Programme Director, G. F. Combe, also Belfast born, and a recent recruit, should be given a post in the feature/topical talks field. Generally, Siepmann recommended staff adjustments and new posts to facilitate the shift in programme emphasis which he proposed. His recommendations did not involve an increase in the establishment.

Marshall accepted much that was in the report but not the recommended closure of his drama department: Siepmann had in fact left the final decision on this to the Regional Director's discretion. Marshall regarded the production of Ulster plays as one of the more important contributions Belfast could make to the development of a regional culture. A year or so later he was to claim that 'a good deal of what was said in Siepmann's report no longer applies'.[68] He listed sixteen important productions intended for transmission between January and March 1938, which he claimed illustrated Linenhall Street's positive achievement. Nine of them, he pointed out, were to be relayed by London (these programmes are marked here with an asterisk).

Week 1   *Dr O'Toole* by J. B. Fagan
Week 2   **Apollo in Mourne* by Richard Rowley, 'Apollo' to be played by Micheál Mac Liammóir of Dublin's Gate Theatre
Week 2   *Quin's Secret* by George Shiels
Week 3   *À la carte* by Mafe Haughton
Week 4   **In the Train* by Frank O'Connor, adapted jointly by Hugh Hunt of the Abbey Theatre and by Denis Johnston
Week 5   *The Enthusiast* by Teresa Deevey
Week 6   *Orpheus and his Lute* by Frank O'Connor, adapted by Denis Johnston

81

Week 7	Not one returns to tell by Denis Johnston
Week 8	*The King of Spain's Daughter by Teresa Deevey
Week 9	Shepherd's Hey, a recorded feature programme
Week 10	*Lillibulero by Denis Johnston
Week 11	*St Patrick's Day programme to consist of recordings in Ulster
Week 11	*Ireland Dances
Week 12	Gone Away by Ethel Lewis
Week 13	*Cathleen ni Houlihan by W. B. Yeats
Week 13	*Riders to the Sea by J. M. Synge, both to be presented by the Abbey Theatre[69]

What is remarkable in this list of plays and features is the contribution of one man, Denis Johnston. For, apart from the programmes credited to him, he also produced the two plays by Teresa Deevey. He was not at the time employed by the BBC as a producer but rather as a feature scriptwriter and researcher. However, his distinction as a playwright was such that Sutthery was prompted to ask him to produce the two plays.

Denis Johnston's opportunity to join the BBC in Belfast arose directly out of Siepmann's recommendation that the production of feature programmes was the richest potential field of programming for Northern Ireland. A scriptwriter and researcher was essential to promote development and it became known that Denis Johnston was interested. Johnston, a Dubliner whose family came from Ulster, was a successful barrister who had gained a national reputation as a dramatist with plays like The Old Lady Says No and The Moon in the Yellow River. He was now, however, contemplating a change in career, being very much attracted by the potential of television. He wished to join the BBC which had begun a television service in London from Alexandra Palace in November 1936. Johnston did not think he would get into Alexandra Palace through the front door, so he decided to try the radio back door in Belfast. There followed a short, highly productive period for the Northern Ireland Region and for Denis Johnston. He wrote a number of feature programmes of distinction which were very successful on transmission and were repeated on television and radio in later years. The most remarkable of these was Lillibulero, hailed on its first performance as 'a landmark in broadcasting in Ireland' and as 'the most ambitious radio programme ever to be produced in Belfast'.

Johnston called Lillibulero a diorama, or radio presentation, of the siege of Derry in 1688–9. The symbolic significance of the event for the Protestant population meant that the subject was politically sensitive. Word got out about the programme before it was transmitted and reached Derry 'with the result that the society known as the Apprentice Boys immediately asked to see a copy of the script. When this was refused they got their Member of Parliament, Mr E. S. Murphy KC, to write to us [the BBC] and press for it. It appears the trouble with Derry is not the usual one of two opposing factions, namely the Protestant and the Roman Catholic, as there is no disputing the fact that the Protestants were besieged and held out till they were relieved, but, on the contrary, some sort of quarrel between the beleaguered Episcopalians and the Presbyterians, each of whom claim to have taken the most important part in the siege itself. The request for a copy of the script was, of course, again refused, but it was pointed out that the author had made a very exhaustive and careful research into the history of the siege, had examined many contemporary documents, etc., and for the moment the enquiries seem to be satisfied.' So wrote Marshall in a report to the BBC Board of Governors. He went on: 'It might have been thought that the siege of a small place like Derry two hundred and fifty years ago should have been forgotten by this time, but this is far from the case, and Mr Johnston says that the real trouble is that the Protestant elements in Derry are afraid that their siege may be "de-bunked" and lose forever its glamorous political significance.'[70]

The radio critic of the *News Letter* considered the implications of the programme and wrote, 'no drama of this type has ever been broadcast in Ulster. The BBC has, in fact, acted continuously on the belief that we take such matters too seriously for entertainment with political implications to be generally acceptable. *Lillibulero* is, therefore, the first local broadcast of its kind.'[71] As a precaution, Marshall and Sutthery invited the press to the final rehearsal. The *Irish News* correspondent wrote an enthusiastic and lengthy feature on the day of transmission:

. . . Whether our fathers were on the side of those who defended Derry or those who besieged it, and whether we think that the version does or does not do justice to the besiegers, we must in the first place applaud the directors of the Northern Ireland Station for giving us in good radio-dramatic form an interpretation of one of the outstanding events in Irish history.

The technique of the piece is excellent. Inside an hour we are given a representation of a siege which lasted for several months, and in more vivid form than could have been done in the most detailed history . . .

No Irishman North or South of the Border who tunes in to it will regret having done so, and many of us look forward to the day when the BBC will give Mr Johnston a commission to write another diorama from Irish history.[72]

George Marshall informed the BBC Board of Governors some time later:

It is interesting to report that from the point of view of programme policy in this region, we have been gradually able to invade the realms of history and religion, subjects inextricably bound up in these parts with politics. Naturally, we have advanced slowly and prepared the ground with a great deal of careful publicity, but that something definite has been achieved is beyond question. Two recent programmes are illustrative of this, and it is hoped that a third . . . [may be added]. The first, *Lillibulero*, dealt with the siege of Derry, which has long been held by the Protestant element in Ireland as an event almost sacrosanct and therefore beyond critical investigation; and yet the *Irish News*, the Nationalist and Catholic daily in Northern Ireland, was loud in its praise of the production and hardly a breath of criticism from any source was heard.[73]

As the radio critic of the *News Letter* remarked: 'The fears of the BBC that the Siege of Derry might be a dangerous and controversial subject for a radio programme were clearly without foundation.'[74]

The second programme which Marshall considered a breakthrough was a play by Hugh Quinn, *Mrs McConaghy's Money*. At least one newspaper critic had presumed that it was the sordid nature of the theme dealt with by the playwright which had caused the BBC to hesitate for a long time before producing it, whereas the real reason was its sectarian nature.[75] The play, which had been successful on the stage in Dublin and in London, dealt with the activities of a Belfast woman who earned her livelihood by insuring the lives of workhouse inmates. It was transmitted and was received with favourable comment. Marshall described it to London as 'a strong play with a definite pro-Catholic leaning, which apparently gave all-round satisfaction to listeners and was certainly one of the best things of its kind which has been done yet'.[76]

The third programme of a more adventurous kind which had not been performed when Marshall wrote to the Board of Governors was *Orpheus and his Lute*. This was a play adapted by Denis Johnston from a short story by Frank O'Connor. 'It involved

Protestant and Catholic elements, Temperance bands and all these imply, and there is a good deal of sarcasm and leg-pulling.'[76] This again was well received.

Marshall concluded: 'In past years programmes of this type would have been sedulously avoided, and the fact that they can now be heard with composure and pleasure by people of opposing creeds is highly significant. Perhaps the impartiality of the BBC is at last being realised and appreciated.'[77] An alternative explanation might have been that suggested by 'Blaris' in the *News Letter* when writing about the reception for *Lillibulero:* 'It has at least shown the BBC that its timidity about dealing with such a subject has been based entirely on a misconception of the Ulster temperament.'[78]

The basic programme policy was not affected. Marshall had always refused to countenance the overtly political and those aspects of culture which he regarded as covertly political. He endeavoured to apply his ban to both communities.

In 1936 the Ulster branch of the Gaelic League requested that, in parity with the provision for Gaelic speakers in Scotland, the BBC should provide programmes in Irish, especially lessons in the language, in Northern Ireland. Marshall refused:

> . . . after careful consideration we decided we could not undertake to do so. The number of Gaelic speakers in Northern Ireland is negligible and, as far as schools are concerned, the proportion of those where the Irish language is taught is quite small and is practically confined to secondary schools. You refer to Scotland, but no doubt you will appreciate the fact that in the Highlands and Islands there is a Gaelic speaking population of about 200,000, and in the universities there are three chairs devoted to the Gaelic language and literature. Even so there are no lessons broadcast in Gaelic although from time to time programmes are specially designed for the Highlands.[79]

The *Irish News* devoted a leader to the BBC's refusal:

> When we state that the decision will cause deep regret among students of the old tongue we are probably putting it mildly. A fair-minded public will be inclined to ask why the authorities in charge of the Belfast studio have adopted this attitude towards the language. Apart from every other consideration one would have thought that the cultural value of the language would have influenced the BBC to set apart at least a short space of time for a talk in Irish . . .[80]

Later in the following year, the BBC did relay part of the Derry Feis in which most of the songs were in Irish. The nationalist press welcomed this departure which was to become an annual event, but it was not the kind of exposure which the Gaelic League had specifically asked for.

An issue which was preoccupying Marshall and the BBC at the same time concerned the Bands Association. In some measure this was also interpreted as a covert political issue, as the bands were Protestant and their normal repertoire outside the studio included a lot of music of a sectarian nature. However, another aspect which concerned the BBC was the quality of their playing: it varied greatly and was generally considered poor. Appearances of the bands were discouraged by the very low fees paid. In order to provide adequate brass band music Godfrey Brown formed a station band from musicians in the BBC Northern Ireland Orchestra, augmented by others drawn from regiments based locally. He used this combination in preference to the bands in the North of Ireland Bands Association. The Association was very upset and made representations to Marshall in Belfast and to Sir John Reith in London but to no effect. In February 1937 Sir Wilson Hungerford, Unionist MP, took up the cause of the bands at an Association annual general meeting:

Unfortunately what we are suffering from in Northern Ireland is that we get on the wireless not what we want to hear but what other people think we should hear. I am at a loss to understand why bands in Northern Ireland have been ignored in this connection. Probably one explanation is that those at the head of affairs in broadcasting for Northern Ireland are people who know little about the conditions and ideals of the people here.

Both the Scottish and Welsh stations have people of those nationalities in authority to arrange their programmes, while we have people, no doubt very efficient in many matters, and, I am certain, anxious to do their best, but who know not Northern Ireland.

We here in the North of Ireland are unique in the fact that our people, particularly our artisans, are keen musicians, and bands are composed of young men, who, after their day's work in shipyard or factory, spend several nights a week practising music, and who also contribute out of their wages a sum each week to pay for the services of a qualified bandmaster to teach them.

Surely it is not too much to expect some encouragement and support? But that is entirely lacking from the organisation that should give them such support . . .

Many of you will have read various letters published recently beseeching the BBC to put our bands on the air but alas! without any result. Yet we have the station director complaining about the lack of support for the special concerts which they give.

Some of our bands are offered engagements, but at what a princely remuneration! Three guineas! And this for a band with 35 players!

The station director complains of lack of support for his concerts. Let me make him this offer: that he should put on one of his symphony concerts and see what support it gets, and allow the North of Ireland bands to run a concert, the same remuneration to be given to both, and that he should take the result as a criterion of what the people want.[81]

Hungerford's intervention stirred up a controversy which had been simmering for some time; he also provided the strategy which eventually led the Regional Director, Marshall, to the negotiating table. The correspondence in the press was prolonged and bitter. The facts of the situation were that the bands had been given seventy-three engagements from 1932 until September 1935, with programmes lasting on average fifteen minutes. Only bands which had gained first place in various musical contests were invited to play. In September 1935 the North of Ireland Bands Association had sent a deputation to the BBC demanding a revision of fees and of the principle on which engagements took place. From that date until the spring of 1937 no further engagements had been entered into by the BBC. Marshall's public explanation of why this was so was scarcely convincing:

During that discussion [in September 1935] the secretary of the Association read out a letter which he had received containing unfair criticisms of the BBC's Northern Ireland Brass Band and its conductor. The BBC felt that it was hardly within the province of the Association – whose members are all amateur players – to associate itself in this way with an unfair criticism of professional musicians who are making their livelihood exclusively by the practice of music. In justice, therefore, to its own players, the BBC asked the Association to dissociate itself from those criticisms before the question of the re-engagement of these amateur bands was reopened. It is the failure of the Association to do this which is alone preventing the BBC from offering broadcast engagements to a number of Northern Irish bands, whose work it would be very happy to encourage, and towards which it entertains nothing but friendly feelings.[82]

As the *Belfast Telegraph* pointed out in a leader, 'If we might seek to interpret the mind of the ordinary disinterested listener, we would say that the reason assigned does not commend itself as being sufficient in itself to close out local bands indefinitely.'[83]

The Bands Association then launched a campaign requesting people to sign a petition and send it to the MPs of the Imperial Parliament. Then, as a further step in their fight for recognition, the Bands Association hired two halls in Belfast, the Ulster Hall and the Grosvenor Hall, for protest concerts on the same night. Posters appeared advertising the concerts with such slogans as 'Come and hear the bands the BBC won't broadcast' and 'Ulster bands for Ulster air'. Tickets for the concerts were sold out.

On the day before the concerts the Prime Minister, Lord Craigavon, intervened as mediator in the dispute. He summoned the Regional Director, Marshall, and the secretary of the Bands Association to a meeting in Stormont. There an agreement was thrashed out and Marshall conceded that higher fees would be paid. He still held to the principle that only prize-winning bands would be invited to broadcast. The agreement reached in 1937 still holds in 1984! Clearly, in this local variation of the 'highbrows' *v* 'lowbrows' conflict, the 'lowbrows' had won a round.

If the bands which marched in Orange processions could win concessions from the BBC then the Orange Order could press for radio coverage of the Twelfth of July processions. 'The next move', wrote Marshall to the Board of Governors,

was a difficult one to counter. It was a request that a running commentary should be broadcast on the procession of Orange Lodges on the Twelfth of July. The political significance of this event can only be fully appreciated by the Ulsterman, and had the request been complied with the BBC would have been laid open to a charge of partiality and political partisanship – in fact, the BBC in Northern Ireland would thereafter have been reasonably called a tool in the hands of the Government. The request for such a broadcast did not come from any insignificant source, but from the County Grand Secretary of the Belfast County Grand Lodge, and was backed up by a Cabinet Minister, the Attorney General and, finally, the Prime Minister himself. On our polite but firm refusal to broadcast such a commentary, it was some consolation to be told that compliance with the request was hardly expected![84]

That was in 1938. In 1939 pressure was renewed. Again Marshall reported to the Board of Governors explaining in the first instance what the Orange Order and 'the Twelfth' was all about. He pointed out that the procession ended in 'the field' with the leaders addressing 'the faithful':

Naturally, religion is well in the background and politics in the foreground, and for that reason it would be highly dangerous to convey any part of the ceremony over the microphone. None the less, each year an attempt is made to persuade, if not compel, the broadcasting authorities in Northern Ireland to alter their policy by having a running commentary on the procession and a broadcast of the speeches, and a considerable time has to be spent in explaining to Cabinet Ministers and high officials of the Orange Order that such a broadcast would conflict with the BBC's inflexible rule governing such political occasions. This year considerable 'copy' was made of the fact that the ceremony of the Pope's coronation was broadcast, and that therefore Ulster's Protestant ceremony should also be included, and it has not been easy to convince certain people of the quite different significance of each occasion. For the present the matter has blown over – probably because the Prime Minister of Northern Ireland himself refused to take up the case, but it will almost certainly arise again next year.[85]

The Second World War intervened, however, and, as regional broadcasting came to an end for the duration, the question of coverage of 'the Twelfth' was deferred.

The tone of the reaction to the 1939 refusal was, however, ominous. The Executive Committee of the Independent Unionist Association in a long statement said:

. . . we understand that this privilege has hitherto been refused on the plea that this commemoration is a narrow sectarian and political issue. Considering the number and variety of sectarian and political issues broadcast this plea is an insult to the intelligence.

. . . we cannot accept the reply of our Prime Minister that since broadcasting is an Imperial service Ulster people must accept its dictums in a passive spirit. The Northern Ireland section of the BBC draws its revenues from the Ulster people and should cater for Ulster interests. We have recently too much evidence of overlordship of Imperial authorities and too much meekness of our Government and Imperial members of Parliament. The time has come for Ulster people to assert themselves to maintain their just rights and privileges.[86]

The Ulster Evangelical Protestant Society also issued a lengthy statement of disapproval, quoting a letter it had received from Marshall which said,

We have considered this celebration very carefully in previous years and, quite apart from the obvious difficulty of making a programme item out of a procession, we feel that its political significance makes it unsuitable for broadcasting, and inconsistent with our policy in political matters.

The Society, after hinting that 'Romanists' were in control of the BBC and that 'Catholic Action' was active in Northern Ireland, stated,

> . . . We consider that the great Orange Institution, comprising the cream of Ulster from Lord Craigavon down, have a very great grievance against the BBC in our midst, and we certainly mean to go further with this matter, as the great majority of the Ulster people have a right to be heard and their reasonable wishes respected, and we can only express our great disappointment with your reply.[87]

The question of political broadcasts had arisen in Marshall's directorship before 1939. Election broadcasts had been permitted in Great Britain during the 1930s. When, however, an election occurred in Northern Ireland in the winter of 1933, Marshall was advised from London that the BBC was not taking the initiative in Northern Ireland by offering air time to the parties. 'If, on the other hand, you should be approached by the Government or by the Opposition with a definite request to provide such faciliites, their request will, of course, have to be considered. In that case, before committing yourself, we should be glad if you would put forward your proposals for our consideration, based on the most equitable distribution among parties that can be devised in the circumstances. We may hope, however, that the question will not arise, and in the meantime the matter may best be treated as a sleeping dog, and as such allowed to lie.'[88] And it did.

In 1938, however, Marshall consulted Lord Craigavon, the Prime Minister. Craigavon 'was very strongly of the opinion' that there should be no election broadcasts similar to those in Britain: '. . . the reason being that the Opposition is so small and that there are so many conflicting interests, that a very difficult situation was bound to arise. He says, in fact, that agreement would be practically impossible as to who should represent the opposing parties and what, indeed, would be their actual platforms.'[89] The composition of the dissolved House of Commons was as follows: Unionists 37, Nationalists 9, Independent Unionists 2, Labour 2, Republican 1 and Fianna Fáil 1. In the circumstances, Marshall strongly recommended that nothing should be done. So there were no election broadcasts in Northern Ireland before the Second World War.

While Marshall wove what he believed to be a consistent path between the various pressures on the BBC in Northern Ireland and tried to avoid all overt and covert political broadcasting, he also endeavoured to apply the same principle to broadcasting on the BBC network which dealt with Ireland in any way. In this broader sense, however, what increasingly manifests itself is his inclination to line up with the unionist position *vis-à-vis* the Irish Free State/Éire. In 1937 Marshall noted that a programme broadcast by the BBC's North Region in Britain, entitled *The Irish*, included the playing of the Irish National Anthem. Marshall wrote to the Controller of Programmes in London:

> This anthem is not National in any sense of the word, as applying to the Irish, for Northern Ireland is just as much Irish as the Free State. The song in question is called 'The Soldier's Song' and is essentially rebel . . . There is no need for me to emphasise how disastrous it is for a Region of the BBC to radiate a rebel song and to invite listeners to stand while it is played. I need hardly refer you to such words as 'Out yonder waits the Saxon foe'. A broadcast such as this may have its funny side from the point of view of an English listener, but it raises the acutest indignation in the six counties of Northern Ireland, where the Irish have remained loyal. Naturally, there has been an outcry in the Press and the most violent of protests.[90]

A reply was sent to the Northern Ireland Regional Director on behalf of the North Regional Director. It apologised but pointed out that consultation with London had taken place, adding sharply: 'I should like to emphasise that the announcing was duplicated in Erse and 'The Soldier's Song' itself was sung entirely in Erse. It is difficult to understand therefore why listeners in Ulster should have interpreted it as being directed at themselves, particularly as I understand that very few of them understand Erse, which was referred to officially in the Ulster Parliament recently as a foreign language.'[91] He agreed, however, that in future Marshall would be consulted on such matters.

Less than a year later Marshall noticed that another programme was to include 'the notorious "Soldier's Song"'. This time it was to be played on St Patrick's Day. He pointed out to the Controller of Programmes that when he had taken exception to the Irish programme broadcast from the North Region that the Controller had ruled:

> Whenever any department or Region was about to produce a programme involving a subject, of which another department or Region possessed special knowledge and experience, there should be preliminary consultation between them, (see Programme Board Minutes No. 576).

91

In this case we were not consulted in advance and I am sorry to note that while a great amount of publicity has been given in the *World Radio* for 17 March to this particular concert, there is no reference in that journal to our own St Patrick's Day programme, despite the fact that part of it comes from Canada and that it is being taken by the NBC of America.[92]

The Controller of Programmes replied that the concert from Dublin on St Patrick's Day was not organised by the BBC. It was 'the Irish Free State contribution to the series of concerts given by members of the International Broadcasting Union, and it so happens – quite suitably – that the day chosen for the Free State to give their concert is on St Patrick's Day. These concerts are automatically rebroadcast by all members of the Union who can do so. We here, of course, have no say in the composition of this programme . . .'[93] The Controller went on to say that he regretted no mention had been made in the *World Radio* of the Northern Ireland programme for St Patrick's Day.

Perhaps, Marshall was eventually glad of that. For, as he reported to the BBC's Board of Governors, the Canadian contribution was most inapposite.

It has always been a matter of extreme difficulty to arrange a programme for St Patrick's Day, owing to the controversies which are apt to start around the figure of the Saint himself, or the songs or other matter chosen for the occasion. This time it was felt it would be safe to provide a short musical programme from Belfast, with quite innocuous musical numbers, and with the balance of the programme from Toronto, Canada, where there are so many Ulstermen, and where the Orange Lodges are so strong. As it turned out, however, the Canadian part of the programme was a complete failure and had no reference whatever to Ulster; in fact, it was definitely Southern Irish, and consisted of a rather poorly performed radio version of James Stephens' novel *The Crock of Gold*. The Canadian Broadcasting Authorities had several months in which to arrange this programme and were thoroughly primed with the type of thing that was wanted, but the actual contents were not known until three days before the performance, i.e., infinitely too late for any alterations.[94]

Right on cue came the letters of protest:

The Northern Ireland Regional Station had a programme that savoured of that good old Ulster spirit, but I regret that the orchestra failed to depart from high-class orchestrations of the beautiful Irish airs and give something more lively than 'Killeter Fair'. Are these splendid reels and jigs not more appropriate on our festival and more descriptive of our happy temperament? When we went over to Canada we were treated to a fairy tale which seemed to come not from Ulster exiles but from the West coast of Ireland. The worst of all was the programme radiated from Dublin . . . Did the BBC know that the self-styled National Anthem, 'A Soldier's Song', was going to be the opening piece for the 'Eire' programme? It is most repulsive to loyal Ulster to hear it, with 'Who Fears to Speak of '98' following immediately. Who is responsible for its radiation through the Belfast Station either here or in London?[95]

Marshall was not completely deterred by the experience. In 1939 he made another attempt to co-operate with Canada on the St Patrick's Day programme:

Very careful instructions were given to the Canadian Broadcasting authorities to ensure that Northern and not Southern Ireland was represented – in fact it was agreed that a family living in Toronto, who had migrated to Canada some fifteen years ago should exchange greetings and a description of their present life with a family in Ulster. The Ulster portion of the programme was carried out to the letter, but the Canadian was a ludicrous travesty of what was intended, and consisted of some extremely vulgar back-chat followed by a series of personal messages to friends and relatives in Ulster from a number of people who were brought to the Toronto studio without any reference to Belfast whatsoever – in fact, the occasion was merely utilised for gratuitous trans-Atlantic telephone calls from Toronto to Northern Ireland.

Marshall concluded this report to the Board of Governors by observing, 'co-operation with Canada will no longer come within the scope of activities in the Northern Ireland region unless a very considerable change of heart comes over the broadcasting authorities in the Dominion'.[96]

In the course of 1938 an opportunity occurred which enabled the Northern Ireland Region of the BBC to tie up its relationship with its nearest neighbour. Dr T. J. Kiernan, Director of Broadcasting of Radio Éireann, was planning an outside broadcast of a Catholic ceremony at Saul, Co Down, in Northern Ireland, with his own equipment and commentator. He asked for the BBC's agreement and co-operation. It seemed that this request provided an excellent opportunity to establish reciprocal arrangements for outside broadcasts in each other's territories, and John Sutthery, Director of Programmes, travelled to Dublin to negotiate. From the BBC Northern Ireland's point of view there were two advantages to be gained. In the first place, BBC gear, engineers and commentators could in future operate in the twenty-six counties and secondly, under a gentleman's agreement, each broadcasting organisation would keep the other informed of its programme intentions in the other's area.

Sutthery explained the first advantge in some detail to London:

As you are aware, there are a number of events of first-class importance which take place in Éire each year and which are in most cases broadcast by Radio Éireann. The trouble is, however, that owing to this organisation's shortage of money, equipment and experience, a relay of their broadcast is rarely satisfactory. For example, they have no broadcast huts at all and work either in the open or from motor-cars. They have insufficient staff to send a programme man to an important OB and generally, proceedings are not at all what we would pass as up to the BBC standard.

The Cork Grand Prix and the Phoenix Park Grand Prix Motor Races are both shows of absolutely first class importance, but are handled by commentators who have been rejected from here as unsuitable, and a system that we could not permit. The Dublin Horse Show is perhaps the most important event of its kind in the world, but is not very satisfactorily handled . . .

We have been hoping for a long time that it might be possible to broadcast some of the major events in Éire with our own gear, engineers and commentators. This was obviously out of the question as things used to be, as we could not easily get a permit to take our gear into Éire and also we had so much to gain and they so much to lose . . .[97]

Dr Kiernan of Radio Éireann got a special general permit for customs clearance for the BBC. Ironically, the BBC had little to do in return for there were no customs difficulties for Radio Éireann entering Northern Ireland.

Marshall and Sutthery were acting beyond their powers in conducting these negotiations and the BBC in London was very annoyed.[98] In the course of a fairly acid correspondence Sutthery revealed the significance of the other aspects of the negotiations:

It is clearly understood between Kiernan and myself that no broadcast will take place in the other's territory without the full permission of the resident director. You should, however, appreciate that it would need special steps taken by the Northern Ireland Government to prevent Kiernan broadcasting from Ulster, if he should choose – which he will not – to proceed in the face of the Northern Ireland Regional Director's veto.

I would like to assure you that the most thorough consultation with our

Government was made before these negotiations were proceeded with and that there are no difficulties to be anticipated in this quarter.[98]

This arrangement was allowed to stand by the BBC in London. So it was that by June 1938 Marshall had manoeuvred himself into a position where he had to be consulted about all programmes produced by the BBC on Ireland and where effectively Radio Éireann could only operate in Northern Ireland with his permission. He was moving close to the position, which he achieved during the Second World War, where he could profoundly influence, if not dictate, BBC policy in and towards Ireland.

The staff in Linenhall Street had three and a half years, after the Lisnagarvey transmitter opened, in which to put a regional policy into effect. During 1937 and 1938, Denis Johnston wrote a string of features and plays which were designed to implement such a policy. These included *Stentor* a programme in celebration of the 200th anniversary of the Belfast *News Letter*; *Death at Newtownstewart* which recounted the course of events in which the brutal murderer of a bank clerk was brought to trial in 1873; *Weep for Polyphemus,* an account of the domestic problems of Dean Swift; *The Parnell Commission,* a dramatic reconstruction of the trial which exposed as forgeries letters published in *The Times* which had sought to damage Parnell; *The Birth of a Giant,* a description of the building of a large ship in Harland and Wolff's shipyard from drawing office to launching. When to these are added *Lillibulero, Orpheus and his Lute* and *Not one returns to tell,* a most effective 'ghostly adventure', Johnston's contribution in less than two years was striking. *The Birth of a Giant* involved a new dimension in broadcasting; included in the programme were recordings made in the shipyard. These were made possible through the visit of a new BBC recording van from Britain. The reflection of the region through broadcasting had now become possible in a more realistic and spontaneous way. The recording van toured Northern Ireland in the summer of 1937. It gathered material for a feature in the National Programme Series *Summer over the British Isles.* As a result, impressions of the famous Ould Lammas Fair at Ballycastle were heard all over the United Kingdom. The first full-length programme made by the recording unit for the Northern Ireland Region was of a ceilidh in a country cottage in Co Tyrone, transmitted on 15 October 1937. Unfortunately, the van had to return to Britain and Belfast did not get its own mobile unit until the middle of the war.

In the same autumn the Northern Ireland BBC executives made a determined drive to win the co-operation of their listeners. They wished 'to absorb and then give expression to Ulster culture'. They were reported as wanting 'original Ulster airs, people with acting ability, not necessarily stage experience, ideas for features, programmes and radio discussions, and Ulster plays of all types suitable for radio'.[99] These were essential, they emphasised, if they were to succeed in carrying out their aim of establishing a closer relationship between the station and the listening public. The Belfast Directors had often in the past appealed for authors to come forward but this was a determined drive. They went on to organise competitions for short stories.

An earnest of good intent was a scheme announced 'to preserve for all time the wealth of folk and traditional music of Northern Ireland'. The BBC secured the services of the Ulster musician, Norman Hay, and gave him the task of co-ordinating 'a group of musicians who were to orchestrate the traditional music of the countryside'. The team included Charles Brennan, Joan Trimble, Howard Ferguson and Redmond Friel. 'The question of what is an Ulster air is bound to arise, but it should be understood that there will be no attempt at invidious distinctions. Naturally, traditional music in Ulster is of all sorts and origins; some of it will be found to have come from Scotland, some of it from the South of Ireland. The qualification, apart from intrinsic merit, of music coming within the scope of this work is not only its origin, but its adoption by the people of Ulster.' The results of Hay's work and that of his colleagues were broadcast from time to time in a series called *Airs of Ulster*. The whole scheme was regarded by the BBC as 'part of its function in reflecting the life of the region to foster such work as the preservation of music which is essentially part of the country's heritage'.[100]

In the autumn of 1938 the Northern Ireland Region launched an Ulster radio drama festival, intended as a retrospective review of plays which were typical of Ulster. The festival was carried by the London Region as well and for the sake of London listeners the Ulster dialect was toned down. Two plays a week were offered over a period of six weeks, including C. K. Ayre's *Wee Moiley Cow*, and *The Unlucky Baste;* Rutherford Mayne's *The Drone*, George Shiels's *Insurance Money* and Jack Louden's *The Ball turns once*. At the press conference to launch the festival a reporter suggested that listeners might welcome a play such as Louis Walsh's *The Auction at*

Killybuck, a fairly crude presentation of the clash between the Orange and the Green. He was told by a BBC executive that 'because of their religious and political touches such plays might perhaps cause offence to numerous people'.[101]

In talks too the BBC studiously avoided controversy. The radio critic of the *Northern Whig* took Linenhall Street to task over the issue:

> The BBC is always a little eager to avoid controversy, a weakness for which I can see no excuse. Why this terror of offending someone, of hurting the feelings of some delicate suburbanite? . . . Are we afraid of treading on someone's toes? People's toes should not be so sensitive. My own beliefs and cherished opinions are constantly offended whenever I go to the cinema or to lectures, and whenever I read newspapers. Yet I and thousands like me do not go a-wailing to the authorities demanding that those with whom we disagree be silenced lest they do irreparable harm to our souls.[102]

It was, however, to take more than a decade before the BBC in Northern Ireland began to admit the possibility of debate. Even then, the basic division in Northern Ireland's society was not at first on the agenda.

One initiative was taken in this period in the field of music that proved controversial in the long term. It occurred after the Directorship of Music in Belfast changed hands in 1937, when Godfrey Brown retired and was replaced by Walton O'Donnell. The new Director had a background in military music, having been Director of the BBC's Military Band in London for the previous decade. He was widely and affectionately known as 'Bandy' O'Donnell. When he arrived in Belfast, he made a strong commitment to the development of music in the region. He stated that he strongly favoured the encouragement of native music and said he would devote particular attention to the work of promising Ulster composers. 'I understand,' he said, 'that quite a lot has been done in the matter of research in folk music which may be made suitable material for an orchestra. It is essential, however, I believe, that local composers should follow the Northern Ireland folk tune idiom.'[103] From the BBC's own orchestra a player emerged who offered original orchestrated arrangements of Irish dance and song tunes. Henry McMullan, then the experienced Ulsterman on the BBC's staff, recounted what happened: 'Bandy came to my office one day and said, "You know David Curry has got a group and they are

97

playing what he calls Irish dance music and he wants me to audition it and see whether it would make a programme"'. Bandy said he knew nothing about Irish dance music and therefore invited McMullan to come and hear it. McMullan did not know much either. 'I knew the ceili bands because we used them all the time. So I went up and talked to David and his group played a couple of things and when I was asked what I thought of them I said, "I like them and they are eminently saleable"'. McMullan added, when asked if they were genuine: 'They are sort of genuine. They are a rather sophisticated ceili band operation which I am quite sure will go down well in England.' So began *Irish Rhythms* which were to prove the most successful programmes ever produced on radio in Northern Ireland. David Curry arranged and composed the music, conducting it himself for over thirty years. *Irish Rhythms* was relayed to Britain constantly and taken by broadcasting systems in Europe and elsewhere in the world. Henry McMullan recalled: '*Irish Rhythms* came under a good deal of attack because, of course, it was suggested that it wasn't representative of Northern Ireland. Various pressures were put on to get it stopped because it was giving a wrong impression of Northern Ireland and because it was claimed to belong to a "foreign culture"'.[104] It should be said that Curry was also attacked by the traditional musicians who maintained that his arrangements were a perversion of purity.

The retirement of Godfrey Brown in 1937 marked the end of an era in the history of the BBC in Northern Ireland. He had worked tirelessly from 1924 to provide musical programmes and to build the BBC's Orchestra. He had, through the Orchestra and through the Philharmonic Society, made an enormous individual contribution to the musical life of the region in the 1920s and 1930s. He was highly regarded by the BBC in London, and Reith in his diaries recorded an appreciation of him.[105] The success of the Orchestra, judged by attendance at public concerts, was uneven during his time. The packed houses at weekly concerts gave way in the later thirties to less frequent and less well-patronised functions, although occasionally, as, for example, when Elizabeth Schumann performed with the Orchestra, hundreds had to be turned away.

The achievement of the BBC in music in this period did not go unchallenged. The music critic of the *Belfast Telegraph*, 'Rathcol' (the Ulster musician, Norman Hay), was a consistent critic of the Corporation's activities and policies. He wrote from the point of

98

view of an u̇...·ᵗ d elitist. 'Music is no longer the cherished mistress of the connoisseur. It is now the handmaid of the million . . . It is the age of the wireless and the gramophone: is the world the better for it? Is there a real growth of music among the millions?' 'Rathcol' diagnosed the disadvantages of broadcast music as:

The imperfect, uncertain transmission . . . The eternal insistence on music without ceasing, which is breeding a race who hear without listening, or else who, listening, have but rarely the power to appreciate. The daily and nightly onslaught of trash. The slow but sure killing of home music-making . . .

'Rathcol' again and again expressed a resentment:

Are we going to go on accepting tamely all that these mightly pundits of superior English stock in the BBC devise for the good of our soul's good? 'Is Ulster sleeping?' asked an eminent literary man visiting Belfast [St John Ervine] – a man whose reputation is almost worldwide and who, when invited to broadcast, had his script ruthlessly 'cut' and tampered with. Is Ulster, indeed, sleeping?[106]

'They have blossomed forth,' 'Rathcol' wrote four years later, in 1939,

as the self-appointed mentors of Ulster musicians. They have a lofty desire to propagate Ulster music, always provided that they have not merely a finger, but both hands in the making of the pie. Witness the present position of the Belfast Philharmonic Society, which, as I have already pointed out, is within the octopodous grip of the BBC even to the extent of having to satisfy that totalitarian body as to the choice of the music it performs. How long is Ulster going to stand for this dictatorship?[107]

'Rathcol' in his attacks on the BBC did at times reveal the details of negotiations which perhaps the BBC would not have wished to have made public. He endeavoured to show that the original sixpenny concerts in 1930 were a deliberate attempt to undercut alternative commercial arrangements. In 1939 he disclosed that when the BBC was asked by Belfast Corporation to continue its concerts in the Ulster Hall it had insisted on a range of higher prices because the concerts had been losing money. The BBC, so 'Rathcol' stated, had in any case suggested that 'it was desirable to cater for a wealthier class of audience, one official actually hinting that an audience of the evening-dress order of society ought to be cultivated'. The Belfast Corporation refused to countenance either this suggestion or the price rises. 'Rathcol' then praised the retired Godfrey Brown for his efforts to provide an alternative series of concerts but alleged that when the BBC was asked to allow some of its players to perform with the alternative orchestra, it responded with 'a blank refusal'.[108]

'Rathcol' may not have been an unbiased observer but his critical appraisal of the BBC's role needs to be taken into account alongside the positive, more appreciative assessments which were common.[109]

There was one field in which the pre-war BBC made little progress in Northern Ireland, that of schools' broadcasting. In one of his last reports to the Board of Governors before the outbreak of war, the Regional Director tried to account for the failure. In the first instance he suggested that the reorganisation of the educational system subsequent to the establishment of Northern Ireland had impeded the introduction of the new medium. Then the reception of the programmes off air had not been good for some time. A weak signal came from Daventry and the early demonstrations of wireless in the classroom for teachers had been complete failures. The reputation established then had been hard to repair. Marshall offered his third reason: 'Northern Ireland, being a self-contained unit with a two-thirds Protestant and loyalist majority, has always been more concerned with questions of politics and religion than anything else, as well as a strong predilection for everything pertaining to the six counties of which Northern Ireland is composed. Those, therefore, connected with education in the Province have always retorted to the Corporation's suggestions about the use of wireless in schools that Ulster topics should be provided for the scholars, and that until this is done, little or no progress will be made.'[110] Marshall had, during the late thirties, organised a number of demonstrations and conferences and these had, on the surface, seemed to go well. However, the number of schools in the region using broadcasts had scarcely reached one hundred by September 1939.

There was, perhaps, another reason which inhibited the advance of schools' broadcasting in Northern Ireland. Laurence Lynch, a Catholic science teacher, had attended one of the BBC conferences and afterwards wrote in the *Irish News* a long critical article on his experience: 'Looking at the programmes listed for the coming year, I read that the talks to children will include one on "The Succession of Life on Earth", another on "Evidences of Evolution", again another on "Causes of Evolution" and still another on "The Ancestors of

Man"'. Mr Lynch wrote of 'this travesty of education' and then launched into a diatribe against the theory of evolution which took up almost thirty inches in the newspaper's columns. He concluded, '. . . it is obvious that the BBC has departed very far from the ABC in its apparent desire for good. In so doing it is making it impossible for all teachers to welcome its efforts to help in the work of education, and depriving particular schools of services to which they have a right.'[111] If such an attitude was prevalent, and it probably was, Catholic schools in Northern Ireland at the time were unlikely to become avid users of BBC broadcasts.

Throughout 1939 the British Broadcasting Corporation was preparing its plans for what it would do on the outbreak of war. By the spring it had finalised its arrangements for the staff: the posts of those who were called up would be held open for them until their return; those who volunteered for the armed forces would be similarly treated provided they requested it. All such BBC employees, conscripted or volunteers, would be entitled to have their service pay supplemented where necessary to bring their earnings up to the level of their BBC pay.

As far as the BBC itself was concerned the war plan was to disperse the production centres so that they would be less likely to be attacked from the air. All transmitters were to be synchronised on two wavelengths; if they remained transmitting independently on local regional wavelengths they would effectively provide enemy aircraft with distinctive radio beams by which they could plot their way to targets. This synchronisation was to have one immediate effect: regional broadcasting would end for the duration of the war. The Northern Ireland regional service would close, like other regional services. Another incidental consequence of the fact that enemy aircraft could use local transmitter signals in this way was that Radio Éireann would become useful to them. In order to prevent this the BBC picked up and relayed Radio Éireann over a consider-able portion of the British Isles during the early years of the war. The Irish Government was not told of this arrangement for some time.

In September 1939 war was declared. Almost the whole Northern Ireland Orchestra immediately joined up and other members of staff were transferred to England. On the last night of transmission, Henry McMullan, then Assistant Director of Programmes, remembered:

I was in the little news studio in what we called 'the extension' – that part

101

which had been added to the original linen warehouse in 1934 and included the Regional Director's office and a canteen. There was nobody in the building except me, the commissionaire and the engineers. The last broadcast consisted of a series of announcements. I remember the last of all being a request for anyone with nursing experience in Northern Ireland to register. This was, of course, because of what was thought to be the imminent threat of bombing. 'Good night! Good bye! Regional broadcasting is coming to an end until the end of the war.' I remember going down the stairs and getting into my car and that was the first time I had ever driven at night with the headlights almost completely blacked out. It was most eerie. I drove back home in a state of utter depression.[112]

In spite of the closedown, the building of the new Broadcasting House next door went on and was completed in 1941. It was a firm indication that the BBC intended to return to regional broadcasting.

For those very few who worked in the BBC in Northern Ireland before the Second World War and who were to experience life in the new Broadcasting House after it, the earlier period had some characteristics which clearly distinguished it from later times. The style of life in Linenhall Street was amateur, although in the studio the fact that all broadcasts were live and scripted imposed a rigid discipline on performance. It was a discipline to some extent welcome, for the programme staff was almost entirely English and Scottish and felt alien and insecure. They were also grateful that politics were excluded from broadcasting, although somewhat inevitably they tended to support the Unionist regime because their existence in Ireland depended on it. The ethos of their programming was middle-class and Reithian in that they believed that the audience could be improved as well as entertained. The reliability and correctness of the BBC's values was vouchsafed in 1933 by a young Church of Ireland cleric who was one day to become Archbishop of Dublin. The Reverend Alan Buchanan in a broadcast Sunday address, pleaded,

... in the name of God, I ask the film producers if they are trying to destroy our modern civilization by the same habits and practices as wrought the downfall of Greece and Rome. If I have used the courtesy of the BBC to attack another interest I apologise sincerely. But this is not an attack. It is an appeal, I appeal to the cinema industry to produce programmes as wholesome and up-lifting as the BBC itself . . .[113]

The pre-war staff had good intentions and sought earnestly to give the best that local resources and budget constraints would allow.

They endeavoured to reflect the region and encouraged talent with this end in view. It should be remembered that there were few of them. In 1924 there was a Station Director and three assistants or producers. In 1939 there was a Regional Director and fifteen assistants.

An assessment of what the Belfast staff achieved is available from an unusual source. In 1944, Deasun O'Raghaille, a young Cork science graduate with an interest in radio, published a booklet entitled *A Listener's Opinion* in Tralee, Co Kerry. He wrote of Belfast:

Before the war this station was, in many ways, doing much more for Irish broadcasting than the stations on this side of the Border . . .

The Belfast Station encouraged young Irish writers, which is more than Radio Éireann has done. They broadcast several series of 'Irish Tales', and in selecting these tales, they selected the stories on their merits alone, no matter what side of the Border they came from, and whether the writer had made a big name in writing or no.

They introduced new ideas into the broadcasting of Irish ceilidh music. I am not competent to say whether these changes were orthodox from the point of view of Irish music, but from the ordinary listener's point of view they transformed what was becoming the monotonous beat and steady rhythm of Irish dance tunes into lively airs and sparkling melody.

These Irish tunes as played in Belfast were called 'Irish Rhythms' and became world famous . . . why should change in form be deplored? Surely if the music be really alive it must change with the times. At any rate, Radio Éireann gave no sign they had seen any change . . .

I could quote many other instances of the Belfast Station beating Radio Éireann at its own game, as it were, and making a better hand of serving the Irish public. For instance, some years ago a comparison drawn between the St Patrick's Day features broadcast from both stations reflected anything but favourably on our own service . . .[114]

Deasun O'Raghaille may have been using the Belfast stick to beat the Dublin ass — the subtitle of his booklet was *Improvements needed in Radio Éireann* — yet there is no doubt Linenhall Street had a creditable record as an Irish station.

Reflections of two who worked there are significant in many ways. Henry McMullan recalled in 1974 that broadcasting in Belfast before the war 'bore no resemblance to life as we live it now in the BBC. It was a question of somebody putting their head around the door and saying "The Orchestra is on the air in two minutes and we can't find the announcer". I would hastily don my dinner jacket and rush up to the studio – I mean literally people wore dinner jackets in case somebody arrived in a dinner jacket and one would appear rude if one wasn't in one too. We all kept dinner jackets in Linenhall Street. When I say "all", there weren't many of us.'[115]

Ursula Eason, a young Londoner who came in 1932 to run *Children's Hour,* remembered in 1983:

> It never occurred to me that I might not be welcome, provided I could do the job. I did get a number of letters criticising the fact that I was English and my accent, saying they couldn't understand me and why didn't I speak plain English. But what I felt was very wrong was that I should pretend and try to put on a local accent. I would use local words, like 'throughother' and 'scunner'. I was aware that quite a lot of the stuff we were doing was quite outside the local audience and that we must draw more material from the Province but it was quite hard to find writers . . . I was very keen to do a lot of folklore programmes, traditional stories and the great sagas. I remember doing a three-part drama on Cuchulainn. I would have liked to have done more. Of course, what we didn't do in *Children's Hour* were stories about the present day in Ulster. That was to come after the War.[116]

A notable characteristic of pre-war broadcasting was that every word spoken over the air had to be scripted, including of course *Children's Hour.* Ursula Eason commented on this tyranny of the script which is quite alien to broadcasting today:

> Yes, I would entirely agree that it was a tyranny now. I would not have at the time because I was nervous. I think I was more nervous because I was not a native of the place. I had to understand the difficulties, the prejudices and the divisions from the outside. For an outsider it was extremely difficult. So that the script to me was a lifeline, a safety piece. But what a lot of poor broadcasting, actual performances, as a result.[117]

Henry McMullan felt that the prescribed use of scripts was only a tyranny for some:

> I think it was absolutely true in case of somebody who wasn't used to script reading. Of course most of our actors – you have to accept that there was a group of actors in Northern Ireland who appeared a great deal, possibly too frequently, but they were the best of the acting talent – they became completely acclimatised . . . The most important thing about broadcasting then was that it was live. I always felt that when tape recording came into studio and video-tape recording into televison a bit of flash went out of the performance . . .[118]

104

McMullan, who became Head of Programmes in 1945, felt on his return from war service that regional broadcasting had to change from what it had been before the war. He put it this way in 1974: 'There was a feeling among the people I worked with then that we must stop sitting on one side of the fence and sit on top of the fence and get everybody to play with us.'[119]

4

The War Years and After

After closedown on 3 September 1939 Linenhall Street was a fairly empty place. The Regional Director, two programme staff, an administrator and studio engineers remained in and around the premises. The programme people were Ursula Eason, who had just been made acting Programme Director having been assistant, or producer, in charge of *Children's Hour* since 1932, and James Mageean, drama assistant. As they were the only producers permanently in Belfast until the end of the war, the number of programmes produced there was small.

At first there were none. From September until the New Year there was no production whatsoever. The ostensible reason why Belfast was not asked to contribute to either the Home or Forces Programmes was that the lines to Britain were 'chancey'.[1] The Post Office could not make them available with any certainty because of the war. The radio link had ceased to exist once all BBC transmitters were synchronised. Contact with the rest of the system had to be by telephone or post. When the Northern Ireland Government wished to have announcements made over the air to the population of the region, the text had to be telephoned to Glasgow and read out from the studios there. Ursula Eason recalled:

> One felt totally isolated. I was not used to being Programme Director. I had done *Children's Hour* and that was all, apart from an occasional evening programme. What should I do? How could I prepare for when we would start again? Not knowing if the War itself would start or what would happen, I wasted those first few months. The Regional Director felt the same way. We were not able to record or we might have recorded a few plays and had them on ice for when they were wanted. Our link was entirely with the lines and we hadn't got any lines . . . We just followed the news, read the monitoring reports and tried to keep in touch. I felt terribly sorry that people in Northern Ireland couldn't be reflected in any kind of way. Not that very much was happening here. Everything was waiting, waiting . . .[2]

It is difficult to say why Belfast was allowed to continue as a production centre. Marshall, the Regional Director, had himself recommended that it should cease to be so and that he himself be left on his own to look after the interests of the Corporation. He could oversee the building of the new Broadcasting House and maintain liaison with the Northern Ireland Government. London clearly dithered for some time about what to do.

By December it had become apparent, however, that the Post Office could provide lines through Glasgow, which would be available twice a week provided three weeks' notice was given. There was, however, a real reluctance in Head Office to involve Belfast in programming. 'There is a good deal of programme policy mixed up with the line restrictions in programmes from Northern Ireland,' wrote a BBC executive, 'so I would be careful how much . . . you pass back to Northern Ireland.' When it was discovered that lines would be available, he added, 'I learned that Assistant Controller (Programmes) was rather upset because he had hoped that the line situation would eliminate Belfast! . . .'[3]

Now that it was possible to begin production again, talks, outside broadcasts and only a very occasional studio programme were all that could be attempted. Ursula Eason reflected years later, 'It was quite hard to get material accepted because some of it was not of a very good standard and because we were a very small region. It was really only news that was wanted.' The tiny staff, however, were determined not only to justify themselves but also to ensure that Northern Ireland was reflected on the Home and Forces Programmes. 'People across the water in Britain simply did not know Northern Ireland, unlike Southern Ireland which they knew was neutral.'[4] It was not surprising, therefore, that one of the first programmes from Belfast was a talk on 'Ulster's Part in the War', given by the Prime Minister, Lord Craigavon.[5] Production gradually picked up and during the three weeks from 3 to 23 March 1940 the Belfast studios produced the following:

2 Cinema Organ Recitals (Home)
2 Variety programmes from the Empire Theatre (Forces)
2 Talks (Home)
1 Association Football Match (Forces)
1 Northern Ireland Entertainments National Service Association (NIENSA) Concert (Forces)
1 St Patrick's Day Programme (Home)

1 Contribution to *Children's Hour* lasting 30 minutes (Home)
1 *Irish Rhythms* (Forces)

The last three were studio based. *Irish Rhythms* was provided by David Curry who kept an orchestra going through most of the war and was given frequent engagements by the BBC. Thus the Irish Rhythms Orchestra was to be a participant in the St Patrick's Day programme which was offered to Head Office as early as January. Ursula Eason's detailed proposals were accepted without enthusiasm.[6] The eventual broadcast was castigated by the radio critic of the *Glasgow Herald*, and the views he expressed were shared by BBC executives:

'Gallumfry' . . . the St Patrick's Day programme from Northern Ireland, certainly lived up to its title, which means a mixture. A set dance and a reel, played by the Irish Rhythm Orchestra, an inconclusive little playlet, a contralto solo, and a choral hymn by the Queen's Island Male Voice Choir were flung at the listener in a rather 'take-it-or-leave-it' fashion, no attempt being made to bind the mixture together.

The fact that the programme began five minutes late owing to the exuberances of *The Dream of Gerontius* did not prevent it ending a minute or two before its time, so that sympathy with the producer on that count proved unnecessary. Altogether one felt that Northern Ireland had not wasted much effort on the broadcast . . .[7]

The fact that the programme had been made in the Belfast studios, however, served an unexpected purpose. It meant that the studios were not available when Radio Éireann sought to hire them to make a St Patrick's Day programme in Belfast for its own listeners. Marshall, the Regional Director, had an immediate excuse for refusing the request of his opposite number in Dublin, Dr T. J. Kiernan, but he was determined not to co-operate in any case.

Since the outbreak of war relations between Northern Ireland and Éire had steadily deteriorated. The Unionist Government regarded the south's policy of neutrality as treacherous and favoured non-co-operation with the régime. The British Government did not share this Unionist view; on the contrary, it endeavoured to encourage good relations. Its purpose was to secure an accommodation with Dublin or to persuade the Irish Government to enter the war. The British Government desperately needed the naval bases in Éire which it had handed over to de Valera as a gesture of friendship in 1938.

'The Treaty Ports' of Cobh and Lough Swilly would enable it to conduct the war in the Atlantic much more effectively.

So when the Dominions Office, which was responsible for conducting the British Government's relations with Éire, learned of Dr Kiernan's request for studio facilities in Belfast, it was very keen that the BBC should accommodate him. Marshall, who took his line from Stormont, obstructed. Consultation inside the BBC went as high as the Director General who let it be known 'that he did not wish any pressure to be brought to bear on Mr Marshall and that the studios are not to be lent to Kiernan (whatever the Dominions Office may say) unless Mr Marshall himself changed his mind about it.'[8] By this time Kiernan had made a second request. He would like studio facilities at any time 'to suit Belfast's convenience' for a broadcast version of a parlour game. Marshall's interpretation of this inquiry was that Kiernan wanted studio space 'for a team of about ten or more people who would undoubtedly be Irish Nationalists who would be selected by Éire'. This request could not be dismissed as the first had been on the grounds that the facilities were not available. The Home Office was consulted; it contacted the Home Department in Northern Ireland and got a negative answer, 'having regard to the present situation'.[9] Marshall was asked to deal with Kiernan on a friendly informal basis. He was told that 'in turning down Kiernan's request, he should not involve either the Home Office or the Dominions Office, but say that he felt obliged to consult the Northern Ireland authorities and that, as a result, he did not feel able to accept responsibility for arranging such a broadcast in these times. (Again, it was stressed that it was undesirable for Marshall to present the case as if he had had special *orders* from the Government ruling out such broadcasts.)'[10] So Marshall telephoned Kiernan and completely mystified him, as he gave no hint that the Northern Ireland Ministry of Home Affairs was behind the refusal.

Marshall had no sooner dealt with this than he got a request from within the BBC for studio facilities on St Patrick's Day. The Overseas Service wished Sean O'Faolain, the Cork author, to give a talk from Belfast. Marshall could not accede to the request, having turned down Radio Éireann. In order to be consistent he had to insist that O'Faolain must broadcast from a studio in Britain; this O'Faolain did, although it was at very short notice.

Marshall was very annoyed with the Overseas Service over the incident and seized the lateness and inopportuneness of the request to ask for a new and more precise version of the ruling which had been given in 1937 that he should be consulted in all cases where BBC departments were considering programmes on Ireland. He recalled once again the case of the singing of 'The Soldier's Song' which he had brought up then and he cited two recent instances of 'provocative' statements in news bulletins. He admitted these 'would probably seem childish to the average Englishman, but in this Region are looked upon as of paramount importance'. He pointed out, 'we live on the spot and are conversant with the problems peculiar to Ireland – problems which cannot be understood by anyone living across the water'. Marshall came to the point:

'. . . what I am anxious to ensure is *prior* consultation, that is, reference to this Region before any commitments with Dublin are made, or in fact, any plans put in hand which might either directly or indirectly impinge on Northern Ireland and thus cause friction which, particularly at the present juncture, might result from apparently trifling causes. The activities of certain lawless people are giving the Government of Northern Ireland a great deal of anxiety, and we have to exercise the greatest possible care to avoid saying or doing anything which might add to its difficulties. The present situation may prove to be more serious than the average person thinks, and I would therefore urge that I be kept informed in advance about any projected contacts with Eire or programmes dealing with it . . .[11]

Marshall's appeal was received sympathetically and the Controller of Programmes issued the following memo to all senior members of BBC staff:

RELATIONS BETWEEN EIRE AND NORTHERN IRELAND

19 April 1940

Relations between Eire and Northern Ireland are at the moment extremely delicate, and without going into all the political complications, I should like you and members of your staff to realise that they must be careful about (a) any arrangements to do with programmes from either country, and (b) any reference in their own programmes to either country.

The following should be adopted as working rules:

1 No commitment for a broadcast from Northern Ireland should be entered into without prior reference to Northern Ireland Director.
2 No commitment for a broadcast from Eire should be entered into except through Assistant Controller Operator, who will be responsible for prior consultation with Northern Ireland Director.

3 No programme dealing with either country should be prepared without reference to Northern Ireland Director.

4 Reference to either country in news bulletins and elsewhere should be carefully watched.[12]

Marshall had now found a role and significance for himself. He may have had nothing to do from the outbreak of war until January 1940, and very little to do from then until April, but from that month forward he was forever busy. He expected to be kept informed of all BBC programmes which had anything whatsoever to do with Ireland. In case he was not informed he listened assiduously to his radio and if he missed any item undesirable from the Northern Ireland Government's point of view he could always be told about it by one of the Cabinet Ministers whom he met in the Ulster Club, where he lunched every day.

In the meantime, the Dominions Office was seriously looking into the question of improving relations with Éire. It asked the BBC if Nazi broadcasts to Ireland could be jammed and if it was known how many people in Éire listened to BBC broadcasts. The Dominions Office wondered if items of special Irish or Catholic interest might be stressed in order to win a greater audience. It made one inquiry which directly concerned Belfast. It was forwarded to Marshall.

Whether it would be practicable to introduce a Gaelic period into the programmes broadcast from the Belfast Station, ostensibly for the benefit of Gaelic speaking people in Northern Ireland and among the Irish population of English and Scottish cities.[13]

Marshall replied:

I do not quite understand what the Dominions Office mean by the introduction of a Gaelic period into the programmes broadcast from the Belfast station, because they ought to know by this time that there is no separate programme from Belfast. Quite apart from that, however, you might point out that there are no Gaelic speakers in Northern Ireland, by which I assume is meant Erse or Irish, and the Scottish items in Gaelic certainly fall on deaf ears as far as this area is concerned.

From another point of view, however, it would be most unwise to introduce the Irish language into programmes from the transmitter in Northern Ireland, as this would certainly bring a great deal of criticism from listeners in this Region. Surely all items in Irish should be reserved for Athlone.[14]

Soon after, the war began to go very badly for Britain on the Continent and on the Atlantic. Greater efforts were needed to entice

111

Éire into the war; de Valera was even offered the end of partition as the price of his involvement. The Northern Ireland Government was not, of course, party to these negotiations.

The Ministry charged with the task of conducting propaganda during the war was the Ministry of Information and although its relationship with the BBC was somewhat amorphous, it was in a position to direct the BBC to carry out its policies. The Ministry of Information, in pursuit of the Government's Irish objectives, consequently issued the following directive to the BBC:

> It is generally inadvisable to engage in controversy or propaganda about the Partition of Ireland. If, however, there is important Irish news which makes it inevitable that the question will be raised, the point to be consistently made is that Partition is a problem for the Irish themselves to solve: the British Government would be ready to accept any agreement reached by the different sections of the Irish people. In other words, the agitation against the British Government and people on this point is made at the wrong address.[15]

As the British Government pressed for a policy of rapprochement with the Irish Government and people to be expressed in part through broadcasting, Marshall found himself in a position to frustrate its endeavours. He shared the view of the Northern Ireland Government that the British Government's policy amounted to appeasement. He was determined that nothing in programmes on the Home and Forces services would be allowed to offend the Northern Ireland Government or the unionist majority and as a consequence he, in effect, operated on their behalf.

Marshall had the power and interfered all the time in programme plans and scripts with a view to altering or suppressing them in the Northern Ireland interest. When programme makers failed to follow the required procedures he alerted the Controller of Programmes, as, for instance, in July 1940, when he received a request to book James McCafferty, a well-known singer from Derry who had given many performances from the Belfast studios before the war. McCafferty had, in fact, already been approached by a producer and asked to submit a list of songs he would be prepared to sing. Marshall refused to do anything because he had not been consulted about the intended programme. He pointed out to the Controller that McCafferty had already been used by the same producer earlier in the year without his knowledge. 'As you are well aware it is not only the question of programmes, but also the artistes into whose antecedents we have now to enquire very closely, and although it happens McCafferty's credentials are in order, this does not absolve compilers of programmes from consulting me in advance.'[16] Marshall requested that programme staff be reminded of the need for prior consultation with him. Within a short time, however, Marshall, with a certain air of triumph, was able to inform Head Office that henceforth travel permits would not be issued to artistes resident in Northern Ireland and this ruling was 'absolutely rigid'.[17]

Later in the year, in November 1940, two instances of programmes concerned with Ireland which gave rise to controversy permitted Marshall to intervene and strengthen his hand. The political commentator, Commander Stephen King-Hall, gave a talk on *Children's Hour* about the combined defence of both parts of partitioned Ireland. His observations were not far removed from the concepts which were being aired in Whitehall at the time. His broadcast provoked a strong reaction in Belfast: there were letters in the papers and the Northern Ireland Government made representations in Whitehall and complained to the BBC's Director General. The Controller of Programmes responded to Marshall, who had pointed out that he had not been consulted, that it was none of his business as King-Hall's talk was a news talk. Marshall fought back, quoting the Controller's circular to programme staff: 'Northern Ireland Director should be consulted in advance on *any reference whatsoever to Ireland in our programmes.*' He pointed out that already earlier in the year he had asked that news talks about Ireland should be referred to him because of 'an unfortunate news talk to schools on Irish affairs which offended the Nationalist party here . . . I would submit with respect that I am in a better position to judge of the effect of such a talk in the region, than either an executive in the Talks Department or certain people in the Ministry of Information, and the fact remains that the talk did give grave offence to the Northern Ireland Government, as well as to many other people.'[18]

At the same time as the King-Hall controversy was going on, another arose. It was prompted by a programme entitled *Music from Éire* given by a well-known quartet. Some of the items broadcast infuriated listeners in Northern Ireland. Marshall had not, of course, been informed about the programme, so he tackled the producer:

Actually I know that it is difficult for you and others to appreciate the reason for such consultation but, even in a programme of straight music,

113

the touchiness of people in Ireland is such that we frequently have to delete songs and other musical items from our programmes, and in fact, it is a constant worry to us here to have to spend so much time on such an apparently trivial matter. Such songs as, for example, 'The Minstrel Boy' offend certain sections of the public, while 'The Boyne Water' offends another and these are two examples out of many.[19]

Marshall was very much aware that Éire's neutrality had heightened unionist sensitivities and sectarian attitudes generally. In December, the Controller of Programmes backed down and issued a directive, No. 47, to all programme staff that they must consult Marshall on all Irish programme matters. He pointed out that this included last-minute topical talks and 'music (e.g. Thomas Moore's songs)'.[20]

It would not have been surprising had those who made programmes in London and elsewhere felt increasingly, as they were to in somewhat similar circumstances after the war, that programmes on Ireland or referring to Ireland in any way were simply not worth the trouble. The BBC was, however, under strong pressure from the Ministry of Information to produce programmes designed to encourage listening in Éire.

The Ministry of Information began to push the matter. 'Will you consider whether there is anything the BBC can do which it is not now doing to attract Irish listeners, i.e. Éire listeners. Both this Ministry and the Dominions Office are anxious that as many Southern Irish people as possible should be led to listen to British programmes, and particularly British bulletins,' wrote the Director of the Ministry's Broadcasting Division to the Controller of Programmes, BBC.[21] Marshall was duly asked for suggestions; his reply was totally negative. The Controller felt that the BBC would have to do better than that but the programme boards failed to come up with worthwhile suggestions, although one proposal put forward was ultimately to be acted on. It was felt that an Irish programme close to a news bulletin might attract Irish listeners and hold them for the bulletin.[22]

In January 1941 the Ministry for Information indicated its determination that the BBC programmes for St Patrick's Day should be of real worth and should appeal to all Irishmen.[23] Ursula Eason, unknowingly, offered a similar Northern Ireland based programme to the one so poorly received in the previous year. It was not what Head Office had in mind. Marshall, however, held out: 'Any St Patrick's Day feature in the Home and Overseas programmes should be confined to Northern Ireland from which we could present something appropriate to the occasion, but not along the lines suggested by the MOI. If Éire must be represented then the programme should, I suggest, be taken from Dublin, where I assume a special St Patrick's Day programme is being arranged, but there again we must have the script in advance.'[24] What was eventually proposed was a joint programme with Radio Éireann which included outside broadcasts from the Empire Theatre in Belfast where Jimmy O'Dea, the Dublin comedian, was appearing, and from the Abbey Theatre in Dublin where the microphone would pick up the final act of an Ulster play which was being performed there.

Before it was even broadcast, this joint programme was bitterly attacked in Northern Ireland. Under the title, 'More Appeasement', the *Northern Whig* devoted a leader to it:

We invite the attention of our readers to the curious programme for St Patrick's Day which has specially been arranged by the BBC. It is to consist of a joint entertainment from Éire and Northern Ireland and will ignore the political frontier. There is no sort of hint that Ulster is fighting side by side in the War against Germany and Italy while Éire is nominally neutral, but is actually aiding the Empire's foes in a number of ways . . . The pretence is that Ireland is united, that Éire is still part of the British Empire, that in fact all might be well were it not for the recalcitrance of Ulster. This is the short-sighted spirit of Munich all over again . . .[25]

The Northern Ireland Government was protesting behind the scenes about 'shaking hands with murder'.[26] On the night, the timing in the programme went wrong: in Belfast, the microphone picked up an unsuitable sequence by arriving too early at the Empire Theatre and in Dublin it came up during the interval with the pit orchestra playing some execrable music. Fortunately the programme was saved from complete disaster by other items. Marshall was not put out, remarking that 'we did not wish to collaborate with Éire at all'.[27] The *Irish Times* radio critic was quite enthusiastic but that may have been more for political than artistic reasons.[28]

The negotiations for this programme, especially those in Dublin, had been carried out for the BBC by Denis Johnston, the Dublin playwright who had joined the Corporation in 1937. Johnston had been sent to Dublin in July 1940 to explore the possibility of providing talks from there for the BBC's Overseas Service. He had been set a considerable task because he had to persuade the Éire authorities to let him do it, Radio Éireann to provide facilities and then to get the scripts passed by the Éire censors, by Marshall in

Northern Ireland and by the British censors. He was constantly under Marshall's surveillance because Belfast was meant to be his base. Johnston knew Marshall of old from his period in 1937 and 1938 when he was features writer for the Northern Ireland Region. Since that time he had been with BBC Television until the War closed it down and thereafter had been the BBC's liaison officer with broadcasters from the United States stationed in Britain. Although he had to censor their despatches, he was popular with them and in fact, on being sent to Dublin, he was invited to prepare talks from there for the US radio networks.

In February 1941 a meeting took place in London at the Ministry of Information attended by top Ministry of Information officials and BBC executives, with Denis Johnston present. The Ministry's policy of addressing programmes to Éire and Éire citizens was discussed. It was felt that if, as under Directive No. 47, programmes were referred 'invariably to Northern Ireland they would quite frequently conflict with the wishes of the Northern Ireland Government, whose wishes the Northern Ireland Director is bound to consider. The development of programmes for Irish listeners from London would be considerably simplified if it could be divorced from considerations of Northern Ireland policy.' It was concluded that a Ministry ruling to this effect should be obtained before there was a commitment to Irish programmes on any scale.[29] It had become quite clear that the Ministry of Information's view was not that of the Northern Ireland Government and that reference to Marshall in Belfast was not desirable.[30] Marshall was somewhat alarmed.[31]

The Ministry of Information began to press even more determinedly for programmes for Éire, and it was leaked to the BBC that a directive was on the way.[32] Denis Johnston's role and advice were considered essential. It was also made clear that if the BBC needed Irish speakers and artistes for programmes, travel restrictions would be removed for them.

Johnston was pushing ahead with the arrangements for his own talks from Dublin and at the same time was furnishing a range of programme suggestions aimed at fulfilling the Ministry of Information's policy objectives. Inside the BBC another Dublin man, Lynton Fletcher, also produced an elaborate memorandum of similar suggestions.[33] Marshall became aware that things were happening in which he had no part, so he wrote to the Controller of Programmes, copying the letter to the Director General, 'You will recall that it was agreed that, before anything of this sort was done,

I was to be fully informed of the proposals and given an opportunity of consulting the Northern Ireland Government in order to discover their general attitude to the scheme.'[34] Marshall was, however, still kept in the dark. The expected directive from the Ministry of Information that programmes for Éire must be provided had arrived.

At the same time Belfast was administered a severe snub. Ursula Eason had made strong representations that there should be a special talk to mark the twentieth anniversary of Northern Ireland's foundation with the new Prime Minister, J. M. Andrews, as speaker. The proposal was firmly rejected. Comments behind the scenes by senior BBC executives included: 'I do not think in these days we want to stress the tragic division in Ireland itself' and 'I'm inclined to leave the Ulster–Éire stew alone for the minute'.[35]

The discussions within the BBC ranged over a variety of formats for a regular Irish programme. Some advocated a magazine-type programme which would include serious informational items; others favoured pure entertainment. When the Northern Ireland Prime Minister learned that the argument was running in favour of the former and that its title would likely be *Irish Magazine*, he wrote immediately to the Director General:

I have no very precise information as to the scope of the new programme, but it seems to me that the term 'Irish' implies that the material will cover both Ulster and Éire, and I am reinforced in this by information which I have received that Mr P. Whelan has called at our Ulster Office in London and asked for our co-operation and to be supplied with Northern Ireland material. I understand that references to Ulster Regiments are to be included in the programme and that the object of the broadcasts will be to interest 'Ireland', both North and South, and Irishmen everywhere, in the war effort, by telling them and the world how Irishmen are helping in the present struggle.

This, in my view, would be an insidious form of propaganda which would entirely misrepresent the position of Northern Ireland in the United Kingdom and would slur over the neutral and most unhelpful attitude which Éire has taken up during the war.

I feel sure that, if I am correctly informed of the position, you would not approve of any such proposal, and I feel strongly that steps should be taken to put a stop to propaganda of this character in whatever quarter it may originate.

Andrews added in his own handwriting, 'Why not leave Éire "to plough her lonely furrow"?'[36]

117

Marshall followed this up with a letter to the Director General which concluded:

> The Prime Minister did not wish to go over our head direct to the British Government but, if we can honestly say that the matter is one which we cannot settle, or, in other words, is for the Ministry of Information to decide, then I think that we should make that clear to the Northern Ireland Government, who could then take further steps, if they wish to do so.[37]

The Director General, Ogilvie, who, as a previous Vice-Chancellor of Queen's University, was very familiar with the local scene, replied to the Northern Ireland Prime Minister, saying that the BBC had on reflection decided to confine the programme to material which was fundamentally of Éire interest. 'You ask in your letter: "Why not leave Éire to plough her lone furrow?" We have long felt, however, that we ought to concern ourselves, not so much with Éire, as with those loyal men and women, tens of thousands of them apparently, who, leaving Éire, have joined His Majesty's forces here and elsewhere in the Empire have thrown their lot – plough-teams, lives and all – with our common cause.'[38]

Andrews came back:

> My opinion, for what it is worth, continues to be that, as Éire stands out of the War and refuses even to lend the Ports, she should be left alone. I am speaking of the Empire's interest, for I am firmly of the opinion that a policy of appeasement which has never succeeded with Éire never will succeed and that it is only through strength that she will be got to change her ways.[39]

Andrews clearly persuaded Marshall to add a further gloss in a memo to the Director General. Marshall said that the Prime Minister hoped the programme would be clearly signposted as being for those 'members of the Forces whose homes were in Éire and that that did not mean the people of Éire as a whole.' Marshall went on:

> I feel that he is perfectly logical in this respect, but that it will be extremely difficult to devise a programme limited in this way, and perhaps therefore it might be better to abandon the project entirely rather than to attempt what may prove to be impossible. I certainly agree with the PM that a policy of appeasement is quite useless with Éire – in fact, I told the Controller of Programmes – when it was originally mooted that a programme of this sort would have no effect in helping to achieve the results which apparently the Ministry of Information have in view.[40]

The BBC pressed ahead, having now decided that the Irish programme would have a variety entertainment format. Participants who were suggested were John MacCormack, Jimmy O'Dea, Barbara Mullen – later to be of *Dr Finlay's Casebook* fame – and Delia Murphy. Jimmy O'Dea and Harry O'Donovan were anxious to take part. O'Donovan was to script and Joe Linnane was to compere, besides helping with the production. The programmes were to be made in the BBC's wartime production centre in Bangor, North Wales. *Irish Half Hour,* for that was to be its title, was carefully sold to official Irish circles in advance. John Betjeman, then serving as British Cultural and Press Attaché in Dublin, provided the definition of the purpose of the programmes: it was 'a series which would keep alive among soldiers serving away from home the sense of Irish nationalism in the broadest meaning of the term'.[41] The United Kingdom's Representative in Éire, Sir John Maffey, much approved of the project. The Radio Éireann authorities, although cautious, were enthusiastic and were anxious to be as helpful as possible. Theatrical circles in Dublin were keen because for them the *quid pro quo* was that British artistes were to be allowed to travel to Éire for stage appearances for the first time since the war began.

The producer, Francis Worsley, wished to include 'a few words of Erse, which would be enormously appreciated in some quarters'.[42] He also wanted to know if Delia Murphy was *persona grata,* it being rumoured that she and her husband, Dr T. J. Kiernan, now transferred from the Directorship of Radio Éireann, were pro-German. The Controller of Programmes referred these matters to Marshall in Belfast who immediately consulted the Prime Minister. Andrews replied to Marshall:

> In the first place, I cannot understand what is the underlying aim to be achieved by broadcasts on the lines suggested and particularly by including in them greetings in Erse which is a language expressive of separatism. I have no hesitation in saying that there would be considerable resentment in Northern Ireland if Erse were spoken during the broadcasts. It occurs to me also to mention that, as I understand these programmes are intended for loyal Irishmen in the British Forces, I cannot see why greetings should be given in a language which is so little understood.
>
> Secondly, I am satisfied that our people generally would take the strongest possible exception to the inclusion in any of these broadcasts of a lady alleged to be pro-German in her sympathies.

My view is that the Ministry of Information's aim should be to endeavour to produce a public feeling in Éire in favour of the Allied cause as opposed to the present anti-British attitude. I feel that the policy which the Ministry now seems to be adopting will be taken as weakness and to mean that Britain recognises that Éire is justified in maintaining her policy of independence and of opposition to the British Empire.

I hope that the Ministry will reconsider the whole position.[43]

As a consequence, Irish was not used and Delia Murphy was not invited to take part. However, the BBC paid no attention to the suggestion that it should reconsider the whole position.

Irish Half Hour went on the air, and Marshall kept a close eye on it, with scripts sent to him in advance. He began by criticising the signature tune on the grounds that 'the use of "the Minstrel Boy" is not universally approved of in Northern Ireland'. In January 1942 one of the early scripts did not reach him before transmission and he immediately complained to the Controller of Programmes:

. . . I am sorry I did not see it in advance as, had I done so, I should have certainly deleted the compere's words at the beginning, 'It's all yours Ireland'. It was agreed, as you know, that Northern Ireland should be excluded, but to refer to Éire as Ireland is entirely wrong and gives the very impression in the North which we wish to avoid. Apart from this, however, several people have complained recently that the programme is called *Irish Half Hour* instead of 'Éire Half Hour' and only last week the Prime Minister wrote to me to the same effect. Éire is the official name of the twenty-six counties and I think that as the programme is intended for loyalists in the British Forces whose homes are in Éire and not in Northern Ireland, it should be given the correct title.[44]

The Controller of Programmes brought Marshall's complaints to the Control Board and then wrote to the *Irish Half Hour* producer:

. . . it was agreed that we could continue to use the adjective 'Irish', but must drop the word 'Ireland' and substitute 'Éire'. I imagine, therefore, that you will drop such references altogether, as Éire is scarcely a romantic word and does not bring tears to the eyes like the mention of 'ould Ireland'. Of course, you need not edit songs about shamrocks and little bits of heaven, which may have the word Ireland in them.[45]

Marshall was not satisfied and kept returning to the demand that it be called 'Éire Half Hour' and not *Irish Half Hour*. *Irish Half Hour*, regardless, continued for years thereafter and outlasted the War. When it had to be dropped for a short time in February and March 1942, because Jimmy O'Dea was not available, Sir John Maffey, the

UK Representative in Dublin, took the opportunity to express his high appreciation of the programme and to bewail its disappearance, however temporary. At the same time a meeting in the Ministry of Information discussed the British Government's policy towards Irish programmes and in consequence the Director General of the Ministry wrote to the BBC, 'The Government is in favour of cultivating the goodwill of Éire listeners by indirect means such as *Irish Half Hour* and other programmes not primarily addressed to them'.[46] The letter was eventually copied to Marshall in Belfast.

Of course, Marshall never relaxed his vigilance. In September 1941 Denis Johnston, who was normally careful not to fall foul of Marshall, received a strongly worded memo. It happened that in a talk for the Overseas Service he referred to Dublin as 'the Irish capital'. The disc had been played by mistake on the Home Service and so Marshall had heard it. Johnston parried Marshall's complaint by asserting that what he really said was 'It is the Éirish capital'![47]

Another Dubliner, John Irwin, had been sent over to his native city to report to his superior, the Director of the Empire Service of the BBC, on the situation there. He made contact with Johnston and came to some firm conclusions. In reaching them he was helped by the fact that he had had experience of Belfast where he had been a producer for a while before the outbreak of war:

May I then, as I feel strongly about the matter, be forgiven for some *lèse-majesté*. Northern Ireland Director who at present seems to have the right to veto on everything in connection with Éire and broadcasting is really in a false position, as is Johnston, who as a junior member of staff based on Belfast has on occasions virtually to act as our Éire representative. Johnston is most sympathetic to the difficulties caused to the Northern Ireland Director by broadcasts from Éire, and is confident that if allowed to deal with the matter himself – not necessarily with any special title, simply to be treated as a responsible person – he could to a large extent avoid matter which would embarass Mr Marshall, who is in the unhappy state of being a target for Stormont and members of the Ulster Club, both of which bitterly resent anything which doesn't suggest that all the people south of the border are cowards. How much easier the Northern Ireland Director's position would be if he were in a position to say – which would be true – 'I really don't know anything about that wretched country of Éire, and so far as the BBC is concerned it is handled by another man altogether'. I think the fact that Johnston has got anything at all out of the country under the extraordinary difficulties he has to work in is a miracle. For example, he had talked Kiernan into allowing the

BBC recording van to collect material in Éire, and when reporting this achievement to Northern Ireland Director was somewhat shocked when NID commented that 'we had been specially asked to conserve our supplies of discs'. And again, when for political reasons Johnston was asked to repeat his programme *The Parnell Commission* on the fiftieth anniversary, he found it a little hard to be denied the right to import really good actors from Éire by the Northern Ireland Director who limited him to two, and after a fight granted three, the remainder of the cast to be made up of the rather scratch and unknown actors of the North. Johnston has no sense of grievance at all, and is prepared to go on under the present arrangement, but prophesied that sooner or later the difference between what the Ministry may want and what the Northern Ireland Director will allow is going to cause him to have a serious embarrassment.[48]

Marshall's refusal to allow Johnston to use any more than three actors from Éire was a matter of personal policy. He referred to it on another occasion, offering a revealing explanation:

Since the outbreak of war, we have, to a great extent, given up bringing artistes from Éire to Northern Ireland . . . because we do not feel that it is consistent with our policy to make use of artistes from a neutral country and also out of consideration of the views of the Northern Ireland Government.[49]

Irwin's report was taken up by the Director of Empire Services and his recommendation pushed with determination. John Betjeman wrote separately to the Controller of Programmes suggesting strongly that Denis Johnston should be freed of Marshall's surveillance and brought directly under the Controller's man- agment.[50] It is as well Betjeman's communications were never seen by Marshall as they would have confirmed his worst suspicions; Betjeman had taken to opening and closing his letters in Irish. Others in the BBC took up the cudgels on behalf of Johnston but to no avail. An important reason for their failure was the fact that Johnston had another BBC role; he was war correspondent in Northern Ireland and therefore was required to work in close association with Marshall, although this role was fairly inactive until the United States troops arrived in January 1942. Thereafter, the BBC's broadcast letters from Dublin were often written and spoken by another Irish author, Donagh McDonagh, who was not on the BBC staff.

Of course, various departments in the BBC, especially those concerned with news, deeply resented Marshall's 'claim to sovereignty over any piece of material relating to the whole of Ireland'. It was felt that 'the position is not a valid one in which he is able to exercise a censor's faculties'.[51] Pressure of time in the newsrooms and the distance of Belfast from London did from time to time frustrate him but for the most part Marshall continued to play his censorial role throughout the war.

The Ministry of Information's persistence and that of the Dominions Office meant that he lost battles on occasions, as with *Irish Half Hour*. In January 1942 John Betjeman suggested that there should be an *Irish Brains Trust* session on St Patrick's Day; the Controller of Programmes told the programme's producer that he thought this ought not to be a cross-border affair. He had no wish to have the programme stigmatised by the Northern Ireland Government, as the previous St Patrick's Day cross-border effort had been, as 'shaking hands with murder'.[52] Ursula Eason, the Northern Ireland Programme Director, had as usual other suggestions to make; one of which, a talk by a Northern Ireland Cabinet Minister, was quickly dismissed. Betjeman had the Dominions Office on his side and pressure was put on the BBC. The BBC resisted. One executive wrote, 'I cannot conceive how the BBC could contemplate an *Irish Brains Trust* without accepting as a first principle that it was walking with open eyes into trouble'.[53] The Northern Ireland Prime Minister got to know of the proposal and immediately made representations against it.

It is difficult to know where the Northern Ireland Prime Minister got his information. It is tempting to believe in this and in other instances that Marshall told him and that they worked out together what they would do. In any case, the BBC went ahead with its *Irish Brains Trust*, the contributors invited being St John Ervine, the Ulster playwright, and L. A. G. Strong, a literary figure from the south. The Controller of Programmes told Marshall that with such equal representation of north and south by such well-known people, 'I really cannot believe that anyone can object'.[54] The third guest was not Irish. The Controller's judgement proved correct and the programme went ahead without incident.

Notwithstanding this reverse on such an intervention, J. M. Andrews made further efforts to influence BBC programmes. In one instance he clearly overreached himself. In a remarkable letter to Marshall dated 16 March 1942 he complained that an extract from Eric Linklater's *Cornerstones* had been read as a postscript after the nine o'clock news and that this had referred to the glorious deeds of British regiments and to the part played by the Dominions but 'no mention was made of Ulster's regiments . . . or of the part which we are playing in this War. These slights to the people of this part of the Kingdom make my task very difficult as I am expected to see that Ulster is not forgotten. Of course, it may be said that the BBC are not responsible for what Linklater wrote, but they are responsible for the postscript.' Andrews went on to ask 'whether it is part of the appeasement policy which desires that the two Irelands should be regarded as one, notwithstanding that we here are in this War to the fullest extent that British ministers will let us be, while Éire is standing aloof and greatly adding to our Empire's difficulties and dangers'.[55] The Controller of the Home Service could not contain his astonishment and impatience when he received a copy of Andrews' letter from Marshall. He replied at length, suggesting sharply that, although the Linklater piece did not, for example, include a specific mention of Canada's contribution to the war, 'we would be surprised if we had any protest on this ground from the Canadian Government'. He added that on the night in question Northern Ireland had not been forgotten because there had been a transmission of *Irish Rhythms*![56]

The pressures on Marshall directly from Head Office and indirectly from the Ministry of Information were so great that when Radio Éireann asked in August 1942 if it might broadcast a programme from St Mary's Hall, Belfast, using its own compere and OB equipment, he agreed. The programme was *Question Time*, with Joe Linnane of *Irish Half Hour* fame, as compere. It was immensely popular in Éire. In the course of the programme Joe Linnane asked a competitor to name one of the world's great compilers of fairy stories. The competitor answered, 'Winston Churchill', and the audience broke out into loud cheers and laughter. Thereafter every time this competitor came to the microphone he was enthusiastically applauded. Unionist listeners were outraged, the more so as the Radio Éireann officials seem to have connived at his answer and not to have gonged it as wrong or inappropriate. Indignation boiled over into the Belfast newspapers and questions were asked in Westminster. Marshall felt vindicated in his stance and publicly disowned any BBC responsibility. A special meeting was called in the General Post Office, London, to discuss what action should be taken. (The Post Office had been responsible for leasing the lines to Radio Éireann.)

'At that meeting,' Marshall wrote afterwards, 'I put forward a suggestion, which was essentially adopted, that I should make a friendly agreement with the Éire Broadcasting Authorities that we would not make any requests for broadcasts from each other's territories, that is, Northern Ireland or Éire, for the duration of the War, but, at the request of the Éire Minister of Posts and Telegraphs, this was eventually limited to a period of six months.'[57]

Marshall was determined that he would not initiate any requests for facilities, especially outside broadcasts, because he might thus encourage Radio Éireann to seek reciprocal arrangements in Northern Ireland. Outside broadcasts, as the Belfast *Question Time* had proved, were particularly risky. Marshall was appalled to discover that Radio Éireann had been approached without his knowledge. The BBC's Deputy Director of Music, on a visit to Dublin, had arranged for a broadcast concert with the Trinity College Choral Society. He did not notify Belfast about it and elaborate preparations went ahead inside the College. When he learnt about the outside broadcast engagement, Marshall immediately sought to change it to a studio-based operation in Radio Éireann instead. This was quite unacceptable to the Trinity College Choral Society as its secretary, William Ewing*, explained. The largest studio was too small for the choir and in any case the tradition of the oldest choral society in the British Isles was to sing only on the university campus. Ewing tried to use some important contacts in Northern Ireland to force Marshall's hand but to no avail. Marshall, determined not to create an outside broadcasting precedent which Radio Éireann could exploit, cancelled the broadcast.[58]

Soon afterwards Radio Éireann asked to be allowed to broadcast a concert from St Mary's Hall, Belfast. Marshall learned from the Post Office that lines would not be available on the required date and so was able to inform the Director of Radio Éireann that this was the case. The Post Office was most unhappy that this should be quoted as an excuse on any occasion and insisted that it must not in future because normally lines were available to Dublin.[59] A further Post Office conference was called. Marshall proved again and again reluctant to put on paper the reason for his opposition to outside broadcasts by Radio Éireann from Northern Ireland. He eventually explained himself:

* W. T. Ewing was subsequently to be the one and only Registrar of the New University of Ulster, 1968 – 84.

125

... when Radio Eireann has broadcast from Northern Ireland, it has invariably been from a centre controlled by the Nationalist (Roman Catholic) party, which is not in favour of the war effort and, thus, such broadcasts throughout Éire only serve to strengthen the belief that this minority party in Northern Ireland is active and gaining strength and that thus the day when partition will be abolished is fast approaching. The Northern Ireland Government is naturally not in favour of activities of this sort, which only add to its difficulties and I feel, therefore, that it should be consulted in advance of any future meeting with the GPO.[60]

The Controller of Overseas Services replied to Marshall on this last point and by implication indicated the anomalous position which Marshall had come to occupy as a broadcaster.

... insofar as the Northern Government is concerned our feeling is that it is for the PMG, in the light of discussion at the proposed meeting, to raise with the Prime Minister of Northern Ireland the question of political desirability of whatever action is decided on. It would hardly be right for the BBC virtually to represent at such a meeting the views of the Northern Ireland Government. In brief, the BBC either grants or withholds facilities desired by Radio Éireann in accordance with whatever high political policy is notified to us by His Majesty's Government.[61]

Nevertheless, Marshall was sent by the Post Office and the BBC to see the Minister of Posts and Telegraphs in Dublin. He reported:

In regard to the OBs, the Minister told me, with a twinkle in his eye, that he quite understood the General Post Office's reason for their inability to provide lines for a concert from Belfast in September and, I think, he fully realises the position as it affects this Region. He is quite willing to continue the so-called 'gentleman's agreement' until the end of the war, but pointed out to me that the Nationalist party in Northern Ireland, whom he refers to as 'their people', are very pressing about having entertainment, etc, broadcast from Belfast and that he naturally does not like to turn them down flat. Under present circumstances, however, he said that, if any further pressing invitations were received, he would let me know privately without committing himself and be willing to accept my guidance as to what ought to be done, and I think, therefore, that we may assume that no further difficulties are likely to arise. When the war is over, the whole question can be re-opened.[62]

Marshall's role within the BBC in preventing broadcasts which might offend unionists was consistent and persistent. In 1943 the Shamrock Club was opened in London, for Irish servicemen and women, whether they came from the north or the south. Captain

126

Shane Leslie, a cousin of Churchill's and member of the Irish landowning class, had played quite a part in its establishment and asked if a concert on the opening night could be broadcast. The matter was referred to Marshall who referred it to the Northern Ireland Prime Minister. Andrews wrote, 'Your views entirely coincide with mine. This organisation exists for the purpose of urging a united Ireland. I have, of course, no objection to their founding a club for the use of volunteers from both the north and the south, but I would strongly object to a broadcast giving the impression that Ireland was politically united in any way and that, in this war, north and south were equally helpful. Such propaganda I cannot describe as otherwise than dishonest and I cannot imagine the British Broadcasting Corporation being party to it'.[63] Andrews' objections prevailed and there was no broadcast. His smear on the Shamrock Club was somewhat typical.

If that was the reception for the Shamrock Club, the outcome of an application later in 1943 from the Gaelic League for coverage of a celebrity concert which it was proposing to hold for its sixtieth anniversary in Glasgow was predictable. Marshall wrote to the Scottish Programme Director, 'Personally I think that you should abandon any idea of broadcasting this celebrity concert and I may say that in this connection I consulted the Prime Minister of Northern Ireland who is of the same opinion. For your information the Gaelic League has always been of a political character . . . and I am anxious, as no doubt you are yourself, that nothing should be broadcast which would, in any way, offend our listeners in Northern Ireland'.[64]

It was 1943 and the war was going better for Britain. With the change in national fortunes came a shift in government policy towards Éire, a shift which was to ease the tension between the Ministry of Information and the BBC in Northern Ireland. The incident which brought the change to light was a General Election in Éire. In June, A. P. Ryan of BBC News had the idea that a fairly full coverage of the General Election would provide an opportunity 'to bring Éire into our broadcasts' as the Ministry had said it desired. He suggested this to the Minister himself, Brendan Bracken, Tipperary-born and partly educated in Limerick. Bracken turned the suggestion down 'in the most emphatic terms' – 'The public would be horrified if they heard anything from the BBC about De Valera and those lousy neutrals: people of Irish stock overseas are heartily ashamed of Éire's attitude . . .' Without the Minister's approval a newsman could not be sent. Ryan commented, 'Mr Bracken's decision is worth remembering for the future in case his Ministry returns to the attack and asks us aga n to do more for Southern Ireland'.[65] The Ministry did not, in fact, push any more. Courting Éire was no longer necessary.

Programme production from the Northern Ireland Region continued at a low level throughout the war. Indeed fewer programmes were produced in 1942 than in 1941. *Irish Rhythms* continued to occupy much of the time allocated to Belfast programmes. In the eyes of the Belfast staff this was unfortunate because, as the Programme Director, Ursula Eason, wrote in 1943 to the Director of Programme Planning in London, 'these light music programmes do not reflect the life of the region in the way we would like to'.[66]

The BBC's concern to respond to the pressure of the Ministry of Information for programmes directed at listeners in Éire had given Marshall and Eason an argument for equal representation in programming for Northern Ireland. 'Now that the *Irish Magazine* programme which is largely devoted to Éire is underway I would like to ask again whether we could not be given space say once a fortnight for a programme devoted exclusively to Ulster,' Ursula Eason wrote to the Controller of Programmes in July 1941. She wanted a service programme, a short bulletin in which official announcements and regulations could be explained. The claim was modest. The existing programmes which performed the same function in Britain were unsuitable for Northern Ireland listeners for a number of reasons. One of Eason's arguments threw into question the whole pre-war policy in Belfast of using English announcers almost exclusively. 'It is a fact that a number of people here, particularly in country districts, find the English announcers difficult to understand. They even complain that the news is very difficult to follow and I say this not from one or two isolated cases but because it is continually mentioned. I feel that a local person would be far more widely listened to . . .'[67] So in the autumn of 1941 began a service programme called *Today in Ulster* which had a ten-minute slot once a fortnight.

In October 1942 the Northern Ireland Director of Programmes put forward a plan for a more ambitious local programme, an *Ulster Magazine*. She indicated the possible range of contents and reminded London that before the war a similar type of programme, *Ulster*

Weekly, had been very popular with the region's listeners. She was looking for an evening slot in the Home Service. She pleaded that there was a strong feeling of isolation in Northern Ireland and a need to maintain contact with the many Ulster people in Britain, and mentioned that the Regional Director had recently had a long conversation with the Northern Ireland Prime Minister, who felt strongly that the region should be as well treated as Scotland.[68] The Director of Programme Planning replied with the warning that the magazine format was a difficult one to bring off and that a good deal of experience and skill were needed to produce it. Nonetheless he suggested a sample of what was intended should be recorded and sent to London.[69]

In the meantime the British Forces Overseas Service invited Belfast to contribute a monthly half-hour music programme which was to include a three-minute local news bulletin for Ulstermen in the forces in the Middle East, in North and West Africa. The programme began as *Six Counties Half Hour* but when the Northern Ireland government heard of it, it intervened and the title was changed to *Ulster Half Hour.* The programme was transmitted on shortwave and so was scarcely heard in Northern Ireland.

The Belfast producer, James Mageean, worked on the trial magazine for the Home Service and it was eventually despatched to London. There, senior programme executives listened to it and their assessments were extremely critical. Val Gielgud, Head of Drama, wrote, 'This example would have done no credit to broadcasting in the year 1925. Unless a little harp *obligato* between items can be regarded as such, it has no presentation of any kind . . .' He took each item apart and concluded, '. . . apart from its possible stimulation of local patriotism, in the worst sense of that word, I see no justification for this programme in any circumstances'.[70] The Director of Programme Planning reported back to Belfast that the standard of the programme was far below what was acceptable and suggested that the whole project be dropped. Neither Eason nor Marshall were prepared to do that. In April 1943 the Regional Director wrote to the Controller of Programmes and once again quoted the representations made to him by the Northern Ireland Premier. Andrews had pointed out that Northern Ireland had nothing comparable with *Irish Half Hour* despite the fact that it was in the War and Éire was not. Marshall wrote, 'As I have pointed out more than once anything that is done in the direction of appeasement and conciliation of that country should not be on the expense of Northern Ireland whose government and people are better able to judge the effects of such a policy than those in London and elsewhere.'[71] On this occasion the Controller of Programmes gave in. The service programme *Today in Ulster* was dropped and *Ulster Half Hour* in the much-condemned form went on the air on the Home Service in July of 1943.

The new Northern Ireland Prime Minister, Sir Basil Brooke, who had ousted Andrews, inaugurated *Ulster Half Hour*. He said the monthly series aimed 'to bring a breath of Ulster to all our people who are separated from us, to hold fast the link between us and our friends old and new all over the world, and to interest others who do not know us yet and make them wish they did'.[72] The programme was welcomed but every transmission ran into criticism, sometimes sharp and bitter. This ran along familar lines: 'I listened to the *Ulster Half Hour* on the BBC last week. A Southern song spoiled for me an otherwise splendid programme. I fail to see why such a song should have been included when the producer had so many good Ulster songs from which to choose.'[73] Another theme was the thorny one of Ulster accents. The magazine format saved the programme from complete condemnation, however, because there were usually one or two items in any particular transmission which merited praise.

Tommy Thompson, a humorist who had often appeared in Belfast programmes, pleaded in mitigation that *Ulster Half Hour* was made on a shoestring: '... it would be interesting to compare the sum allotted to the producer of *Irish Half Hour*, in which there is Jimmy O'Dea, who I am sure will be offered more than two guineas a show (rehearsals extra), supported by two paid script writers, full cast, variety orchestra and guest artistes (with the 'e' please) and the sum allotted to the producer of *Ulster Half Hour*, for from what I know of Northern Ireland, the pay was none too generous, and from what I have heard recently, I would be inclined to rename the present series as *Ulster Half Paid*.'[74] There were probably other reasons for what the radio critic of the *Northern Whig* described as programmes which were 'uneven and badly blended, and would be better for greater concentration on one subject'.[75]

Ulster Half Hour went on until after the war, endlessly subject to criticism. In April 1946 at a Unionist Party meeting one member 'hoped the Northern Ireland government would make representations to the BBC to have that programme more truly reflect the life of Ulster'. The Prime Minister also spoke, using the occasion to say he would like to have the BBC under the authority of the Northern Ireland Government.[76]

Altogether, despite the efforts of Marshall, there was dissatisfaction with the way in which Northern Ireland was treated during the war on the Home and Forces programmes. A special correspondent in the *Northern Whig* asked, 'What is happening to the BBC in Northern Ireland? What purpose does it serve? . . . Surely the time has come for Northern Ireland to demand, and demand vigorously, that she be given in the BBC programmes a part commensurate with her importance.'[77] One letterwriter in the paper asked, '. . . why not an Ulster Broadcasting Station under the complete control of the Northern Ireland Government?'[78] Another returned to an old bind: '. . . of the entire staff engaged in Ulster broadcasting, how many are Ulster born?'[79]

Such demands inevitably raised questions about the kind of programmes a broadcasting service staffed and controlled by Northern Ireland people should offer. Unionists never addressed these questions seriously but the Catholic and nationalist *Irish News* did attend to the deeper cultural issues which the BBC confronted in Northern Ireland:

> If . . . the BBC is anxious to present the North as a separate area with an identity of its own, we may be sure it finds itself in a quandary . . . In the long run, if there are to be more and better broadcasts about this area, they will inevitably expose the Irish background and prove that not even the North can live down its past, however much it may want to do so. If it were merely a British shire it could have no grievance against the BBC. But not being a British shire, its ability to establish its identity depends not so much on Orange balladry as on the heritage it shares with the rest of Ireland. Partition has given it no literary standing; won for it no new culture, and supplied it with no rights to establish a separate nationality.[80]

A feature writer in the *Irish News* returned to this topic a year later in November 1944:

> . . . politically, then, the BBC operates in a country called Northern Ahland, musically it has a habit of going all 'broth of a boy', 'When Irish Eyes are Smiling', 'The Rose of Tralee', 'Macushla' – these are some of the Ulster classics I heard the other afternoon from Ormeau Avenue in a programme labelled *Ulster Half Hour*. In brief, the old *Punch* cartoons of Irishmen, tailcoats, shillelaghs, caubeens, and all, are being refurbished, translated into terms of electrical frequencies, and pumped out through a transmitting station known by the good Irish name of Lisnagarvey.

131

The Belfast building is, in fact, erected on a shaky foundation that has produced the cracks at Stormont. When it broadcasts the bright lilting arrangements of Irish dance music by David Curry, or its orchestral arrangements of Irish airs (the two best things it has done), it contradicts itself by drawing on the whole cultural background of Ireland. In an Irish national broadcasting system such items would reinforce and brighten the national programme as a whole; in the Northern Ahland programme they merely stick out like pieces of new cloth patched into a shoddy garment, and like pieces of new cloth on a shoddy foundation they end by tearing the foundation to tatters.[81]

As the number of items in *Ulster Half Hour* which were drawn from the broader Irish context increased, a correspondent in the *Irish News* asked why the programme should not be called *Irish Half Hour*. It was, of course, such tendencies which provoked Sir Basil Brooke and other unionists.

Access for programmes made in Northern Ireland to the Home and Forces programmes during the war was so limited that close attention was focussed on the content of those few which were transmitted. The argument about content highlighted Northern Ireland's cultural problems more sharply than in pre-war years. The promised return of regional broadcasting at the end of hostilities inevitably prompted questions about the way Northern Ireland would be reflected and about how cultural issues would be faced when there was much more programme time available.

At the end of 1944, the Director of Publicity, Kenneth Adam, visited Belfast and disclosed the Corporation's post-war plans in broad outline. From the press point of view his most important news was that regional broadcasting was to return. The new Broadcasting House, which newspaper reporters were wont to refer to as 'the white elephant of Ormeau Avenue', would soon serve the purpose for which it was built.

For the Regional Director the detailed plans for Northern Ireland, which he received a few weeks later, were a profound disappointment. The major change from pre-war days proposed for his region was that it would have to share a wavelength with another region. The BBC had only a limited number of wavelengths because of international pressure and agreements. The smallest region had as a consequence to be denied a wavelength of its own. The partner allocated to Northern Ireland Region was North-East England and so the BBC staff in Belfast had to negotiate regularly with their counterparts in Newcastle-on-Tyne a division of the limited time available for locally-produced programmes on the Home Service. Each region was saddled with the products of the other; Geordie had to listen to what was intended for the Lagansider; the man from Enniskillen had to hear what was meant for the man from Durham. Marshall at first believed that this was likely to be a temporary arrangement and publicly suggested that this was so. This shared wavelength arrangement on 285.7m, far from proving temporary, lasted until 1963. It meant that production in Northern Ireland was restricted and the extent to which the life and culture of the region could be reflected through broadcasting was limited. The staff would be small, and a decision of the Director General that the Northern Ireland Orchestra would not be restored meant that it would be smaller still. It was no wonder that behind the scenes in London Northern Ireland began to be known as 'the half region'.

If Marshall lost out in the planning for the postwar era he also found himself being divested of the power he had acquired during the war over the BBC's Irish programming and over BBC-Radio Éireann relations. The process had begun in July 1944, when, on the orders of the Director General, he lost all surveillance of news to do with Ireland. 'We are not . . . required,' wrote the Assistant Controller of News, 'to consult the Northern Ireland Director over, e.g., an obituary notice about De Valera, or over despatches from a special correspondent (should the time arise for sending one to cover political or other developments there) or over the handling of day-to-day news items.' The Assistant Controller added: 'I am sure you will agree that in working to these rules we should always keep NID as far as possible in the picture. We should tell him, if time allows, when we are sending a man over to either part of Ireland, to use him as the natural first point of enquiry in any news point concerned with Northern Ireland.'[82] The news service was freed of an incubus which it had always deeply resented.

A measure of the resentment which Marshall had engendered in other programme areas may be judged from an 'off the record' note which John Irwin wrote in September 1945, while working for the North America Service on a programme about Ireland.

There is one point which we should be aware of and that is the position of the Northern Ireland Director. A ruling was issued during the War that no broadcast could come from Éire without his approal. I imagine that this may have been rescinded since; with the end of wartime security, radio has again 'no frontiers', but we should certainly regularise this position

133

because I know from personal experience that Northern Ireland Director's touchstone as to a programme's suitability is the opinion of his fellow members of the Ulster Club. This hot-bed of Orange fascism considers any programme which does not vilify the people of Éire as unsuitable for the BBC. I should imagine that as the programme would be solely broadcast on shortwave to America we should be free to use our own discretion and avoid the impossible censorship of the members of the Ulster Club . . .[83]

The position was 'regularised', as Irwin called it, on 15 August 1946. The Senior Controller issued a directive to the effect that 'liaison between the BBC on the one hand . . . and Radio Éireann and Éire on the other will in future fall into the normal field of Overseas liaison, which will be the channel for programme offers in either direction, for requests for facilities and for communication on all other matters'.[84] Marshall's role was quite explicitly restricted to direct relations between the regional service now called the Northern Ireland Home Service and Radio Éireann. Marshall had no choice but to accept the directive's terms. His only comment was: 'as the views of the Northern Ireland Government do not necessarily coincide with those of the Government of the U.K. in regard to Éire, I think it would be advisable to let me know of any major arrangements in contemplation which might cause irritation in this region.'[85] He did eventually fight back. He waited until he had enough evidence, as he thought, of bungling and inefficiency on the part of the Overseas Service in its dealings with Radio Éireann and then sent a detailed memo in which he implied that if the BBC worked through the Belfast office it would do better. The Director of the Overseas Service at first reacted mildly: 'it is not surprising in the circumstances that he should seek to discredit arrangements which operate under a directive which he clearly dislikes'.[86] His patience was soon lost when Marshall persisted: 'I begin to find it very difficult to comment with restraint on such partial and tendentious statements as are contained in his last memo.'[87] The Overseas Service then found that Marshall was impeding its normal operations through Belfast and accused him of being 'wilfully provocative and obstructive'.[88] The outcome was a further directive firmly excluding Marshall from all but a narrow local role.

There remained one dimension of Marshall's wartime influence: his ability to manipulate cross-border outside broadcasts. In the course of 1947 Radio Éireann sought co-operation over some outside broadcasts which it planned in Northern Ireland. The Northern Ireland Programme Director endeavoured to intervene and persuade the BBC's Overseas Service that it should insist that agreement to such broadcasts should always be subject to the BBC in Northern Ireland receiving notice of Radio Éireann's intentions. It was pointed out that Radio Éireann made no such condition in respect of BBC OB units operating in Éire from Northern Ireland. Belfast's suggestion was rejected out of hand.

Regional broadcasting began again on 29 July 1945. The absence of even half a wavelength before that date enabled Marshall to declare that there would be no General Election broadcasts that year. Thereafter, the limitations imposed by the shared wavelength provided an excellent excuse, if needed, for having no election broadcasts. It could with justice be argued that to inflict Northern Ireland political issues on Geordie listeners was unfair.

Marshall renewed the pre-war practice of giving a Director's talk to the listeners on programme plans and on general Broadcasting House matters. He explained the shared wavelength arrangement and gave details of the schedule of local programmes. There was to be a nightly five-minute news bulletin, except on Sundays, supplemented by a fortnightly news commentary; a Saturday sports bulletin; regular plays, beginning with Patricia O'Connor's *Highly Efficient*; a weekly *Children's Hour* programme; a monthly religious service from church or studio and a weekly programme of hymns; the restoration of regular talks for farmers and one special feature, *Atlantic Bridgehead*, a history of Ulster ports during the war written by Denis Johnston.

It was not an ambitious regional schedule but that was in some measure due to the fact that the programme staff was still the same as in wartime, apart from some part-time assistance from talented people like the actress Cicely Mathews, who was already gaining experience of *Children's Hour*. Ursula Eason was loath to press ahead with the appointment of new producers before a new Programme Director was appointed. She knew she would be surrendering the temporary post which she had held throughout the war and hoped she would be transferred to schools' broadcasting in London. Her successor, she felt, should have a free hand.

A crisis was brewing in one area, news. The Director General had decided to promote the autonomy of Regional Directors in this area. He advised each Director to negotiate an arrangement with an individual newspaper reporter for a short daily bulletin with the permission of his editor. The effect of this would be to break the longstanding contracts with the news agencies by which they nominated the journalists who would undertake the work. The Council of the Newspaper Society did not like the change and prepared to fight it. Trouble loomed, but Marshall in Belfast was not affected for some months. His arrangement with R. Beattie, a reporter on the *Northern Whig,* lasted until February of the next year when he found himself blocked by both the *Northern Whig* and the *News Letter.* Until then, however, Marshall's news bulletin was safe and on 30 July he gave Beattie a very significant instruction: 'The news should be drawn from the Six Counties of Northern Ireland and should be confined to Northern Ireland only.'[89]

One programme area in which Marshall could begin regional broadcasting with a certain amount of satisfaction was religion. He had a year earlier persuaded the Catholic Church to send a representative to the Religious Advisory Committee; he and his predecessors had tried to achieve this for twenty years. The Church's original refusal had been related to its policy of non-co-operation with British institutions in Northern Ireland but in recent years it was much more concerned about the fact that any sermons or addresses which its clergy gave would be censored by a representative of the Archbishop of Westminster. When it was agreed that the English archdiocese would waive this right, the Catholic Church in Ireland's objections were finally removed. Monsignor A. H. Ryan then joined the Committee. Three years later he was joined by a second Catholic representative, the Very Reverend C.B. Daly of the Queen's University, Belfast.[90]

Regional broadcasting could only progress when new staff were appointed. Henry McMullan, who had been Assistant Programme Director in 1939, returned from war service and was appointed Programme Director. Sam Hanna Bell, who had some part-time experience and was already a successful author, was appointed as features assistant or producer. These appointments boded well, for both men were of Ulster stock, a requirement which Charles Siepmann had highlighted back in 1936.

In October 1945 the BBC celebrated its coming-of-age in Northern Ireland, and the Northern Ireland Prime Minister, Sir Basil Brooke, struck a note of regional pride:

There is no disgrace in being provincial. Give me the good red blood of a province that has a mind of its own, for we here are lavishly endowed with both character and imagination – and the language with which to express them. The best of us has been broadcast, the best of our native drama, music, industry, history and our church worship. Our great occasions, those stirring moments in our national life, have been shared and honoured in homes up and down the country. And every broadcast from Ulster is an ambassador . . .[91]

In the surge of hope and expectation for the new regional service the radio critic of the *Irish Times* saw much that the Belfast station had done well. He praised its achievements in music, drama, talks and in the fair showing it gave to poets and short-story writers. However, he likened BBC policy and the Northern Ireland station to a timid rider and . . .

a very spirited horse which he rides on a tight rein, and whose ration of oats is kept on the short side. Out of a weekly total of 121 hours of listening time, the Northern Ireland station provides programmes for about five hours and although the quality of the programmes is of the very highest standard, one feels that much good radio material is going to waste because of the excessive canniness of station policy . . . There is no sign of the Northern Ireland station serving as a forum for the discussion of social, political and religious problems. Why, if it is the BBC's policy to make the Northern Ireland Service 'an alert, living thing'*, should there not be such features as *The Week in Stormont*, discussions on such questions as Sunday entertainments, immigration from Éire, and religious teaching in schools . . . It may be that such a policy will stir up trouble for the station. Suppose it does; suppose that occasionally an MP at Stormont lays down a barrage against the station; suppose that there are letters of protest in the papers and hostile resolutions passed by obscure societies. What about it? . . . with a little courage the Northern Ireland station could make a great contribution to the solving of Ulster's problems.[92]

The challenge thrown down by the *Irish Times* critic was one which the Northern Ireland Regional Director was unlikely to pick up with enthusiasm. He had after all systematically endeavoured for more than thirteen years to impose a policy of non-controversial broadcasting. Yet even he was not totally immune to the opening up of broadcasting which was going on in the BBC across the water. If a measure of controversial discussion was to be allowed, then he would define the basic political parameters. Marshall declared in public that 'BBC programme policy in Northern Ireland is not to

* A phrase from an article on the BBC's plans for post-war broadcasting by the BBC's Director General in the *Radio Times*, 29 July 1945.

admit any attack on the constitutional position of Northern Ireland'.[93]

So when the recording van went out to cover specially arranged public debates in the towns of Northern Ireland a necessary consequence followed. Early in 1948 a series called *Free for All* was launched. One of the first programmes was recorded in Londonderry, entitled *The Future of Derry*. Derry was then, as now, a distressed area. Marshall reported as follows to the BBC Board of Governors:

> The city has the highest unemployment figures in Northern Ireland, and it has undoubtedly been very hard hit by partition, since it has been cut off from the West of Ireland from which it drew much of its trade. As a result the discussion was extremely critical of the Northern Ireland Government and of the situation in general, since very little had been done in the way of starting new industries to keep the city alive in the last ten years. *Much of the discussion naturally ranged over the constitutional question, and this was deleted in the recording.* What was left, however, was sufficiently critical in tone to displease both the Unionist minority in Londonderry and the Government of Northern Ireland.[94]

The BBC received support for this broadcast from an unexpected quarter. The new Northern Ireland Advisory Council of the BBC expressed the view of a majority of its members at its fourth meeting that 'if uncomplimentary remarks about any locality were made during a recording of these public and unscripted debates, then it was no function of the BBC to suppress them'.[95] What the Council did not know, of course, was that all references to partition had been erased from the recording. But it ought not to have been surprised for at the same meeting, the chairman, Sir Henry Mulholland, had ruled discussion of partition out of order when members tried to suggest that it was a proper subject for local broadcasts.

This remarkable decision caused concern in BBC Head Office. The Senior Controller wrote to Marshall: 'I think you should make clear at the next meeting that while the Chairman if he wishes is entitled to rule out of order consideration of the matter by Council, the BBC itself does not accept the position that it is not able to deal with current constitutional questions if they are matters of public interest.'[96] Marshall hastened to reply: 'I note what you say but it has always been our policy in Northern Ireland not to broadcast anything which could be interpreted as assailing the constitutional position of the Province. Several months ago I discussed this particular point with the Director General who, in a subsequent memo dated 9 October 1947, directed me not to embark on anything which would almost certainly arouse the political passions of our listeners here and we therefore have not attempted to arrange any discussion on such questions as Dominion Status or the Abolition of the Border.'[97] The issue was not raised again with Marshall, perhaps because he had only one more meeting of the Advisory Council to go before retirement.

The Council had been established as a consequence of a Government White Paper of July 1946, which had followed naturally from the Westminster Government's commitment to regional broadcasting. To help promote the reflection of the regions in programmes it was recommended that each region of the BBC should establish 'an Advisory Council . . . broadly representative of the general public of the region'. Members were to be chosen 'for their individual qualities and not as representative of particular interests'.

This task of selection caused Marshall much anxious effort. He informed the Director General: 'I have consulted numerous people, including the Prime Minister, and I think my list is a representative one. You will note that I have included three Nationalists, which, I would say, is about the right proportion . . .'[98] In view of the fact that the Council had a total of twenty members, including ex-officio members, three was a gross under-representation. The proportion did, however, change and improve. His choice of chairman was significant. Sir Henry Mulholland was the Northern Ireland Prime Minister's brother-in-law and he had been speaker of Northern Ireland's House of Commons from 1929 to 1945. So he was a reliable sheet anchor. By all accounts he had to be: participants recall, although the minutes do not mention, heated exchanges between the Unionist MP Harry Midgley, and the Socialist/Nationalist MP Hugh Downey. The Council, however, was drawn for the most part from professional middle-class people, noted more for their respectability than for their controversial views.

The Council had no power; it was merely required to advise. It could, however, ask questions and probe into programme matters, including content and planning and in time it was to prove a liberalising influence. In the early days, during Marshall's Directorship, it raised the question of the shared wavelength, the restoration of the BBC's Northern Ireland Orchestra and the promotion of schools' broadcasting in the region. It also pressed for a programme series on *The Week in Stormont* and for audience research to be extended to Northern Ireland.

The BBC Board of Governors wished to be seen to be taking the Regional Advisory Councils seriously and so considered all matters of major moment raised by them. The Board encouraged Marshall to press the matter of schools' broadcasting with the Northern Ireland Ministry of Education. There was a clear need to do so, for the number of registered listening schools in the region in November 1946 was only seventy-three. With regard to the shared wavelength the Governors offered sympathy and an explanation; they were to go on doing the same for years. The other issues raised by the Council were not carried to the Board. Nevertheless, the Belfast staff took note of them and attempted to get some action on them.

In the early months of 1946 Broadcasting House began to fill up with staff. New appointments were made and demobilised former staff returned. They came back to an impressive building, very poorly equipped, much of it a shell. Some studios had been lined with temporary kapok mattressing for acoustic reasons and, by 1946, it was beginning to smell. What equipment there was, was out of date, apart from that for outside broadcasting. There was also a recording van which had been acquired at the time the United States troops came to Ulster, and had been much used by Denis Johnston, the BBC war correspondent in Ulster, before he was transferred to Southern Europe.

Among the appointments in 1946 was that of C. L. Frankland, a journalist from Yorkshire who had served in the Information Office in Stormont. He was made news assistant and he arrived just in time, as the local newspapers had refused to co-operate in furnishing the nightly five-minute bulletin. Henry McMullan, with Frankland, proceeded to create an alternative system for producing news, the basis for today's extensive news network. They arranged for various local organisations – the Government and Belfast Corporation particularly – to provide the BBC with the same information that they normally supplied to the press. Frankland had contacts with reporters all over Northern Ireland and, as they were not party to the Newspaper Society conflict with the BBC, they were free to co-operate as stringers. Belfast city presented a problem but Frankland tried to tackle it himself. From all these sources the bulletins were compiled.

Frankland proved efficient and effective. One facet of his work was to supply BBC London with regional news. Godfrey Talbot, BBC's Chief Reporter, did a tour of the regions to assess 'what we can get from the regions' in the summer of 1947. He reported on Northern Ireland to the News Editor:

> The main regular stories from Ulster are about shipbuilding (Harland and Wolff are a town in themselves), flax and linen. BBC Belfast relations with the NI Government at Stormont are, of course, cordial and close. A point of note is that we can get nothing out of Belfast about Éire. No one of our Ulster people can touch anything south of the Border.[99]

The ban applied to the fortnightly news talks as much as to the nightly news. *Ulster Commentary* was given by John E. Sayers, from the editorial staff of the *Belfast Telegraph*. Sayers was a very competent journalist and broadcaster, a fact recognised by the radio critic of the *Irish Times*. The critic, however, observed that Sayers was 'a little dazzled by the glory of the Empire; a little over-awed by the wonders of the centre of the Empire; a little over-conscious of the bonds linking his own region to the Empire . . . On the other hand his enthusiasm for anything relating to Ulster traditions, and even Ulster institutions, seems moderate by comparison; and as for ties between Ulster and the rest of Ireland, to these he seems to turn a blind eye.' The critic speculated: 'It may be that his apparent indifference to Dublin and the South is due to station policy and station censorship'.[100] The suspicion was correct.

The evening bulletin was not trouble-free, in spite of its omission of all news from the twenty-six counties. In the summer of 1946 the introduction of the results of important Gaelic games played in Northern Ireland provoked angry correspondence in the newspapers. The decision to include them was made by the Director General, just as the decision to exclude them had been made by his predecessor in 1934. He had taken the advice of the Director of Religious Broadcasting on the issue of reporting Sunday games, who had replied:

> If the political and policy reasons make it right for us to give broadcasting recognition to the sporting events of the Gaelic Athletic Association, then I cannot think that we should do wrong, or offend sensible Protestant Christians, by broadcasting the results of these athletic meetings on a weekday. I do not think that the BBC should, by withholding

141

broadcasting recognition, imply that we disagree with Sunday sports and so refuse to broadcast their results. Whether people play games on Sunday is not, as I see it, our concern, and I do not think we are called upon either to hold Sabbatarian views or to give expression to these views by refusing to broadcast a sports' bulletin on a weekday. To me it seems a straightforward matter of reportage to say, in effect, 'At the meeting of the Gaelic Athletic Association last Sunday the following competitors won: . . .' That would be straightforward recognition of the fact that the meeting took place on a Sunday and that the BBC was reporting the event and its results. I should be in favour of a sports' bulletin on a weekday even if the sports about which we were broadcasting were held on a Sunday. I do think we should be wrong if we were to broadcast the bulletin itself on the Sunday because we should undoubtedly offend a great many sincere Protestant Christians in Northern Ireland.[101]

So listeners heard the results on Monday, by which time they were history, not news.

In April 1948 Frankland ran into a more serious problem. On the evening of the 27th, Belfast broadcast in the regional news a reply to a Stormont parliamentary question on the abolition of the death penalty. The reply had been supplied to Frankland by the Government Press Officer, but the question had not in fact been called and the prepared official reply had been supplied in error. An MP raised the matter in the Stormont House of Commons on the following day, asking for a ruling from the Speaker as to whether the broadcasting of the item constituted a breach of privilege. The Committee on Privileges was required to investigate the matter; in its report, the BBC was exonerated from all blame. The Committee expressed the opinion, however, that 'the existing system for the collection of information relating to Parliamentary news by the BBC is unsatisfactory and that it would be desirable for the BBC to have a press representative at Stormont who would thus obtain first-hand news items relating to the proceedings of the House, thereby obviating the practice of such information being supplied to the BBC by the Government Press Officer who is also a civil servant'. It was sixteen years before this recommendation was acted on. 'In the meantime,' the Prime Minister reported to the House, 'the BBC has asked the Government to continue the present service'; he thought that 'was entirely fair'.[102] The BBC Advisory Council did not agree and stressed the need for impartiality and independence in parliamentary reports which could not be expected from a paid government press officer.

The staff in Broadcasting House in 1946 was set the task of turning the rhetoric of regional broadcasting into programmes. The microphone went out and about, and some of the pre-war formats were revived: *Provincial Journey* toured the towns of Northern Ireland once more; *Village Pictures* was a new variation on the old *Village Opinion*. There were also new outside broadcast series. A most popular one, which was launched in October 1946, was *Up Against It,* a general knowledge quiz which toured the town halls, the BBC providing a team which competed with the local teams. Another outside broadcasting series was *Concert from the Country,* which sought out entertainment talent in villages and small towns.

The BBC ran into trouble when it attempted to mount a *County Ceilidhe* in County Armagh. Intended to be the first of a series, the project excited the angry opposition of the Gaelic League and the Gaelic Athletic Association. The secretaries of a number of branches and related organisations signed a joint letter of protest to the newspapers. They pointed out:

> The term ceilidhe has a definite connotation. It means Irish music, Irish dances, Irish songs and, above all, the use of the Irish language. From past experience of the BBC we know that Irish will have no place in the conducting of the 'Ceilidhe', and from the poster issued locally we see that non-Irish dances are included in the programme. The proposed venture can therefore be nothing more than a complete travesty of all that is commonly understood by the ceilidhe.
>
> We understand that the Northern Ireland region of the BBC contemplates further production on these lines, and we exhort all other Gaelic bodies in the Six Counties to write in protest.[103]

The mobile recording unit had better fortune in this respect as it toured the country making records of Irish folksongs and ballads sung in the traditional style. It provided a notable feature programme, with a script by Sam Hanna Bell, on life on Rathlin Island. It went to ploughing championships and agricultural shows, and began to record folklore and folk memories.

There were at the time some distinguished programmes. On the occasion of the 1,500th anniversary of the foundation of the first church in Armagh, W. R. Rodgers wrote a script on the history of the cathedral and its archbishops. Louis MacNeice, who always sought an excuse to come to Ireland for rugby internationals, produced the programme. The collaboration of the two Ulster poets ensured that *City set on a Hill* was a notable production. Denis Johnston's *Weep for Polyphemus* was revived to commemorate the bicentenary of Dean Swift and *Lillibulero* was produced once again, as was *The Parnell Commission*. Johnston's reputation was enhanced with each new production. Another revival from the 1930s was that of scenes played from *A Midsummer Night's Dream* in the Tyrone accent and introduced by the ever-popular W. F. Marshall.

It was clear nonetheless that Broadcasting House, Belfast, could not live entirely on past glories and so a campaign was launched to find new talent. There was a major competition for new plays, with entry confined to Ulster authors or authors living in Ulster and an impressive 132 scripts were submitted. The real discovery was that of the second-prize-winner Janet McNeill, who was to go on writing successfully in subsequent years. The first prize went to Graeme Roberts whose work was already known to listeners. A really significant change from pre-war days was that very many of the plays entered, including the winners' plays, were not traditional Ulster kitchen comedies.

Drama competition was not confined to adults. Cicely Mathews, who had taken over the Northern Ireland *Children's Hour*, also launched a competition which likewise produced a large entry. She was an enthusiast for children's participation in programming and out of this experiment grew her long-running feature 'I want to be an actor'. Many broadcasting careers began there, as indeed they had in earlier forms of *Children's Hour*.

When the war ended Marshall was only three years from retirement. Although, as we have seen, the period saw the revival of regional broadcasting, he provided neither enthusiasm nor inspiration. He was more inclined to be restrictive and prescriptive, and in his long period of office had become ever more cautious and hesitant about programme innovation. He had become identified with the Unionist regime and with a disposition to use broadcasting in its interests. He was not inclined to reach out to the minority and welcome its culture on the broadcasting scene. Sam Hanna Bell remembers being carpeted by him for having the Belfast Gaelic Choir, a most talented combination, in a programme. Marshall, did, however, defend programmes which attended to the broader Irish culture. 'One set of people complained that too much attention was paid to the South by performing plays, music and poetry drawn from

144

that quarter, but, said Mr Marshall, "we don't really do much of this and when we do, it is entirely on merit. Surely, however, things of this sort, if of the highest quality, are not confined to geographical limits; for, if so, Bach, Beethoven or Mozart would go unheard in the United Kingdom."'[104]

In the weeks before he went, he seemed to recover some part of that wider role which he had exercised during the war. On St Patrick's Day 1948 the Irish Prime Minister John Costello made a speech in which he appealed to the United States and to the countries of the British Commonwealth to assist in the healing of divisions between Irishmen. He called for an end to partition. By agreement with the BBC Overseas Service the broadcast was carried on its shortwave transmitters to the States and the Commonwealth. However, when it was broadcast the speech was substantially cut. The reason offered by the BBC was that it overran the time by six minutes. Costello's permission had been asked for this and he had agreed. The passages removed were mostly those which concerned his attack on partition. The BBC declared that it felt 'there were certain parts of it which were unsuitable for broadcasting', and implied that Costello agreed this was so. The Irish Government Information Bureau denied this emphatically.[105] Some anti-partition passages did survive and the Unionist MP for the Queen's University, Belfast, immediately tabled a motion in the Westminster House of Commons which read: 'That this House deplores the rebroadcasting of passages offensive to Northern Ireland.'[106]

Broadcasting House, London, had once again got its feet wet in Ireland's troubled waters.

In his last report to the Board of Governors Marshall could write,

Director of Overseas Service has agreed that where anything affecting the constitutional position of Northern Ireland is broadcast in the Overseas Service, Controller, Northern Ireland, [the new title of the Regional Director] should be consulted in advance as he is in a position to judge the local public reaction.[107]

The Director of Overseas Service knew, however, that his staff would be consulting Marshall's successor and not Marshall. Otherwise, he might not have agreed to the arrangement so readily. The memory of Marshall's intransigence during the war years was still very much alive.

5

The Professional Touch

The Director General, Sir William Haley, discussed with Andrew Stewart, the newly-appointed Controller Northern Ireland, the distinctiveness of his future role and what he should attempt to achieve:

> Try to extend the area of discussion. Try to get people talking to one another about their problems in Northern Ireland, but remember that you must only do so within the boundaries of public acceptability. Northern Ireland is the only region in the BBC in which, out of exacerbation from broadcasting, people might kill each other and that you must avoid.[1]

If appropriately used, radio might provide a medium through which a dialogue between the two communities could begin. Inevitably the communities would discover the problems which they had in common and to that extent a consensus could emerge. It was too early to proclaim that broadcasting might provide a platform for reconciliation but this was the direction in which things should move.

Andrew Stewart, who was charged with this task, was a Scot. He had joined the BBC in Scotland in 1926 on graduating from Glasgow University. Since then he had had much experience of production, becoming Programme Director in 1935. On the outbreak of war he was posted to the Ministry of Information in London where one of his many duties had been to persuade the BBC to make a determined effort to include items of Irish and Catholic interest in its programmes in order to build an audience in Éire.[2] In the middle of the war he returned to Glasgow to his former post as Programme Director for Scotland.

Inevitably the contrast between Stewart and Marshall was great. Stewart was determined, enthusiastic and ambitious for the BBC in his region. His colleagues found him encouraging and supportive and were all agreed, on reflection years later, that his most significant characteristic was that he was a thoroughly professional broadcaster. He was not inhibited by local experience like the longserving members of programme staff around him, McMullan and Eason. He was not satisfied that because a programme idea had been tried and had failed that it should not be tried again. Stewart had strong political convictions – Northern Ireland was an integral part of the United Kingdom and the task with which the BBC was charged was to serve it as such – but he did not accept that a political debate on radio in Northern Ireland would necessarily be provocative or unproductive.

Within a few months Stewart had encouraged developments which were to broaden the field of political information from the listener's point of view. He was not satisfied with the arrangement reached with the Northern Ireland Government on the reporting of parliamentary proceedings and debates. He was conscious that the Opposition would never be happy if the Government Press Office was the source of information for news bulletins, and had noted their conviction that 'no speaker who speaks against the Government would get fair play'. He therefore made a contract with the Press Association for the full use of its local parliamentary service as a basis for news bulletins.[3]

Moreover, the PA parliamentary service offered Stewart a way out of an immediate dilemma. He found on arrival that the Advisory Council was pressing for a local version of *The Week in Westminster*. *The Week in Stormont*, a report on the week's proceedings in the regional parliament, was not a new idea. Marshall had explored it in 1945 but had dropped it when the Prime Minister and a majority of the MPs who replied to a BBC postal survey opposed the suggestion. Stewart thought he would reopen the project with Sir Basil Brooke and soon learned the PM's opinion:

> The nature of much of the membership of Parliament would put objective, fairminded and non ex-parte treatment out of the question. He was not only referring to Opposition speakers. Since private members could have time in the House, members would ride their own hobby-horses and such a series would lead to them arranging to raise certain matters in which they or their friends could deal with them, and so the arrangement of business and the stress of discussion would move from the House to broadcasting.[4]

The leader of the opposition Nationalist Party, quite independently, gave the same verdict. James McSparran, MP, felt that the urbanity of Westminster was missing at Stormont, and also thought

147

that few Opposition members could write or deliver broadcast talks. Stewart was not deterred. He decided that if the MPs themselves would not report on Parliament then the News Editor would do the job instead, on the basis of the Press Association parliamentary service reports and Hansard. The experiment was tried once every fortnight and although the result lacked vitality and inspiration, the Advisory Council thought it quite adequate.

Stewart was not in favour of Marshall's total ban on the discussion of the constitutional issue and it seemed to him, almost on taking office, that the time was opportune to release the regional news and news commentaries from the ban on reporting and analysing what was going on south of the border. The political temperature there had been somewhat lowered, as far as the partition issue was concerned, with the accession to power of a Coalition Government, less ardently republican than de Valera's Fianna Fáil. John E. Sayers was encouraged to devote complete programmes in the *Ulster Commentary* series to the subject of partition. The leash was not let off entirely though: as Stewart informed the Board of Governors: 'The Northern Ireland News has continued to avoid extremist statements, some of which now threaten violence, and to report the present phase by selecting from the more authoritative and responsible utterances.'[5] Thus, within six months the new Controller had begun to tackle seriously the mandate he had been given by Sir William Haley. He also had talks with the National Union of Protestants (Ireland) which were eventually to lead to the coverage of the Twelfth of July Orange procession in 1952.

It was at this point that George Barnes, Director of the Spoken Word, one of the most senior programme staff, made a visit to Northern Ireland. On his return he submitted a short, comprehensive, perceptive report to the Director General, Haley:

The first thing that struck me about the country is the intensity of political feeling, resentment is quickly taken and bitterly expressed. ('Would you be liberal if rats were gnawing at your constitution day and night?') Neither party, for instance, will trust even its own members to broadcast an objective talk on 'This Week in Stormont'. I was told that this feeling is indigenous and no longer religious, though the line of religious difference follows the political line. It is deepened by parochialism – a cabinet and two legislative chambers ruling a population of one-and-a-half million – and the length and tediousness of the journey to 'the other side of the water'.

The position of the BBC needs examination against this background.

Broadcasting in Northern Ireland is a 'reserved service', one which stems from Westminster, not Stormont. The BBC is constitutionally more independent in Belfast than in London, yet its fear of making a mistake, where the consequence is a fighting matter, has prevented it until very recently from using the microphone as widely as in London or other regions. There is little sense of a 'strong, independent BBC' either among the staff (other than the Controller Northern Ireland) or the Advisory Council. (There was a flap on when I arrived owing to the dissatisfaction of members of Protestant churches with the unanimous advice of the Northern Ireland Religious Advisory Committee to allow broadcasts of the Sacraments, and Controller Northern Ireland had to make clear that the decision was the BBC's.) Thus the desirability of greater freedom in programmes and in the pace and manner of achieving it are difficult matters which cannot be decided in isolation owing to the effect of programmes other than those in the Northern Ireland Home Service, e.g., how Features Department can upset Controller Northern Ireland's relations with Harland & Wolff; why an item taken from Dublin is called *Round Britain Quiz;* and how the nine o'clock news reports the controversy over partition.

In considering this question, the following points need to be taken into account:

a The sharing of a wavelength increases the isolation of both listeners and staff.

b The proportion of licences to total population is low; i.e., it is 23% in Great Britain and 14% in Northern Ireland (though in Belfast alone it is 18%).

c The poor coverage of 285.7m in the west, the Catholic fringe, which is both a fruitful source of programmes and the place most cut off from British influence.

d The absence of Listener Research. This gives newspaper agitation undue importance. Thus, the self-censorship which a negative policy has engendered in the staff is increased by the absence of audience response.

e The staff are not all Ulstermen; where they are, the emotional conflicts and parochialism of the audience affect programme building, but it was significant at Programme Board that the others were against the more liberal use of the microphone.

I talked at length with Controller Northern Ireland and the Head of Northern Ireland Programmes [McMullan] about ways of developing programmes and noted the following points:

1 The standard of journalism in Belfast and of broadcast talk from Athlone is not high, and there is clearly a great opportunity for developing talks.

2 The love of argument is inherent in the audience and should make good programmes when resources are available.

3 *Ulster Commentary* has established itself, and, in the last two months, has demonstrated the ability of the Northern Ireland Home Service to deal objectively with controversial questions. It needs developing, in particular with another speaker of a different political colour and, possibly, a deeper mind.

4 Half the population lives by farming and the BBC could extend its influence by providing a good regional service for farmers, and by making the importance of farming more apparent to the city listeners.

5 School broadcasting: (subject of a separate note).

6 News. This seemed to be satisfactory, and the News Editor was spending two days at Egton House to see how *Today in Parliament* is handled. Whether it can be successfully extended to cover a fortnightly talk about Stormont on the lines of *The Week in Westminster*, but written in the office, remains to be seen.

Programmes

Though Belfast is thirty years behind the English industrial cities, the outlook for cultural programmes is not dim. The present exploitation of folk song, folk stories and light music is better than providing a symphony orchestra which the concert-going public could not support. The acting talent and poetry reading is strengthened by borrowing from Dublin and by the growing amateur dramatic movements amongst groups such as Young Farmers' Clubs, which are bound to produce better acting talent for the BBC in a few years time.[6]

This was the Northern Ireland Region as a senior BBC executive from London perceived it. Stewart saw it all as a challenge, as he recalled twenty-five years later:

Northern Ireland was a fairly untilled field. The staff had some highly experienced old-stagers ... and the rest were mostly post-war appointments who by 1948 had pretty well learnt their trade and it was then a question of applying it. Well, that was the human side ... The gear, the machinery was antiquated and pre-war ... and there was no hope of getting modern equipment, or so I was told. Northern Ireland was way down the list and there were other more important concerns. Everything was governed by Sir Edward Plowden's Committee which allocated supplies. I then learned from Maynard Sinclair, who was NI Minister of Finance, that the Plowden Committee rules did not apply in Northern Ireland ... so I went galloping off to the Director General gladly with this piece of news, which surprised him, and within a few months Broadcasting House, Belfast, was equipped with decent tools with which to do the job.[7]

Andrew Stewart was to be as enterprising and as effective in other aspects of his task. His long experience in Scotland had suggested to him that 'on the artistic side, the kernel of regional activity was an orchestra' and the BBC in Northern Ireland had none.[8] The problem was how to get one.

In 1947 Edgar, or 'Billy', Boucher, had joined the staff as music assistant. The resources which were available to him, without an orchestra, were limited, and were all external to the BBC. He could employ a local band each week, under the agreement reached with the North of Ireland Bands' Association. There were some good choirs in the region and they provided in the studio or through Outside Broadcasts a programme every week; church choirs were also used weekly in OBs. Occasional recitals were possible, limited by the availability of musicians: there were some pianists, a few string players and quite a few singers. In the mounting of recitals, Boucher was much supported by Havelock Nelson, like himself a Dubliner. Nelson had been appointed as an accompanist to the BBC in London and had chosen to be posted to Belfast. Finally, there was traditional Irish music and its practitioners, with David Curry and his Irish Rhythms Orchestra always available to give modern renderings of old dance and song tunes.[9]

It is clear that, musically speaking, BBC Belfast did not suffer from an *embarras de richesses*. As the Controller saw it, Broadcasting House had to have an orchestra: in December 1948 he put the case to London. The point of departure in his argument was a reply which the Senior Controller had sent Marshall in 1945. Marshall had made the case that Northern Ireland lacked a permanent orchestra and that there were public pressures for the BBC to restore the pre-war orchestra. The Senior Controller had written:

> I can see a distant possibility that we might require some time after the War a new orchestra of a particular type, and then might conceivably be led to locate it at Belfast in view of your fine new studios and premises, but I do not myself feel that it would be right to reconstitute the orchestra on the basis of what are really local PR arguments.

Stewart, after six months in Belfast, agreed that PR arguments, to which he had already been subjected, were invalid. 'They stem from a lack of serious musical activity in Belfast itself, and they miss the point which seems to lie in the kind of music which the BBC could draw from Northern Ireland rather than in the symphony concerts which the BBC could present cheaply to Belfast.' Stewart took the collection of the 'Airs of Ulster', some 160 tunes which had been orchestrated by a team of Ulster musicians under Norman Hay in the late 1930s, as the justification for a distinctive music policy in Northern Ireland. The 'Airs of Ulster' had been scored for the pre-war orchestra and for the existing Irish Rhythms Orchestra. 'This collection,' Stewart wrote, 'supports the view that here is one of the fundamentals from which one should work. A characteristic of this music is its cheerfulness unlike the predominant sadness of much of the folk music of the British peoples, and we could add a useful strand to British light music by forming a light orchestra and setting about providing it with arrangements.' 'Light music has always been weak in Britain,' argued Stewart, 'and consequently in broadcasting, where we are largely in the hands of the outside conductor with his "specially augmented" group of players. Their programmes . . . contain little that is fresh or distinctive.' He thought the time had come to consider that 'distant possibility' which the Senior Controller had suggested in 1945. Stewart simply proposed a light orchestra of eighteen players based in Belfast, which could perform in the Home Service, Light Programme and Overseas Services. 'It would draw upon the general repertoire of popular music but would diversify its programmes for these services with arrangements of Irish tunes so giving them a character of their own – in fact, something fresh in light music.'[10]

Stewart had chosen a particularly opportune moment to put forward his proposal. The BBC was in conflict with the Musicians' Union, and outside orchestras, which supplied the Corporation with light music, had very recently ended a strike. The BBC's own symphony orchestras were concerned with serious music and so there was a gap. Stewart astutely argued that the BBC Northern Ireland Light Orchestra which he was proposing would not constitute an extra drain on resources because the fees which were normally paid to outside orchestras for light music could finance it. He would endeavour to find anything extra from BBC Belfast's own resources.

Stewart was authorised by the Director General to explore the possibility. It proved significant that the BBC Music Department was not drawn into the arrangement. By the summer of 1949 Belfast was able to go ahead and recruit an orchestra on a six-month contract, during which trial period it would have to prove itself. David Curry was appointed conductor and fifteen musicians were recruited, including half of his own Irish Rhythms Orchestra. The new Orchestra soon ran into severe criticism from the BBC Music Department. As long as it played Irish rhythms it was unchallenged, but as soon as it ventured into any other light music, it became a target for attack. There was a serious quibble about its entitlement to the prefix 'BBC'. The Orchestra was described as sounding 'like the old fashioned boiled down band of the orchestra pit of 25 years ago'.[11] David Curry was personally described as 'a man with a metronomic mind which is an excellent attribute where the playing of Irish rhythms and dances are concerned, where, in fact, absolute rigidity of tempo is essential. This, however, applied to light music is disastrous.'[12] There was a recurrent theme: 'The style of the Orchestra is identical with that of similar combinations dating back to the mid-thirties.' This critic added, however, 'I am of the opinion that little can be done with the present combination unless someone with a great interest in and knowledge of light music can be appointed to control the destiny of this Orchestra.'[13] David Curry fell ill under the strain of forming the Orchestra and for some time a Czech conductor, Villem Tautsky, took his place. Tautsky licked the Orchestra into shape and proved a great success with the critics. It became clear, however, that some of the problems of the Orchestra lay not in its playing but in the acoustics of the studios in Broadcasting House, Belfast, and in the lack of balance in the arrangement of microphones. While the Northern Ireland Light Orchestra slowly gained acceptance, it long remained the subject of unfriendly appraisal in London. Nevertheless, Stewart, the Controller, had succeeded in giving the region an orchestra. Once he had got it, he was able to co-operate with CEMA (the Council for the Encouragement of Music and the Arts), the forerunner of the Arts Council, in the formation of the City of Belfast Orchestra. For years the NILO was to provide a nucleus of players for the larger public orchestra.

The creation of the Light Orchestra was probably Andrew Stewart's greatest achievement in the four years of his Controllership. Ironically, it was one element in Broadcasting House which could not conform strictly to the new programme policy which he imposed on his staff. He was determined to achieve the complete regionalisation of programmes. If Ulster only consisted of the six counties, it would be called the 'Ulsterisation' of programme production. Stewart's lengthy directive on programme policy* was summarised for the Regional Advisory Council as follows:

An Ulsterman who writes about Ulster is in a strong position; work by authors outside Ulster which can appropriately be performed by Ulster

---

* See Appendix II for the full text.

153

players is legitimate: work by Ulster authors and composers which cannot be performed by Ulster performers is also legitimate as an ingredient of the Regional Programme even if performed by performers from outside the Region.[14]

An ingenious programme series which kept to the letter of the policy, if not to its spirit, illustrates the constraints Stewart was imposing. It was called *Irish Writers*. Well-known authors born in Northern Ireland talked about the work of authors born in Southern Ireland and vice versa. The series ran through the winter 1948–9 and maintained a high standard. St John Ervine spoke on G. B. Shaw, and incidentally provoked a typical Shavian reaction*; Oliver Edwards spoke on Yeats and George Buchanan on James Joyce. In reverse Frank O'Connor spoke on George Shiels; Lord Dunsany on 'A.E.' and Sean O'Faolain on Shan Bullock. The policy was not specifically directed against people from Éire. Artistes visiting Northern Ireland from anywhere else in the British Isles who sought an opportunity to broadcast from the Belfast studios were turned away. Boucher, the music producer, recalls many requests from the South for auditions which he turned down, although in particular cases where he knew they were performers of merit, he informed London about them. The policy of strict regionalisation was not, of course, applied to the new Northern Ireland Light Orchestra. The terms of the agreements which Stewart made with the Light Programme, the Home and Overseas Services were such that the Orchestra could not be confined to Irish rhythms. With this exception, every producer was told 'to cultivate his own garden', the six counties.

Intrinsic to the policy was a stronger emphasis on outside broadcasts and recordings. It was the kind of pressure welcomed by most producers and by none more than the features producer, Sam Hanna Bell. He recognised at the time that 'the voices of men and women describing their daily work, their recreations, their hopes and troubles, are the life and breath of regional broadcasting'.[15] 'Up to this time,' Bell said later, 'the working-class voice had never been heard in Broadcasting House, Belfast. Matt Mulcaghey and Mrs Rooney may have been supposed to represent it in the 1930s but really that was a travesty. We now had a marvellous opportunity to go out into Queen's Island [Harland & Wolff's vast estate], to go

---

* Shaw wrote to St John Ervine, 'Your broadcast was on the romantic side. I never struggle – I am incapable of it. I rose by sheer gravitation.'

154

down into the streets and have people talk about maybe innocuous things but the point is they were real people talking.' The ordinary people of town and countryside 'were an untapped source, a tremendously rich reservoir of material. People were so eager to tell us a story, to sing us a song.'[16]

Sam Hanna Bell's very first responsibility, the production of a programme in the *Provincial Journey* series, was restricted by technical limitations. Larne was the town which was to be dealt with but all the participants had to be brought to the Belfast studios to talk and perform. Subsequent programmes in the series were outside broadcasts, as they had been before the war. 'But . . . the most effective way of collecting programmes from the countryside is the mobile recording unit,' wrote Sam Hanna Bell, and he was happy to surrender *Provincial Journey* to another producer and to take to the roads and boreens. 'The history, character, and day-to-day life of a small community can be recorded in such programmes as *Village Picture,* or the occupations and music of a district can be gathered into a programme such as *It's a Brave Step,* edited, and set in a leisurely descriptive narration.'[17] Bell's enthusiasm easily overcame the difficulties which the cumbersome disc-recording equipment presented.

Recorded programmes, like *Village Picture* and *It's a Brave Step,* could provide a reflection of life in the countryside of Northern Ireland but they could also seize and hold on disc for posterity the oral and musical traditions which were declining and dying. The first series to tackle this task was *Fairy Faith.* The initiative which produced it came from the Northern Ireland Advisory Council where Cahir Healy, the Nationalist MP, expressed some dissatisfaction with the way in which the BBC's Third Programme was sending teams to record the folklore and music of the twenty-six counties and neglecting the six.[18] Andrew Stewart responded to the criticism. Sam Hanna Bell recalled that, 'One day he called me into his office and said, "I've got hold of some money and I want you to go out and look for the heroic tales and myths of Ulster". We were lucky in having the folklorist, Michael J. Murphy about and so I went off to ask him about the suggestion. He said that the heroic myths were pretty dormant and what survived was so corrupted that they were not worth collecting. "But," he said, "there are the fairies".'[19] From that suggestion there followed months of travelling around and recording the tales told by many old men and women. A

155

large reservoir of folklore was built up and from it was distilled the distinguished series, *Fairy Faith*. Professor Delargy of the Irish Folk Lore Commission was enthusiastic about the project and regarded it as 'the most important work in Irish Folklore in modern times'.[20]

In the course of their travels Sam Hanna Bell and Michael J. Murphy became very aware of the presence of much more recent lore than that of the fairies, about the hiring fairs which had been a feature of the Irish countryside until the 1930s. When their task of recording fairylore was complete, they turned to this new field. They found those who had frequented the hiring fairs: booth holders, farmers who had hired young people, and old people who, when young, had been hired. Sam Hanna Bell also recorded a variety of songs about the hiring. The outcome was a feature programme which made an impact on critics and listeners alike. It was to be repeated on a number of occasions and was taken by the Third Programme.

Another by-product of *Fairy Faith* was a BBC project to record the folk music of Ulster. As the BBC was fortunate in the collaboration of Michael J. Murphy, so in the field of folk music it found an expert in Sean O Boyle of Armagh. At first in company with Sam Hanna Bell and then on his own O Boyle went out for a number of years recording the best of traditional music, creating an extensive and valuable archive for the BBC and for the Irish people. Sean O Boyle himself wrote scripts and became a well-known broadcaster, often using his own recordings, as in the various *Music on the Hearth* series.

By the end of 1949 the Northern Ireland Controller, Stewart, could record in his Report for the year the impressive outcome of his policy of strict regionalisation of programmes:

> In addition to all the usual studio productions during the year, some 260 programmes were broadcast from sources outside the studio in the cities, towns and rural districts of the Province ... About twenty feature programmes all written by local authors, treated different aspects of Ulster life and history. W. R. Rodgers's *Return to Northern Ireland* first produced in the Belfast studios for the Third Programme, was repeated in all Home Services, as well as Sam Hanna Bell's documentary on Rathlin Island and his St Patrick's Day feature on life in the Lagan Valley. The series of documentary programmes *Within Our Province* took stock of such matters as exports ... afforestation and the fight against tuberculosis. The Northern Ireland studios provided a play almost every fortnight during the year, all but three of them the work of local writers ...

156

The life, history and interests of Ulster were examined in twelve talks under the title *Our Heritage*. The series attempted an assessment of the fundamentals of life in Ulster at the half-century . . . Another series described some of the great houses of Ulster and the families associated with them.[21]

In the course of 1949, Stewart had had an idea which sparked off what proved to be the most popular programme ever produced on radio in Northern Ireland. As Director of Programmes in Scotland, he had observed the genesis and success of a serial based on the life of an ordinary family, *The McFlannels*, and it occurred to him that an Ulster equivalent would go down well with the local audience. He put the suggestion to his head of programmes, Henry McMullan, who looked for a script writer. He chose Joseph Tomelty, an actor and playwright, who had begun his career writing for radio. Tomelty came up with *The McCooeys*, an ordinary Belfast family of unidentifiable religious background who spoke in the accent and dialect of the city. This everyday story of city folk ran for seven years and only ended when Tomelty was involved in a serious accident. The Saturday evening transmission and its Monday evening repeat were found, when Listener Research eventually reached Northern Ireland, to have had half a million listeners in the region per week. 'What is the secret of *The McCooeys*?' asked Henry McMullan in the *BBC Year Book* for 1951. 'Probably the answer is their normality. The author knows and loves the people he is writing about. The cast finds his lines "read themselves", and the problems and anxieties to which he exposes them are largely the ordinary problems and anxieties which afflict us all. There is a warmth and humanity in the 'McCooey' home which has reached the listener and brought him back week after week to his loudspeaker.'[22]

Stewart's years in Northern Ireland involved important political events which affected broadcasting. In 1949 the Coalition Government in Dublin broke the tenuous link with the Commonwealth. In the run-up to the legislative enactment of the Republic, the BBC in London took action. It reissued the immediate post-war directive which required all liaison with Éire to be conducted through the BBC Overseas Service. The Director of the Spoken Word, G. Barnes, wrote that he was doing so 'since particular care and consideration are needed during the transitional period when the new relations of Éire with Great Britain and Northern Ireland will be hardening. An internal reason for reissue is that the minute was originally drafted at the end of a period when the Northern Ireland Director exercised powers almost amounting to censorship. The situation is now changed and the purpose of the minute is to warn staff rather than free them from control.'[23] The directive suggested that programmes which dealt with the political relations between the two parts of Ireland or with Éire's domestic situation 'in so far as such programmes may be judged to have repercussions affecting Northern Ireland' should be referred to the Controller Northern Ireland for advice. Barnes had an extra paragraph added to the effect that 'heads of departments and programmes should inform the Controller Northern Ireland in advance of forthcoming programmes about Éire or Northern Ireland since he cannot deal with a row which blows up overnight if he is unaware that the programme has taken place'.[24] The requirement was that CNI should be informed and consulted; no one had to listen or to act on advice given. There is little evidence that the Controller had much to do as a consequence of this directive.

The declaration of the Republic resulted in a General Election in Northern Ireland. The BBC in London anticipated this and resolved to offer the major competing parties facilities for election broadcasts, with the BBC to decide what time was available. It was the responsibility of the parties to agree among themselves on the allocation of it. Sir Basil Brooke, the Northern Ireland Prime Minister, was consulted about party political broadcasts and said he was not against them. He was 'rather doubtful, because the argument would probably not be reasonable on either side. It might well be over-emotional, full of personalities, go too far and become a slanging match. On the other hand, it would be breaking new ground and making history.' He indicated that if the BBC offered, say, eight broadcasts, the Unionists would suggest a division of five Unionist, two nationalist and one Labour. Brooke concluded by saying that he 'hoped that the Governors of the BBC would be clear that this was not an election where the issue is between the domestic policies of two major parties, either of which would carry on within a set constitutional framework. The issue of this election was whether a part of the United Kingdom would remain within the United Kingdom or withdraw from its allegiance and join the Republic . . . He would go to the country because the majority in Northern Ireland should have the opportunity of showing unmistakably whether the change in status of Éire meant anything in the

158

nature of what Southern Irish politicians and Northern Ireland Nationalists were claiming. Party broadcasts on such a theme would be unique.'[25]

In due course when Brooke announced the election, the BBC invited the three major parties to a conference to decide on the allocation of eight fifteen-minute slots. The parties leaked the invitations to the papers. The *Belfast Telegraph* announced: 'Party politics will be on radio in Ulster for first time. BBC policy change offers all sides time on air for General Election campaign.' Having given details, the report commented that the extension of party political broadcasting to Northern Ireland 'will represent an important departure. Hitherto the BBC has not broadcast anything which is inimical to the Constitution, but Nationalist speakers will now be allowed to give the anti-partition viewpoint.'[26]

Four days later the *Belfast Telegraph* and other papers published an agreed statement which said, '. . . since the three parties had not reached agreement upon the allocation of the broadcasts and the proportion of speakers to represent each party, no election broadcasts will take place'.[27]

A lengthy detailed account by the Controller of what took place behind the scene survives. It is marked 'secret'. The account is not a transcript but Stewart's own summary of what passed. James McSparran attended the meeting as the Nationalist leader, although he was uncertain how far he could commit his party. He opened the meeting and made two points which in Stewart's summary were:

a That the parties should have the same number of broadcasts so that listeners would have an equal chance of hearing the competing views, but that he did not know if the Nationalists would be able to state their position because of BBC censorship.

b That the Government had all the advantages, for instance, the Prime Minister's manifesto had been summarised in the Northern Ireland news which would not summarise a Nationalist manifesto.

'I at once interposed,' wrote Stewart,

that the BBC would summarise the manifestoes on the day of issue and that, if the parties reached agreement among themselves on the allocation of broadcasts and the order, they would be free to argue their programmes in their broadcasts as far as the BBC was concerned (that is, of course, as far as I could go because what Mr McSparran had in mind was the fact that the government of the country was still continuing and that a delicate and undefined line must exist about how far the

159

Nationalists can go without calling the Special Powers' Act into effect. Mr McSparran was obviously hinting at the possibility of a posse of police waiting at the front door to pick up the broadcaster and it crossed my mind that the posse might possibly pick up the BBC Controller as the official responsible for uttering the broadcast! This was one of the stumbling blocks in the negotiation, although it was almost unspoken).

When it came to hard bargaining, the issue revolved around the Unionist claim to a five Unionist, two Nationalist, one Labour basis as opposed to four Unionist, four Nationalist, one Labour basis put forward by McSparran. Stewart indicated that the BBC could find nine slots. Topping, the Unionist Chief Whip, who was acting for his party, went as far as offering a 4:3:1 arrangement. The negotiations at this time were broken up by the Northern Ireland Labour Party representatives who claimed two broadcasts, while McSparran said that three must be the Nationalist minimum. No conclusion could be reached and negotiations were abandoned with agreement on a statement to be issued to the press. It was Stewart's opinion that if the British Labour Party had not had a representative alongside the official from the local party, the meeting would have ended successfully. The Englishman insisted on two broadcasts, whereas the local man would have settled for one and that would have brought agreement.[28]

Party political broadcasts were thus delayed for a few years more. The 1949 Election was, however, fully reported on the news within the limits imposed by the brief bulletins of the time and this was the first occasion on which such an effort was made in Northern Ireland. Initially, the BBC was faced with the problem that it was denied the co-operation of the proprietors of three Protestant newspapers who, as members of the Newspaper Society, had previously decided not to allow their journalists to supply material to the BBC. This obstruction was circumvented by an arrangement with the Unionist Party Headquarters whereby all important election speeches were sent directly to the BBC. James McSparran, on being approached about Nationalist Party speeches, arranged for the *Irish News* to provide full reports. Frankland, the BBC News Editor, managed to cover the other parties and his news bulletins, constructed with meticulous care, won the commendation of the party leaders for their fairness and accuracy. The BBC went to some trouble to accommodate the Nationalist Party, whose manifesto was delivered late, that is to say within the prohibited final three days before

160

polling day. Stewart, the Controller, took it upon himself to waive the rules and gave as his reasons for doing so:

1 We had agreed to summarise and broadcast the Parties' Manifestoes.
2 We were clear that ramshackle organisation and not crafty tactics had delayed the issue of the Nationalist Manifesto, and in the event, we discovered that Mr. McSparran had had to take it upon himself to draft and issue the document.
3 Because Polling Day was still more than two clear days after 6.10 p.m. on Monday, 7 February 1949.

While this concession did not pass unnoticed by the Unionists it did not arouse any anger. The anger was reserved for the BBC in London which reported a lengthy statement on the Election by the Éire High Commissioner in London. Stewart commented, 'Many Unionists feel that the BBC bought a piece of Éireann propaganda and it fanned the feeling expressed at the Unionist Council's Annual Conference that, whereas the Nationalists had the services of Radio Éireann, the broadcasting organisation of an external government, the Northern Ireland Government had no facilities for reply.'[29]

In the meantime the process of introducing controversy over political topics in other areas of programming was advancing, if slowly. A series of monthly programmes *Opinions Differ* began in halls around the region. Stewart reported to the Board of Governors, '. . . the argument is recorded and edited, partly in the interest of concision and partly in the knowledge that the tense political situation can affect a wide range of subjects. This rules out frank exchange of opinions on some subjects of major local interest, but helps to direct attention towards subjects of general social usefulness.'[30]

The basis on which the talks on public affairs, *Ulster Commentary*, were given was broadened. Sayers was no longer to be the lone speaker. He was well known as a Unionist and so speakers of known Labour and Nationalist affiliations were added and the three took it in turn to review political developments. There had been strong criticism of Sayers but the BBC decision, by chance, anticipated a resolution passed in the Old Park, Belfast, branch of the Anti-Partition League, the alliance of bodies set up to campaign against partition,

That in view of the fact that the BBC in its *Ulster Commentary* programme has allowed time for an 'Ulster' spokesman to explain the

161

'Ulster' attitude towards Partition, the National Executive should demand from the BBC time for a spokesman from the Nationalist minority to give their views and and their attitude towards Partition and the dismemberment of our country.[31]

These things happened in the autumn of 1949. In September 1951 there was introduced 'a monthly discussion designed to bring NI region more into line with controversial broadcasting elsewhere in the United Kingdom. Four such discussions have now been broadcast,' Stewart reported to the Board of Governors,

and they have included two Ulster Unionist MPs, the Secretary of the NI Labour Party and a Roman Catholic with Nationalist sympathies. The NI Labour Party, unlike the Unionists and the Nationalists, has no newspaper devoted to its interests and consequently broadcasting is the only means apart from meetings, of communicating its views. The experiment with the Catholic Nationalist has succeeded so far; while his sympathies have been unmistakable, he had kept to matters of importance for people within Northern Ireland, without confusing local social, economic and industrial issues with constitutional red herrings. This is valuable since the Catholic Nationalist section of the community has a point of view on local issues which is seldom heard or expressed, for in their own press and speeches they habitually distort it in such a way as to suggest that 'Partition' is the cause of every ill. The discussions have steadily improved in quality.[32]

The 'Catholic Nationalist' mentioned by Stewart was the educationalist, J. J. Campbell.

In 1949 the Westminster Government named a committee whose task it was to review broadcasting in the United Kingdom and to advise on the terms of a new charter for the BBC; the committee was under the chairmanship of Lord Beveridge. The committee did not include a representative from Northern Ireland, and this aroused concern in Stormont Castle, where senior civil servants felt something should be done about it. One with a particular personal interest wrote a memo pointing to two areas of concern for Northern Ireland: '(1) The position of the regions in the general scheme of broadcasting, and (2) The development of television.' He suggested representations should be made to the Beveridge Committee on both accounts. His memo then presented observations on both areas of interest:

1 Northern Ireland is regarded as the least important of all the Regions of the BBC and treated accordingly in programme budgets, staffing, and

time allotted in basic Home Service programmes, etc – because of the comparatively small number of licence holders in this Region. As against the small number of local listeners, due weight has never been given, as I see it, to the fact that Northern Ireland is not merely a Region for broadcasting purposes, but a Province with a Government of its own and a place in the United Kingdom which is strategically and politically more important than its proportionate area and population. In times of emergency the Northern Ireland Region is the first to be cut down in staff and programme representation – as during the late War.

Generally speaking, there has been a lack of Government or 'political' support from Northern Ireland making itself felt at BBC Headquarters to back up the claims of the Region. If in the future development of Regional broadcasting Northern Ireland is to be fairly represented, not merely on a *per capita* basis but with account taken of status and prestige in the United Kingdom, continuous and effective interest from Government sources will be needed.

To take one example only where there is room for improvement – there is no School Broadcasting originating from Northern Ireland (although a handful of Schools take School broadcasts from other Regions). Scotland has a flourishing Regional organisation on this side of broadcasting, in which the BBC has a high international reputation. Needless to say we are not in a position to contribute anything to the Schools' programmes taken by other Regions; and yet we complain that the younger generation in Great Britain is brought up in ignorance of the geography, economics, constitution and history of Northern Ireland!

2 Plans appear to be getting under way with increasing momentum for the extension of the Television service throughout Great Britain. Northern Ireland so far is ignored . . .[33]

The author of the memo, A.L. Arnold, appended a note to his Permanent Secretary regretting that Ministers 'still regarded [broadcasting] as a necessary evil'. The Permanent Secretary in response to the memo said he thought that the case for change ought not to be overstated and that all they should seek to achieve was that 'our radio facilities [are kept] on a par with other regions'.[34]

The television issue, which Arnold had mentioned, was a live one. There was a growing demand that Northern Ireland should be included in the plans for UK coverage. Among those who sought to rally public opinion was George Marshall, the former BBC Regional Director, now retired and living in Belfast. He wrote three lengthy articles in the *Northern Whig* under the headline, TELEVISION:

163

PROVINCE MUST PRESS FOR PARTICIPATION.[35] The radio retailers and other interested groups pressed their MPs to lobby the Westminster Government and the BBC. In September 1949 the Lord President of the Council, Herbert Morrison, made a speech in which he seemed to imply that Northern Ireland would have television by 1954. In any event it appeared to most people that it would be only a matter of time before the region got a television service.

So representations to the Beveridge Committee did not need to include television. The BBC Northern Ireland Advisory Council limited its submission to a memorandum on the shared wavelength, requesting that the Region be granted a wavelength of its own.

When the Beveridge Committee reported in January 1951 the recommendations which it made concerning regional broadcasting were of great interest to Northern Ireland. The Committee favoured devolution to the national regions with some form of federal delegation of powers to bodies appointed by the Government rather than by the BBC. 'In each of these national regions [Scotland, Wales and Northern Ireland] there should be a Broadcasting Commission. Each Commission should consist of, say, five persons appointed by the Government of the United Kingdom, including a Chairman who would be a member of the Corporation.' The Committee suggested that while detailed definition of the powers to be delegated to the national commissions should be left to be worked out by the BBC, 'each of the commissions should initiate and decide on a Home Service programme in its region and should have powers in relation to finance, accommodation and staff sufficient to allow this . . .' The Beveridge Committee explained its purpose: 'Our aim in proposing the Commissions is to ensure, first, that each of the three regions, which are also national units, has its own distinctive voice on the ether. It is, second, in the conduct of British broadcasting as a whole to substitute federal harmony for centralising unity in London.'[36]

The Northern Ireland Prime Minister, Sir Basil Brooke, presented a paper to his Cabinet stating that 'The question of giving greater autonomy in the Northern Ireland region raises issues which I think should be considered by the Cabinet.' The PM offered no arguments one way or another, but he provided two facts which were relevant to the debate: for the year ending 31 March 1949 the local BBC's expenditure exceeded its income from licences sold in the Region by £210,000; and the number of licence holders in Northern Ireland per 100 of the population was 13.32 compared with 20.87 in Scotland

and 20.81 in Wales. Brooke concluded, 'I should be glad if my colleagues would consider whether they desire a measure of self-government in the field of broadcasting to be accorded to Northern Ireland or whether they feel that a policy tending to cut us off from much of what is best in the sphere of information, education and entertainment in the world outside would be a great mistake.'[37] There is no doubt that Sir Basil Brooke's concluding remark weighted the argument against a Commission, for it exaggerated the effect of a Commission's work. Whatever the Commission recommended, the bulk of programming would still come from London.

The Prime Minister took the unusual step of inviting the Controller Northern Ireland, Andrew Stewart, to attend the Cabinet meeting which discussed the question of whether to have a Commission or not. Stewart was asked for his opinions. He said that he was very conscious that the Commission would have to be representative and therefore reflect the divisions in Northern Ireland's society. Inevitably, in the circumstances the members would not always agree and the Commission would then split. This split would probably always be on the same lines and as a consequence, the minority would feel constantly put down and the majority would always appear bloody-minded. In the end the representatives of the minority would resign and there would be a public scandal. Stewart then asked what the Commission would control? The answer was not much, he said, because of the shared wavelength and he was able to indicate that recent BBC investigations showed that the BBC had no room to manoeuvre on that question. In addition, there were limited resources in Broadcasting House, Belfast, both of staff and equipment. The annual programme allowance he described as puny. In the programme area the impact of the Commission would necessarily, therefore, be very limited. Yet it would have to bear public responsibility for the Northern Ireland Home Service. In the circumstances the Commission would have to endure perpetual public obloquy. Stewart recommended that the Government turn the offer down for the time being and, when the shared wavelength arrangement ended, when the resources made available to the Northern Ireland region more closely approximated to those of Scotland and finally, when there was some local television production activity, then it should reconsider the question. By then a Commission might have a basis for power and responsibility which was lacking in 1951.[38]

Stewart left the Cabinet meeting after some questioning. A very lively debate ensued in which two Ministers, Harry Midgeley and Maynard Sinclair, argued strongly for a Commission. In the end, however, the Cabinet decided that it would accept the Beveridge Committee's proposal that the Region should be represented on the BBC's Board of Governors and rejected the proposal for a Commission for the time being.

These conclusions were reached independently by all political parties, by the newspapers and by the BBC's Advisory Council. Members of the Advisory Council feared: the dangers of a Commission over-developing regionalism and degenerating into parochialism; that the Commission might dispense with the Advisory Council and bring in autocratic rule; that the Commission could not possibly be as representative as the Advisory Council. One member, Samuel Napier, who was Secretary of the Northern Ireland Labour Party, believed that 'the present BBC organisation in Northern Ireland should be retained from the point of view of maintaining impartiality which was so important. He foresaw very deep waters and feared that a Commission would lead to bias.' The Council was unanimous in rejecting a Commission and in accepting that there should be a Northern Ireland Governor on the Board of the BBC.[39]

A major argument in favour of devolution, in the eyes of the Beveridge Committee, was that it would secure regard for the distinctive cultures of Scotland, Wales and Northern Ireland. The Belfast *News Letter*'s view of this was that, while in Scotland and Wales . . .

> men who disagree on social policies may well agree on the question of 'securing regard for our distinctive national culture . . .' the question of what is our 'distinctive national culture' is itself a matter of political controversy . . . The BBC, under its present system of local guidance, has steered a careful course through our political shoals, and the absence of any serious criticism of it, is its best tribute.[40]

There was a general disposition to keep things as they were. The Dublin *Sunday Independent* hazarded a guess as to why this might be so:

> Many Unionists take the view that the injection of the region's peculiar political conflicts would not improve broadcasting as a service and might well ruin in. Anti-Partitionists and Labourites are naturally afraid of the Belfast station being controlled from Glengall Street and used for Unionist propaganda.[41]

In any event, Northern Ireland had been offered a measure of control of the Home Service, and had rejected it because no one believed that power-sharing would work. The *Northern Whig* summed up:

> Northern Ireland has certain distinctive issues and outlooks which willy-nilly find a reflection of some kind in almost every aspect of communal life. It is desirable that in such circumstances a broadcasting service designed for the whole community should preserve a greater aloofness from possibly controversial matters, should not only be aloof but be known to be aloof, and though in the result it may be less representative of the Province than might otherwise be wished the gain must outweight the loss.[42]

So BBC Northern Ireland was left to evolve its own policies in the region.

There was a new element in the situation however. Northern Ireland had a 'national' Governor who sat on the BBC's Board of Governors. He was and is a government appointee, and as a consequence, the succession of Governors has reflected the complexion of the successive governments in Northern Ireland. The first Governor was Sir Henry Mulholland who had been first Chairman of the Regional Advisory Council. From his time forward all 'national' Governors were automatically Chairmen of the Council. The succession has been, after Henry Mulholland, Ritchie McKee, Sir Richard Pim, Lord Dunleath, Bill O'Hara and Lady Lucy Faulkner. All have been establishment figures. Their influence within the Board of Governors has until recently been constrained by the fact that Northern Ireland has not had a broadcasting council and has always been by far the smallest region. As the 'national' Governors before the demise of Stormont were the nominees of the Northern Ireland government, they were normally expected to represent its interests. There is no doubt that they did, and that occasionally their interventions were effective, but usually this was on the back of unionist public outcry in any case.

The direction in which Broadcasting House, Belfast moved under Stewart's Controllership was towards an ever more determined exploitation of the programme resources of the Region. The search for talent was promoted by competitions in short-story writing, song writing and play writing. A school for radio writers was run in order to develop the skills of feature writing. In production terms there was a growing emphasis on professionalism. Ursula Eason,

167

who did not get away as she wished and remained on after the war as Assistant Head of Programmes, said that Andrew Stewart strove hard 'to make programmes much more professional; a great deal of what we did had been so unprofessional'.[43] Sam Hanna Bell drew attention to the fact that 'unlike most Northern Ireland Controllers Stewart had been a programme maker most of his life and therefore knew about programme making. He would stop you in the corridor and ask about what you were doing and discuss it fully. It could be irritating but mostly it was encouraging.'[44]

Ursula Eason, who was in charge of religious programmes, described how programming in that field was made more professional:

Far too many clergy who had come in before the War were only concerned with what they had to say and never for a moment realised that the pulpit is different from the microphone but we rather brutally after the War shook them out of that. We started auditions of people who would probably give a good broadcast so as to let them find out what they sounded like in front of a microphone. We would collect four or five of them together and they would each bring a short sermon written for broadcasting. Then we would record them and all sit around and criticise each of them on playback. They were very co-operative and began to realise that broadcasting is not just the message – five minutes to say what you have got to say about the whole Christian doctrine, which is what many tried to do – but that manner and style of presentation were most important. They were brought to realise that it was utterly unlike what they normally did in church. There were disasters. People who seemed to be good simply could not project themselves over the microphone, even though they might have more significant things to say than those who could. That's the danger and it's up to the broadcasters to do something about it. Some people we only used in the studio because in church they could not change their manner. There was very much more studio based religious broadcasting after the War than there had been before.[45]

In this drive for more professional broadcasting, Ursula Eason was much assisted by the Religious Department in London. She brought over a member of that Department each time she ran an 'audition school' to help her in training the clergy. She also learned never to mix the denominations in these sessions because this inhibited the trainees.

In the autumn of 1952 it was announced that Andrew Stewart had been appointed Controller of the Home Service and that he would leave Belfast at the end of the year.

Before he left he became aware of the fact that a General Election was in the offing and he wrote a memo to London informing the Director of the Spoken Word of this probability and offered his advice. That advice represents a curious reflection on the outcome of his experience in Northern Ireland. He recommended that the BBC should not 'offer the facilities of broadcasting to the parties on the same terms as in Great Britain'.

Frankly I don't see much point in making this offer for two reasons:

1 It is difficult to see how, under the Charter, we can utter propaganda for breaking up the United Kingdom.

2 Neither of the main parties really wants broadcast propaganda: it is a two-edged weapon and they will almost certainly do as they did last time and get out of the problem by failing to agree on the allocation of dates.[46]

After four years Stewart had obviously changed his mind and had come to the conclusion that party political broadcasts were not to be recommended.

Stewart's Controllership represents the second major turning point in the history of the BBC in Northern Ireland. The first was when the Lisnagarvey transmitter opened in 1936 and brought an end to the period when BBC coverage was effectively restricted to within thirty miles of Belfast. In the three years or so before the war the BBC staff had tried to give expression to the Region but it was in Stewart's time that regionalism could be said to have been realised, despite a shared wavelength and a limited programme allowance. Henry McMullan wrote in the *BBC Year Book* for 1950:

... much has been done – as a comparison between the programmes broadcast from Northern Ireland before the War and the programmes today will show. Then the 'imported' artistes were many and the amount of genuine Northern Ireland material very small. Now the country stands on its own broadcasting feet, with a preponderantly Ulster staff to serve the needs of Ulster people.'[47]

McMullan may have been a little ungenerous to the late 1930s but his enthusiasm for what was being achieved, when he wrote this in 1949, reflected a real change.

6

The Attempt to Create a Consensus

The thirteen and a half years from January 1953 to June 1966 form a distinctive period in the history of the BBC in Northern Ireland. Broadcasting House, Belfast, was occupied by a succession of Controllers who pursued a consistent policy of reducing the constraints on broadcasting which they had inherited. The policy had, in fact, been initiated by Andrew Stewart, although he was not thought of as a liberal. Cyril Conner, who succeeded him, stayed only six months. It was Richard Marriott who was perceived as a liberal and many saw the impetus which he gave in the years from 1953 to 1956 as one which persisted throughout the Controllership of Robert McCall.

Conner, Marriott and McCall were all drawn from the BBC's External Services. To some extent they were drafted to Belfast by the Director General, Sir Ian Jacob, who knew them well from his time as Director of External Broadcasting. None of them accepted the posting with enthusiasm. Conner, an Englishman, had domestic reasons for not wishing to stay. Marriott, another Englishman, only stayed three years. McCall, who had spent most of his life in Australia although Scottish born, passed the final ten years of his broadcasting career and then his retirement in Belfast. McCall gave up the post of Deputy Director of External Broadcasting to become Controller Northern Ireland, possibly for health reasons. His experience of broadcasting was considerable. He had begun his career in Australia but had been invited to join the BBC in 1946. He had served in the External Services with some distinction.

Under the direction of these men the BBC sought to play a constructive role in Northern Ireland. All three hoped to win recognition for broadcasting as an agency for improving relations between the communities, always of course within the given political context. They wished to see open political debate but they remained chary of speakers with extremist views on the grounds that they were divisive. Their conviction was that this dialogue would help the

170

communities discover what they had in common. When current affairs programming developed in the region, social and economic problems were investigated as universal problems and little attention was paid to the separate and often different impact of those problems on the majority and minority communities. The issue of discrimination was scarcely raised. The programme policy consequently accentuated what bound the communities together and neglected or ignored that which drove them apart. The aim again was to create a consensus. It was never enunciated as such; rather, it was pursued pragmatically. Quiet initiatives directed to this end were unlikely to provoke negative reactions and were most likely to win social and political acceptance.

In the first days of the new regime, however, there was uproar among unionist elements of a kind which was to recur on many occasions later. Dr D'Alton, the Catholic Archbishop of Armagh and Primate of all Ireland, returned from Rome where he had been created Cardinal. He was warmly received in the cathedral city and in his speech of thanks he took the opportunity to express his regret that Ireland was partitioned. His speech and the ceremonies of welcome were recorded by the BBC and transmitted on the following evening. The Stormont Government made no objection and regarded the BBC's action as perfectly proper. A violent attack was, however, launched on the BBC by loyalists both in the press and by letter to Broadcasting House. They argued that the BBC should have suppressed the Cardinal's statement on partition, even though it was widely reported in the newspapers. Conner, the Acting Controller, was somewhat taken aback by the attack, for, as he reported to the BBC's Board of Governors:

Curiously enough the reports in the Northern Ireland Home Service Regional News of statements in the Stormont Parliament regarding partition are never criticised. The BBC's policy of impartiality, based though this must be on the premise that Northern Ireland continues to be an integral part of the United Kingdom, is often imperfectly understood by both sides, and the difficulty of a political situation in which the opposition opposes not only the policies of the Government but the very existence of the country as a separate entity calls for constant care in the content and presentation of programmes.

It is true to say that, outside broadcasting, there is practically no interchange of views on any subjects between the two divisions of opinion in Northern Ireland. For some years past the BBC has encouraged both sides to come together in broadcasting. It is a long-term policy with obvious limitations, but progress is being made: in the monthly debate by three speakers on current affairs in Northern Ireland; in the 'open' debates recorded in country halls; and in the critical discussions on *The Arts in Ulster* which have become one of the outstanding programmes on the service. Five years ago in Londonderry it was not possible to combine artists or audience from the two groups of opinion in one hall. In the period under review a joint debate of the most mixed kind on a burning topic 'Emigration and Unemployment' drew a big audience from both political and religious groups. The speakers included (anonymously) one of the more fiery Nationalist members of the Northern Ireland Parliament, who accepted the limitations imposed and made a useful contribution to the discussion.[1]

Speakers were required to stick to the subject of the debate and not to raise the constitutional issue. Such a constraint could not be imposed on party political broadcasts and it became apparent that rather than permit open debate on the constitutional issue the Government party was prepared to block agreement on election broadcasts.

Before Andrew Stewart left, he warned London that a General Election in Northern Ireland was imminent. In the event it did not occur until a year later, in the autumn of 1953. The Board of Governors decided that the BBC would again offer election broadcasting time to the main parties. Richard Marriott informed the Government of this intention through Sir Robert Gransden, Secretary to the Cabinet. Marriott reported that Gransden's 'attitude was most co-operative and friendly, and in theory he supports our making this offer and believes that its acceptance would be a step forward. In practice, from the fear of the consequences, his influence may well be used in seeing that the necessary agreement between the parties is not reached.'[2]

A short time before the dissolution, Marriott confessed to the BBC's Director of the Spoken Word that his 'chief anxiety was that the Nationalists might say something so offensive about the Throne or the Constitution as to bring odium on the BBC, no matter how carefully we explained that we are not responsible'. After the dissolution it became apparent that, while the Unionists and the Labour Party proposed to attend a meeting to discuss the allocation of broadcasting time, the Nationalists would not. The BBC's Board of Governors decided that the Controller should press the Nationalist Party to attend but if its representative did not, then the meeting should go ahead. If the allocation decided by the two parties seemed fair, then the BBC should abide by it. The agreed number of slots should be offered the Nationalists and if they didn't take them, that was it as far as they were concerned. The other party political broadcasts were to go ahead.

In the event, James McSparran did attend, as he had done in 1949. Topping was present for the Unionist Party and there was one newcomer, Napier, for the Northern Ireland Labour Party. Marriott opened the negotiations because no one seemed prepared to start: he suggested four Unionist broadcasts, two Nationalist and one Labour. Topping immediately 'stated categorically that this was unacceptable, and that 5:2:1 was the least he could consider'. McSparran thought there should be a 50/50 division of time between Government and Opposition as a matter of principle but conceded that he would accept the BBC's formula. Marriott reported, 'The attitude of McSparran throughout was, unexpectedly, entirely reasonable and he made no claims that anyone could seriously call unfair.' It was known beforehand that Labour would be content with one broadcast, for they had no seats in the dissolved Parliament. Marriott observed, 'It was evident from the outset that the Unionists were determined either that no broadcasts should take place, or that they should be in a proportion which at least one of the others would find unacceptable.' Topping stuck to 5:2:1 and Marriott, in order to keep negotiations open, offered 4:2:½; the half being a shorter broadcast for Labour. Topping said he would have to consult and it was agreed that if the Unionist Party agreed to this arrangement the broadcasts were on, otherwise they were not.

Marriott reflected, when he learned that the Unionists would not agree, 'It is clear to me now that it is the Unionists who do not want to broadcast and are quite happy to keep the others off the air even though the others are willing to agree to what I think an impartial person would say was a reasonable allocation.'[3] Marriott felt frustrated and was determined that next time there would be election broadcasts.

The General Election of 1953 was covered in Regional News as fairly and as impartially as it had been in 1949. However, a new dimension was added to media coverage of the event: BBC Television *Newsreel* carried a short report on the campaign and its results. Some people in Northern Ireland were able to watch the bulletin.

For television had arrived in Northern Ireland in the spring of 1953. The network service was relayed by a temporary low-powered transmitter and the signal could be picked up over an area which was somewhat less extensive than that served by 2BE in 1924. Undoubtedly the arrival of television in this temporary form was dictated by the wish to provide a service in time for the Coronation ceremonies in June of that year. The royal occasion, it was felt, would stimulate the sales of sets and of licences. It was clear in the circumstances that this transmitter would simply relay programmes and that there would be little local production. A film unit was nevertheless recruited for the region and it was given a modest task: to shoot film for a fortnightly series to be called *Ulster Mirror*. These programmes, each lasting fifteen to twenty minutes, were at first transmitted to local viewers when the network was off the air but soon they were regarded as good enough to find a place in the network schedule. They did not, in fact, provide the first glimpses which viewers in Great Britain had of Northern Ireland. Two programmes had already been transmitted. The first was *Pattern of Ulster*, of which the Acting Controller, Conner, said, 'a good deal of supervision and discussion has been necessary to ensure that the picture shall maintain a sense of proportion between the thatched cottage and the very modern techniques and achievements of the country'. Conner told the Northern Ireland Advisory Council, 'there is obviously a tremendously important field of possible publicity for Northern Ireland in the new Television Service'.[4] The other travelogue shown on the network before the start of *Ulster Mirror* was a film in the *About Britain* series, presented by Richard Dimbleby.

Of the *Ulster Mirror* series, Richard Marriott reiterated the point that it 'may be able to give some useful publicity for Northern Ireland in the United Kingdom'.[5] This was an expectation of television which was to grow. The Unionist Government and the unionist majority did not envisage that the new medium would have anything other than a positive, promotional role.

For thirty years BBC schools' broadcasting, while it achieved world renown, made little impact on the schools of Northern Ireland. The Regional Advisory Council had expressed its concern that this was so at its first meeting in 1947 and although, strictly speaking, schools' broadcasting did not fall within its remit, successive Controllers were willing to waive the rules in order to have the

Council's support in their own efforts to promote the educational programmes. Schools' broadcasting was the concern of the School Broadcasting Council, a representative body which had virtually an executive function in the field. Northern Ireland had three representatives on the Council, one each from the Ministry of Education, the Association of Education Committees and the Federal Council of Teachers. This trio, especially the inspector from the Ministry, had made some efforts to promote the use of BBC programmes in the schools. By 1953 the number of registered listening schools had reached 500. This number, it was rumoured, would constitute a turning point. Northern Ireland would be given a national council or local committee of its own and some local production.

J. J. Campbell, who had a professional interest in education, gave notice of his intention to raise such issues at the Regional Advisory Council. The Acting Controller, Conner, contacted the Education Officer for the North-West of England, Stephen Murphy, who had been required by the School Broadcasting Council to include Northern Ireland in his area of responsibility. Conner put Campbell's questions to Murphy and invited him to attend the next Advisory Council meeting.

Murphy, a former teacher who was later to become the British film censor, wrote a lengthy confidential memo in reply in which he analysed the Northern Ireland situation in some detail. Murphy was well aware that the Advisory Council had favoured schools' broadcasting all along and that it had pushed the notion that 'a courageous policy . . . would do something to heal Northern Ireland's wounds. Surely, by now, the argument went, we can stand a scholarly and objective study of Irish history.' Murphy commented too on the expectations of many people in educational circles in Northern Ireland that a council and local production were immediate possibilities. The obstacles to such developments, he revealed, were the region's own representatives on the School Broadcasting Council. Stuart Hawnt and A. C. Stanley held firmly to the view, he said, that 'it would be a mistake to regard Northern Ireland as in any way different from England'; productions from Great Britain were all that the pupils in Northern Ireland's schools needed. The Ministry's inspector by contrast was simply opposed to the creation of any body which would not be directly under the Ministry's control.[6]

175

All three put forward to the School Broadcasting Council a paper which made the following points:

a there is no case at present for a Northern Ireland Council.
b there is no case at present for special series.
c more programmes using Ulster material should be incorporated in normal output.
d to this end, they asked for increased membership of the programme sub-committees . . . .[7]

Murphy was quite certain that the three representatives were not 'representing'. He wrote, 'In my view there is a very wide demand from the teaching profession for a Council and for special series. Dr Hawnt, I know, did not consult his fellow-directors of education in any way, or he would have found that five of the seven disagreed with him quite strongly.' In the circumstances, with the hopes and expectations of many in the educational service being sabotaged by their own representatives, there was little chance of serious progress. The percentage of listening schools at the time was only 30% compared with 60% in Wales, 70% in Scotland and over 70% in England. Most observers believed that until there were some locally produced series in the output there would be no dramatic rise in the percentage. On the Regional Advisory Council, J. J. Campbell was quite unaware of the source of the impasse in the way of local developments, but urged that more Northern Ireland material should be included in the London-made programme series, which of course coincided with the advice of Northern Ireland's representatives on the School Broadcasting Council.

The interest which the Advisory Council had expressed in a schools' Ulster history series as early as 1948 was to be sustained, but in 1953 J. J. Campbell expressed the view that the time had come for such a series to be broadcast to the general listener. The BBC accepted the suggestion and established a small committee consisting of Professor T. W. Moody of the University of Dublin, J. C. Beckett, Reader in Irish History at the Queen's University, Belfast, and J. J. Campbell himself, to advise on the structure of a series of talks and to suggest the names of historians who might give them. *Ulster since 1800* drew from the expertise of a number of historians belonging to the new movement in Irish historiography which had developed since the mid-1930s. The approach was objective, scientific and not dictated, as earlier approaches had often been, by overt political commitment. It is not without interest that at the same time

Professor Moody prompted Radio Éireann to launch the Thomas Davis lecture series which was to play a similar role in the Republic to *Ulster Since 1800* in Northern Ireland. The Northern Ireland series did not become a regular feature of BBC radio programming as the Thomas Davis lectures have become in the Republic but it was so well received that a second series followed, dealing with the economic and social history of Ulster.[8]

While the BBC thus sought to encourage Northern Ireland listeners to take an informed, rational view of the past of the region in which they lived, it also tried to find a programme format which would permit a reasonably balanced discussion of current problems in Northern Ireland. None of its experiments had been particularly successful until in January 1954, a regional variation of the popular network programme, *Any Questions* was launched, entitled *Your Questions*. It had a panel of speakers – most of whom appeared regularly – and a chairman. The questions came from the floor but none of the argument. 'The intention was to provide a forum for open discussion on subjects of every kind which had particular point in Ulster, including the most controversial.'[9] The programme caught the public imagination and became even more popular in Northern Ireland than the network version. It was increased in length and became peripatetic, appearing in centres throughout the region. The platform speakers on the first occasion were John E. Sayers, J. J. Campbell, J. C. Beckett and Charles Brett. The chairman was Desmond Neill of the Queen's University. All were to become well-known personalities as a result of their many appearances. While this team by no means agreed with one another and indeed sometimes hotly disputed issues, there is no doubt that they all occupied the middle ground. More extreme views only occasionally came from other speakers who joined the platform party. The general tone was moderate and civilized. This may be illustrated from the hundredth edition of the programme which began with the question, 'how do we get sectarianism out of politics?'.

> J. J. Campbell: Well, there is a very simple way, when asked how you can cut it out, cut it out. Simply like that, make up their minds that they want to cut it out. Now, of course, a politician when you talk to him about a thing like this will say, 'you know I agree with you on this matter but I have to deal with my constituents and I have pressure groups in my constituency who would make it very awkward for me if I

	didn't beat the big drum at times and wave the flag and so on'. I think that it is time they ceased to take notice of such pressure groups because they represent a minority of the people of Northern Ireland. The majority of us here do not want sectarian bitterness. Secondly, I think that the press should cease to take note of and to publish accounts of bitterness in speeches whether they come from politicians or from anyone else. I think, for example, that a man of God, a clergyman of the Christian Church, who contributes to bitterness in our midst is a man who should not be noticed by any newspaper. His actions and his speeches should not be noted and that applies to teachers and to professional men of all kinds . . . We should have a truce to party slogans, a truce to slogans on walls, a truce to flag waving and then we'd cut out sectarianism. (Applause)
J. E. Sayers:	Well, really this is the first time that I've known my friend Campbell to be so facile. Let me answer first for newspapers: our duty is to report what exists and I don't think any service is given to Ireland by suppressing people who express themselves in a bitter way. I think that is merely disguising the situation. But to look at this thing more broadly, I think he is also facile in saying that sectarianism has merely to be cut out. I can only quote the example of the Republic of Ireland which represents the ideal of the Nationalist Party in Northern Ireland and it professedly lays down that it is a Catholic Ireland. Now there's sectarianism for you and my answer to this question would have been, before I heard Campbell speak, to say that the English constitution names no religion but produces a society and an ideal in society of social and economic betterment and that is, I think, all that you need.
J. J. Campbell:	I think that this question refers to Northern Ireland and what can be done inside Northern Ireland. I have maintained, and this is now the hundredth edition of this programme, since the first edition when I appeared, that our difficulty here is the border within, the border between the two sets in our own community and not to worry about anything else. We want to live in peace and harmony and let's cut out the bitterness. (Applause)[10]

The Northern Ireland Home Service was trying to do its best! Other BBC services were naturally not so concerned and the unionist majority remained as reactive as ever to what it deemed provocations transmitted by them. On four occasions in March 1954, incidents occurred which led to protests from listeners, viewers, newspapers and the Northern Ireland Government. Two were associated with programmes to celebrate St Patrick's Day, the first following a familiar pattern. Wilfred Pickles conducted a *Have a Go* programme from the London–Irish Society and in the course of it 'The Soldier's Song' was played. On television, the editor of *Panorama* at the last minute, having lost his prearranged St Patrick's Day item, filled in with a travel film, *Ireland – Land of Welcome*. Effectively, it promoted tourism in the Irish Republic and there was no mention of Northern Ireland.

Both instances generated anger. With regard to the film BBC executives felt, 'The complaint about us is mainly jealousy that it did the Éire scenery so proud.' The editor remarked, 'I did not know that St Patrick was more an Ulster saint than an Éire one.' He apologised to the Director of Television who was annoyed that the Controller Northern Ireland had not been asked for his advice beforehand. The Director General ruled, in relation to future St Patrick's Day broadcasts:

> . . . The celebration of St Patrick's Day is only justified in BBC broadcasts in virtue of the relationship of St Patrick to Northern Ireland, which alone places St Patrick in the same category as St George, St Andrew or St David. From our point of view there is no more significance in St Patrick as the patron saint of the Irish Republic than there is in the patron saint of any other country outside the Commonwealth . . .[11]

Towards the end of March unionists again found cause for incitement in a broadcast on radio and in one on television. In a religious programme, *Lift up your Hearts*, the Catholic bishop of Leeds, later to become Cardinal, John Heenan, made the statement: 'We are so used to tolerance for minorities in England that we take it for granted. They don't elsewhere – in Spain, for example, and Northern Ireland – but their intolerance is as nothing compared with the savage treatment of believers where active Communists are in control.'[12] As soon as the programme was over protests began flowing into Broadcasting House, Belfast. Lord Brookeborough, the Prime Minister, immediately sent a telegram of protest to London:

> On behalf of the Northern Ireland Government I protest strongly against the unjustified attack on Northern Ireland in Bishop Heenan's *Lift up*

179

your Hearts broadcast today. I must request immediate repudiation by the BBC.[13]

The BBC broadcast an apology in its next news bulletin regretting that such a statement should have been made in a programme intended for encouragement and worship. A BBC official in Belfast said:

> The passage was interpolated into the script after the script had been agreed to by the Head of Religious Broadcasting, the Rev Francis House, and after the producer had left the studio. It was written in pencil. The BBC is no way to blame.[14]

The Bishop described it as 'last minute inspiration' and strongly resented the terms of the BBC apology and indeed questioned the need for it. He stressed that he had not mentioned the Government of Northern Ireland and commented, 'That they took it to mean themselves suggests an uneasy conscience.' Meantime, protests continued from the Unionist Party, the Orange Order and various other Protestant organisations. The *Northern Whig* devoted a leader to the affair.

The next row concerned a film, *The Promise of Barty O'Brien*, which showed 'by means of a fictional story how electrical power was brought to an under-developed bog area in the Republic of Ireland with the help of American Aid. It is, of course, a propaganda film for the development of rural districts generally and is one of a series about the application of practical aid in European Countries.'[15] The basic objection to the film was that viewers in Great Britain might have thought that it was about Northern Ireland. The Director General, Sir Ian Jacob, rejected this firmly and added, 'To exclude such productions from broadcasting would in my opinion be unfortunate. While therefore I am sorry if the showing of this film should have given offence, I do not myself believe that the film is one which should not have been shown.'[16] Brookeborough persisted:

> ... The notice in the *Radio Times* referred to the film as one about 'an Irish farming family' and unless the film itself made it clear that it gave a picture of farming life in Southern Ireland I am afraid an unfortunate impression will be created in the minds of viewers in Great Britain who are unaware that there are two distinct elements in the 'Irish' scene.
> I know how difficult it must be for you and your colleagues in the BBC to hold the scales evenly where controversy is likely to arise, and we are

180

encouraged by your promise to do all you can to see that offence is not given to the great majority of viewers in Northern Ireland.[17]

Pressure such as this, exerted as it was on the back of public reaction, was designed to discipline the BBC. It had the desired effect because, although Jacob publicly rejected the criticisms stirred up by *The Promise of Barty O'Brien*, he wrote to heads of departments:

. . . It is most important that we should not unnecessarily fan the flames of disunion in Northern Ireland. It is difficult here to realise how real the political and religious factors are in that country, and how near boiling point opinion constantly remains. It is, therefore, most necessary that very great care should be taken before programmes dealing with any part of Ireland are mounted and that the procedure laid down in this matter should be followed in every instance. Decisions will in this way be taken with our eyes open.[18]

The procedure was the one which originated in Marshall's wartime days and required that the Controller Northern Ireland should be consulted on all programme plans to do with Northern Ireland or the Republic of Ireland. Marriott, the man burdened with this role, had a realistic attitude to the situation:

The problem here, of course, is that Northern Ireland is an integral part of the Corporation's network, but the regional office can control only its own output, it is a physical impossibility even to detect in advance from the whole output of the BBC matters which might conceivably be offensive to particular sections of the population in Northern Ireland.

The wide publicity given to the events in March had in fact focussed attention in the the BBC on Northern Ireland and in so far as is possible precautions have been taken to avoid the same kind of problems arising in the future. At the same time, taking account of the possibility of human error among so large a staff, it is impossible to guarantee that other mistakes will not occasionally be made.[19]

In the period from 1953 to 1966 radio was eclipsed by television, although it happened more slowly in Northern Ireland than elsewhere. The audience remained loyal to the older medium. There were a number of reasons, one of which was the relatively lower incomes of the population of the region, which meant fewer people could afford to buy television sets. Another reason was that television for long lacked any significant local component whereas radio continued to supply a regional service. The abiding interest of the Northern Ireland audience in its own radio programmes was attested by Listener Research from the time it arrived in 1954. The Northern Ireland Home Service was in fact more popular in the region than the Light Programme, reversing the pattern elsewhere in the United Kingdom. More people in Northern Ireland turned on the regional news than in any other region. This regional loyalty reached its peak with *The McCooeys* which in its time proved more popular than any other programme in any other region. Doubtless people in the North-East of England, who were forced to receive the series because of the shared wavelength, would have found this hard to credit.

After Joseph Tomelty's accident in 1957 and the consequent demise of *The McCooey's*, the BBC in Belfast tried very hard to find a satisfactory replacement. *The Carlisles* by Janet McNeill had already been floated. It recounted the daily lives of a Northern Ireland professional family, a counterpart of the network *Mrs Dale's Diary*. It left the audience cold. Even less successful was *At No. 5* which dropped down the scale to the same social level as *The McCooeys*. It failed because it was regarded primarily as a means of informing the audience about the public services to which they were entitled and the author's characterisation of those who lived in 'No. 5' suffered as a consequence. *Mrs Lally's Lodgers* was the last attempt to replace *The McCooeys*. Written by Jack Loudan, it won quite respectable audiences but never the affection and acclaim bestowed on Joe Tomelty's fictional family.

The McCooeys had one by-product, however, whose individual success almost equalled that of the parent programme. James Young first appeared as a character in the serial but was soon singled out by the broadcasters as a comedian of unusual quality. He was given a programme of his own which, under a variety of titles, continued throughout the 1960s. Young was the Belfast equivalent of Dublin's Jimmy O'Dea. Like O'Dea, he had the rare talent of being able to make fun of both sides of the sectarian divide in Ulster without offending either. What he did offend was middle-class propriety. Members of the BBC's Regional Advisory Council found his 'vulgarity' hard to take. Members of the BBC staff were more concerned about the difficulty of finding scriptwriters for Young, who did not write his own material.

Finding writers of all kinds and at all times had posed problems for the BBC in Northern Ireland. Its search had opened careers to quite a variety of talents but not every writer welcomed the opportunity.

The novelist Anne Crone felt that, 'Regional broadcasting has in one way done Ulster writers a grave disservice . . . The great excuse for regional broadcasting is that it should offer programmes that have the flavour of a particular region. Only too often this comes to mean, so far as Northern Ireland is concerned, a perpetuation of certain types which are simply clowns and of a dialect and humour that are not always characteristic . . . The would-be writer in Northern Ireland who paints his fellow creatures here as not so wildly different from his fellow creatures a hundred miles away and using an idiom and an accent not greatly at variance from theirs, runs the danger of having his script refused.'[20]

Doubtless some authors were constrained to write about regional stereotypes but a number were discovered who wrote original radio plays which enriched regional drama. Janet McNeill, Graeme Roberts, John D. Stewart and Sam Thompson all had their particular successes, both on radio and stage. And not all their plays were narrowly regional.

Reflecting the region was the special task of feature producers. Sam Hanna Bell sought to capture the distinctive qualities of the men of the Belfast shipyards in the programme *The Islandmen*. In order to build up his portrait in sound, he made over 200 recordings. Although *The Islandmen* won much appreciation, there were still those who, like one member of the Advisory Council, questioned the veracity of the accents and of the dialect. Sam Hanna Bell produced other notable feature programmes in these golden days of radio. One, *A Kist O'Whistles*, was an account of the bitter controversy which surrounded the introduction of the organ or harmonium into the worship of the Presbyterian Church of Ireland.

Feature producers and all those who went out and about for programme material were able to transform their programme-making in the 1950s. Methods of recording improved beyond recognition. At first tape replaced disc in the mobile units and the lighter, less cumbersome equipment meant that production teams could more easily reach remote places. Then the portable tape recorder enabled the interviewer or recorder to gather material anywhere he or she was capable of going. It wrought a revolution in most areas of broadcasting. Robert Coulter, who became agricultural talks producer in Belfast in 1953, indicated what it meant for him:

> The previous way of preparing a programme had inevitably been in the studio which made two things likely to happen: a) one used experts, speaking with a high degree of knowledge but not necessarily broadcasting

in the proper sense, b) one used farmers, practical men from the land, who like others found coming into the studio a terrifying experience and who were inhibited by the whole system. With the coming of the midget tape recorder one could go to their place, to their farm, to their byre, to their pigs, where the broadcaster was the intruder, and they were at home and therefore they talked freely and easily, being on their own spot, in their own way of life, their own things around them. The effect of this was quite extraordinary because lots of people who had no interest in brucelosis, cocciliosis or any of the other 'oses' found these men talking in such a vital way from their own direct experience . . . that broadcasting on farming became widely listened to. We were also able to go into magazine treatments, so, instead of taking a straight long piece on grassland management, we could have a five or six item magazine which was lively and worth listening to. It was a great experience because not only the farmer felt better but the broadcaster himself got deeper and deeper into the way of life of country people rather than into the technicalities of farm radio . . . They always said that farmers learnt most by looking over the hedge and there was something in this recording technique of nonscripted interviews which was a kind of looking over the hedge. So that even in educational terms it brought improvement as well as being friendlier, easier and more relaxing to listen to in the farmhouse and elsewhere.[21]

As one technological advance enabled the radio broadcaster to improve the programmes, another enabled him to improve the quality of the signal. For years Northern Ireland listeners had been promised that very high frequency channels would eventually not only end the interference and fading which they experienced on medium wave but also remove the inconvenience and limitations imposed on local regional broadcating by the sharing of the wavelength with the North-East of England. When VHF broadcasting was introduced, it was in association with television. The VHF transmitters were installed in the television transmitting stations. This coincidence had two effects. In the first instance, VHF arrived with a very much more expensive medium and so resources were not made available to expand regional programme production on the new radio channel. For long, the difference between what was offered on medium wave and on VHF was only a ten-minute news bulletin as opposed to a five-minute one and one light musical programme. In the second instance, VHF broadcasting began in the region in 1956, as television started on its way to win the mass audience. Inevitably the significance of the shared medium wavelength diminished as more of the audience moved over to watching the small screen. By January 1963, when the sharing ceased and Northern Ireland got a medium wave channel to itself, the event was almost unnoticed. The major gain to the listener then was not additional regional programmes but a rescheduling of existing programmes to more satisfactory times and the removal of some programmes emanating from the BBC's North Region, to which the Northern Ireland audience had never really objected, and their replacement by London programmes.

The television signal in Northern Ireland had to come from a temporary transmitter for more than two years. At last, on 21 July 1955, the new Divis Mountain transmitter overlooking Belfast was officially opened. Its signal covered eighty per cent of Northern Ireland's surface and potentially reached two-thirds of the population. In subsequent years this coverage was extended through a series of satellite transmitters until the whole population could receive BBC television.

Divis came on air only two months before Independent Television began operations in Britain. The new competition had an immediate impact on the BBC Northern Ireland. It was decided that the network schedule could not afford to keep *Ulster Mirror* in a regular slot. Instead the film unit in the region was required to supply six half-hour documentaries per year. Some of the films produced to this order were good enough to be shown on the network a number of times. They included *Family Farm,* an account of rural life in Ulster, and *Rathlin Island,* a glimpse of a declining community.

The first live television transmissions from Northern Ireland were made possible by the visit of a mobile Outside Broadcasting unit in November 1955. The development of a permanent live transmission facility had to wait two years, when a small sound studio was adapted for the purpose. From it a five-minute programme, *Today in Northern Ireland,* was produced on weekday evenings. The slot was solemnly divided in two: the newsroom produced two-and-a-half minutes and the general producers were responsible for two-and-a-half-minute features. The precedent set lasted for more than a decade. The sharing remained as the length of the programme increased. There was at first no film, only still photographs. The production team did eventually attempt a 'lash-up' film operation and showed the same enterprise on the Twelfth of July 1958, when they used the studio cameras to make a programme of the Orange procession marching past Broadcasting House.

A purpose-built studio came into commission on 20 February 1959, enabling the television staff to mount a weekly programme named after it, *Studio Eight*. It was usually a magazine consisting of various topical items but sometimes the programme was given over to other purposes. The experiment was tried of transferring the radio programme, *Your Questions* to the television studio. It was not very successful. Sometimes documentary films filled the slot and occasionally musical programmes. Initially, *Studio Eight* posed the problem long familiar in regional radio: Broadcasting House, Belfast, had to 'opt out' of a network programme in order to find space for it. With some viewers this was not a popular move, as they resented losing what they regarded as a 'better' programme. This audience resistance was to restrict the expansion of regional television. Programme planners and other broadcasting executives at the time used to say that the problem would be relieved when the BBC got a second channel.

Studio Eight had only established itself when the BBC in Northern Ireland was faced with an official competitor for the first time. For decades, it is true, Radio Éireann has constituted an alternative service over much of the region, used particularly by listeners in the nationalist community, but this was accidental and unofficial. On Hallowe'en 1959 the BBC in Belfast was confronted by Ulster Television. This company, which had won the contract to provide Independent Television in Northern Ireland, consisted of a number of interests drawn from the entertainment and newspaper world. The Belfast *News Letter* had played an important role in its creation. Its only serious rival for the franchise was Northern Ireland Television Ltd, based in part on the *Northern Whig*. Ulster Television succeeded because its support was more broadly based in the community. That is, more influential people from the minority backed it than backed Northern Ireland Television Ltd.

As elsewhere in the United Kingdom, the arrival of Independent Television brought a rapid rise in the sale of television receivers and licences. Very soon the new service captured a larger audience than the BBC, as happened in Britain. The significant and direct rivalry between Broadcasting House and Havelock House was over locally-produced programmes. UTV launched a weekday magazine *Roundabout* which took a while to make an impact. When it did, the competition became intense. One consequence was that each broadcasting organisation reached out in an ever more determined way into both the Northern Ireland communities for programme material and sought to broaden the dialogue between them. Ulster Television explicitly declared that it was in the business of reconciliation and bridge building. As a commercial concern, of course, it was addressing the whole population with no intention of alienating part of it. Whatever its motives, Ulster Television accelerated the process of liberalisation going on in Broadcasting House, Belfast. It also permitted the BBC in Northern Ireland to demand and to obtain much increased resources in equipment and programme allowances with which to meet the competition.

From 1956 onwards into the early 1960s Northern Ireland was subject to an IRA campaign. News coverage of the acts of violence was limited on the broadcast media: news bulletins were short and current affairs broadcasting in the region did not exist. Ulster Television did not have a newsroom until October 1962, eight months after the IRA had called off its campaign. Robert Coulter of the BBC recalled:

> . . . the IRA were at first almost theatrical desperadoes in people's minds. The Londonderry radio transmitter was blown up on the same night in 1956 as the other ten or eleven incidents took place which started the violence. There was the same atmosphere in Derry as elsewhere. There were these strange and rather alien figures who had been responsible for outrages against the whole community. It wasn't split then. Most of the blowings up took place along the Border and news coverage was a pure 'fire brigade' operation of going with the Army to the site, of photographing the damage and the RUC men who happened to be around. It was a very literal kind of coverage. Just sheer straight reporting without comment or interpretation. It was only when the thing began to take a more sinister turn – the early outrages were not anti-personnel – and they started booby-trapping empty houses on the Border that people began to divide more and more in their minds again. There was still, however, nothing significant about the coverage of the time beyond pure newsreel pictorials.[22]

IRA activities in the period failed, however, to win significant support in the minority community and for that reason were abandoned. Their effect on the unionist community was inevitably to strengthen intransigency and to make the BBC's self-appointed task of bringing the communities together more difficult. As the Controller, Robert McCall, reported to the Board of Governors:

Broadcasting in Northern Ireland has been working under some difficulty since the outbreak of the IRA campaign of violence in December. The majority of our listeners are quick to take offence if the BBC attempts to 'inform or educate' on the problem of the Partition of Ireland. Even Irish music has become suspect to the Unionist part of the population, and the reflection of some factual news has been described as propaganda for the Republic. Complaints on television coverage of news or inclusion of Irish items – unless they emanate from Northern Ireland – are also a matter of comment. In the circumstances, with an audience quick to take offence – suffering perhaps from rather stretched nerves – the BBC in Northern Ireland has tried to preserve a sense of balance, and on the whole has, with the assistance of the other departments of the Corporation who seek our advice, steered a reasonable course. It is not easy, when tempers are high, to induce a sense of proportion in an audience anxious to find some way of expressing its irritation.

Nevertheless this was the period in which there was a breakthrough, this time as a result of a Northern Ireland General Election. Parliament was dissolved on 27 February 1958. Once again the BBC offered election broadcasting time to the main parties. To the meeting to seek agreement on the allocation of time came: Brian Faulkner and W. B. Douglas – Unionists; Sam Napier – Labour; and Patrick McGill, J. G. Lennon and Edward McAteer – Nationalists. The Controller, Robert McCall, wrote an account of what transpired:

Mr Faulkner (Chief Government Whip) began for the Unionists by saying that his party would agree to take part if they had six of the eight broadcasts; they didn't care who had the other two. They had had thirty-eight out of the fifty-two members of the House and they were not prepared to accept an allocation of less than six of the broadcasts.

This attitude was quickly challenged by Senator McGill for the Nationalists. He said that the periods should be allocated 'on the basis of population'. He answered a Unionist query by frankly stating that this was population based on religious adherence – Protestant and Roman Catholic.

Mr McAteer (Nationalist) said that if this was the Unionist approach the meeting was not worth while. The debate continued haphazardly until McAteer said that five Unionist, two Nationalist and one Labour would be correct. The Unionists flatly refused to consider five broadcasts.

At this stage the Unionists were insisting on six and Nationalists on two broadcasts. Napier (Labour) looked forlorn and grim. I enquired whether it would ease the situation if I could make available a ninth broadcasting period. In this case, the Unionists said, they would have to have seven of the nine broadcasts. Mr Douglas, the Secretary of the Unionist Party, declared 'we don't care what happens to the two broadcasts we don't have.'

This obviously interested the Nationalists who asked leave to withdraw for consultation. Senator McGill returned shortly to invite Napier (Labour) to join them.

Returning fifteen minutes later McGill announced that the Nationalists and Labour had reached agreement and that the Nationalists would have both broadcasts. Before proceeding with the allocation of broadcasting times I asked Napier to formally indicate that he was in agreement.

Napier said he disagreed with the decision but didn't see what he could do about it. It was noticeable that the Unionists had been taken aback by the announcement of agreement.

I pointed out that this was not, in fact, an agreement by the three parties at the meeting; it was an agreement between two of the parties represented. Napier said he had only agreed unwillingly that Labour should be left out. He didn't really agree.

The Nationalists then had a whispered consultation and suggested that, since they believed strongly in free speech, they should give Labour part of one of their periods, i.e., five or ten minutes out of fifteen. I said that I could not agree to one party 'sub-letting' all or part of one of its broadcasts to another party. If a period were split in this way it would result in a total of nine broadcasts and the Unionists had already insisted on having seven out of nine.

The Unionists, needless to say, hastened to support this ruling; the Nationalists protested and Labour was despondent.

It appeared that the meeting was at stalemate and that history was about to be repeated – there would be no election broadcasts.

On enquiry Douglas (Unionist) repeated that his Party was quite unconcerned with what happened in the two broadcasts they did not have. This led to another consultation among the Nationalist representatives. Eventually McAteer said, with some heat, 'I suppose the only thing we can do then is to give one to Labour and take one ourselves'.

Napier did not delay in announcing that this would suit the Labour Party admirably. I asked the meeting then to confirm that the Parties had in fact reached agreement. There was no doubt that the Unionists were surprised and discomfited by the way things had turned out, but, with the others they signified assent.

The Nationalists exploded with some bitter comments on 'the dictatorship methods of the Unionists'. The meeting broke up; the representatives rushed their several ways to organise speakers and scripts.[23]

In this way agreement on election broadcasting in Northern Ireland was reached for the first time. All programmes were transmitted on the Northern Ireland Home Service and were repeated on the same evening, in sound only, on the television channel after closedown.

Apart from a hiccup in the Westminster General Election in the following year, 1959, when the Unionist Party refused to accept the arrangements made by the main parties at Westminster, election broadcasts have been held ever since.

In 1961 the Unionist Party initiated negotiations with the BBC and the other political parties long before the next Northern Ireland General Election was due to take place. The parties met and had little difficulty in dividing seven broadcasts on each medium between them. The agreed basis was four Unionist, two Nationalist, one Labour on radio and on television. The Independent Television Authority arranged that Ulster Television would carry the BBC television broadcasts.

Henceforth the political debate could be open over the air. The way had undoubtedly been prepared by *Your Questions*. The Northern Ireland audience, and the politicians, had become used to hearing opponents express their views in public, for politicians of all parties had at one time or another opportunities of speaking freely on the *Your Questions* platform. The producer, John Boyd, had steadily and successfully worked to broaden the range of speakers and the nature of topics raised.

It was much less easy for unionist opinion to accept criticism and slights in BBC network programmes.

In 1958 *Tonight*, a current affairs television programme, turned its attention to Northern Ireland. It had been developing investigative journalism in a style inherited from the journal *Picture Post* on which a number of its reporters had served. The presenter Alan Whicker was sent to look at life in the region. He used the local camera crew and during his stay maintained close liaison with Broadcasting House, Belfast. He gathered material for a number of reports and the first of these was transmitted on 9 January 1959. The contents of the programme were summarised the next day by the *Northern Whig:*

> The film opened with Mr Whicker standing, microphone in hand, before a dismal-looking City Hall, and describing Northern Ireland in general as a place where the policemen all carried revolvers, where public houses were open from morning to night, and where betting shops, legalized, were carried on off the main streets.

190

Northern Ireland, he said, was a strongly loyal part of Great Britain where there was no National Service. Then the cameras, after displaying close-ups of police revolvers, turned to dirty back-street walls bearing such slogans as 'No Pope Here', 'Ulster is British', 'To – with the Queen', and 'Vote Sinn Fein' . . .

After listing famous Ulster generals who 'practically ran' the British Army during the last War and stressing that Northern Ireland people were 'intensely religious' – he showed hundreds streaming into chapels – Mr Whicker, or rather the cameras, presented shots of dirty-looking streets and alley-ways, posters advertising cowboy films, and corner public uses.

The greater part of the film dealt with the fact that betting had been legalized here and quite a number of the punters were interviewed in bookmakers' premises. Most of those interviewed were unemployed, nearly all were regular punters, and each had his own views on the subject of betting.[24]

Shortly after the programme concluded complaints started pouring into Broadcasting House, Belfast: '. . . a spokesman there said the Corporation had had to deal with "millions" of these throughout the evening'.[25]

The *Northern Whig* and other Belfast papers received many telephoned complaints. The Chairman of the Northern Ireland Tourist Board said the film was 'very damaging' to Northern Ireland and one which showed the 'most sordid' part of life in the region. 'Some of the Province's beauty spots should have been presented,' he said, 'and although Parliament Buildings had been flashed on the screen for a few moments, as well as the statue of Lord Carson in Parliament grounds, there had been no comment on these. They had not even been named . . . The statue of Lord Carson looked something like a scarecrow.'[26] The Minister of Education complained in a similar manner.

One correspondent, having gone through the common complaints, went on:

It was stated, however, that Sunday in Belfast is really a day of rest, which everyone will agree is true, but in regard to the part of the film showing people going to church, well, in all my life I've never seen such a motley crowd. Most of the women wore head scarfs, many of the men had no collars or ties, and it was very evident that these people were not entering a Protestant church.[27]

The Belfast *News Letter* devoted a leader to the programme in which it complained:

. . . there was no reference to the city's industries, to the general bearing of the citizens or to the fact that without the loyal help of Northern Ireland it is doubtful whether the Allies could have won the War against Hitler's Germany.[28]

Letters poured into the *Northern Whig*, the Belfast *News Letter*, and the *Belfast Telegraph*. The *Belfast Telegraph* found it necessary to summarise most of them presenting the arguments 'pro' and 'con'. It did report the Church of Ireland Bishop of Down, Dr F. J. Mitchell, as suggesting that the BBC had 'done us a good turn by exposing to the people of Ulster a situation which exists here – the plight of the unemployed . . . It is little wonder that these young people take to gambling.'[29] In the Northern Ireland Senate, Senator McGladdery asked the Leader of the House, 'if he was aware of the deep resentment of the public about the programme which purported to give a reasonable view of life in Belfast'.[30] Government Ministers made statements and Westminster MPs indicated that they would take the matter up both in the House of Commons and with the BBC's Director General.

The Regional Controller apologised to the Northern Ireland public, indicating that although he knew the details of the filming and broadly the intentions of the *Tonight* team, Belfast had not been responsible for the presentation or the editing. In a letter to Grace Wyndham Goldie who had overall responsibility for *Tonight* in London, McCall said that he hated having to issue a press statement 'which implied a public chiding to my colleagues'. He offered some background information to the affair and stated his own position in relation to it:

I am not personally worried that there should have been
  a some hundreds of telephoned attacks on us;
  b letters which suggest that there is an inefficient and irresponsible Controller here and that he will be thrown out;
  c slogans painted on the front of Broadcasting House which had to be brushed off this morning. They said 'Down with Whicker' – 'Away with McCall';
  d Thelma, my wife, has been attacked on the 'phone at home. 'Your husband is Controller – Controller of what? You won't be here much longer. We'll see to that.' (Anonymous.)

There's a lot more of this nonsense I could relate. It is all beside the point, personally, and quite absurd. But I report these ridiculous examples of behaviour to underline the singular reactions of which the Corporation has to take into account over here.

Until I came over here and had a couple of years' experience of the place, I could not have comprehended the possibility of such things happening in the United Kingdom community.

Anyway, I believe, that the BBC has, over recent years, been tremendously effective in liberalising the thinking of the Ulster communities.

Obviously, there is a great deal still to be done.

I am sure that there must be the closest contact between this Region and any department which is putting out programmes.

I will fight like a cat, as always in the past, to protect the independence and the integrity of the BBC – no pressures from Government PROs, tourist boards, and the rest. But I must confess that this area needs careful treatment.[31]

The BBC in London decided to quell disquiet in Belfast by offering the right of reply and so two speakers were invited to appear on the *Tonight* programme, one who had spoken for and one who had spoken against the programme. Senator McGladdery and Dr Mitchell, the Bishop of Down, agreed to take part. They were flown to London with the BBC Head of Programmes in Northern Ireland, Henry McMullan. McMullan recalled, 'By the time I got them to London, I discovered that neither of them had seen the programme. So when we arrived, Cliff Michelmore and his team gathered and showed them the programme. They saw it and unhappily they both thought it was pretty fair. This was a frightful situation because they had to attack it, so they did attack.'[32] The BBC withdrew the remaining Whicker reports on Northern Ireland from *Tonight*, and they were never shown. The consequences were in many ways significant. The Regional Advisory Council immediately seized on one: 'a fear that, because of the criticism which their editor had created, Northern Ireland might not be featured again in *Tonight* for a long time'.[33] Members of the Council were to express this suspicion again and again. In fact, *Tonight* did not return for five years and then only at the prompting of BBC, Belfast. The consequence was that Northern Ireland did not feature on the television network, except in news bulletins. Effectively, there was a Westminster rule in the BBC as there was in politics. Questions were not asked because they were the concern of another place. So the greater British public learnt little about what was going on in its own political backyard.

This situation was consolidated by another crisis which took place in April of the same year. On the 25th the BBC showed the first of two programmes from a popular United States network series called

Small World. In these the renowned broadcaster, Ed Morrow, conducted a conversation with celebrities. The two selected for the British audience had Noel Coward, James Thurber and the actress Siobhan McKenna as participants. In the course of the programme, somewhat gratituously, Siobhan McKenna was given the opportunity to sound off about the Irish situation. She attacked the British Prime Minister Macmillan, for his critical comments on de Valera's recent release of IRA internees. She attacked de Valera for interning them in the first place. She described the IRA men as 'idealists' who had only been blowing up customs houses and bridges along the Border. She wanted to know why the British, if they found that partition was no solution in Cyprus, insisted on maintaining it in Ireland.

Official Unionist circles were incensed by the transmission. By this time the IRA campaign had cost the lives of four policemen with many others injured; it had also involved the destruction of much property. The programme had, however, been considered at the highest levels in the BBC and the decision had been made to show it. A BBC spokesman in Belfast said, 'There was nothing to be gained by cutting out the parts likely to be offensive here and pretending they were never said. To have done so would have been to deceive British viewers. The remarks were said and it is as well to know they were said.' Broadcasting House, Belfast, received eighteen protest telephone calls. The public reaction was more muted than in the case of Whicker's report, but the press and Unionist politicians took it very seriously.

The *Northern Whig* devoted a leader to the broadcast:

Northern Ireland may be regarded as unduly sensitive to what is said about it and it may, and does, react more sharply and vigorously than an English or Scottish audience would, but then its situation is different. Ever since its establishment as an autonomous area its constitutional position has been under continuing attack – the BBC should not need to be told that the activities of these murderous 'idealists' are merely another expression of the same antagonism which would submerge the Province in a united Irish Republic – and Miss McKenna's outburst is seen here not only as a reflection on Ulster but as part of that attack.

It is not surprising, therefore, there should be a feeling in many minds here that the BBC treats Northern Ireland less than fairly. In its programmes dealing with political affairs in Britain, the BBC is careful to observe the impartiality enjoined on it by is charter, but where Northern

Ireland is concerned it seems to grope blindly in the dark, unhappily tripping over the same hurdle time after time.[34]

On the day on which this leader was published, Brian Faulkner, the Chief Whip of the Unionist Party in Stormont, resigned his membership of the BBC's Northern Ireland Advisory Council. 'It is quite clear to me,' Faulkner said, 'that the Northern Ireland Regional Advisory Council is not taken into consideration when putting out programmes that are critical of Northern Ireland.' He indicated that he objected to the *Small World* programme with Siobhan McKenna, but that he would not have resigned over 'rather niggling criticism' like that in the Whicker programme.[35] Faulkner wrote in protest to the Director General and to the Controller Northern Ireland. The Northern Ireland Prime Minister, Brookeborough, in the Stormont Commons said that it was a 'damnable thing' for Siobhan McKenna to have been seen to be upholding the IRA on BBC television. He indicated that the BBC's National Governor for Northern Ireland was about to leave for talks with the BBC's Director General in London. Harry Diamond, the Republican Labour MP, responded by saying, 'it is clear from the present protest and previous protests that an attempt is being made to establish a censorship of radio and television as far as Northern Ireland is concerned'.[36] The Unionist MPs at Westminster made it clear that the gravamen of their concern was not that the programme was broadcast but that the BBC had failed to disclaim it and to correct the errors of fact in Siobhan McKenna's remarks. The consequence of the discussions in London was that the second programme in which McKenna took part was not shown and another *Small World* programme replaced it. The *Northern Whig* derived some satisfaction from the fact that Broadcasting House had been 'shaken'.[37]

Robert McCall reported to the Regional Advisory Council, 'These two major events' (he meant the Whicker affair and the *Small World* transmission), 'highlighted the special problems here in Northern Ireland from a broadcasting point of view and also the necessity for close liaison with London. These matters had been taken very seriously there and had resulted in a new directive on the subject being issued to the staff.'[38]

While effectively the BBC in London had been warned off Northern Ireland, the BBC in Belfast somewhat paradoxically was making steady progress in opening up broadcasting. Robert Coulter, who during this period assumed responsibility for regional television production, described the process:

> . . . in the first instance subjects which had been relatively taboo became more easy to tackle and in the treatment of them one was freer – not to express opinions exactly for as BBC producers you had no editorial opinions in theory – but one could question more sharply, one could dig deeper into a subject. Partly this came about because of the very fact that the whole population in Ulster was receiving network television in a new flood and it became used to seeing the harder line of questioning, the deeper inquiry, across the water. It began to accept that it was quite reasonable and proper. I think that helped a lot. We obviously tried to follow that trend. We were learning our own trade and were watching the masters as it were.
>
> Secondly, this did happen, and subjects which were previously difficult to handle became that degree easier and one could take greater chances and the politicians or the public themselves were freer, more willing to meet you half way. They did not want to know the questions in advance as they did at one time. They were prepared to talk freely and off the cuff. This began to ease the situation in programme-making terms.[39]

Among the range of sensitive issues which broadcasting was slow to handle was discrimination in employment. In February 1957 J. C. Beckett raised the matter in the Regional Advisory Council. He said that, 'Broadcasting was the only medium in which certain topical subjects could be discussed temperately.' He maintained strongly that the BBC in Northern Ireland had an even greater responsibility to raise such subjects than the BBC in Britain because 'Northern Ireland did not have any organ for two-sided discussions, such as other parts of the UK possessed.' Professor T. Finnegan thought that 'this was the kind of programme which should be kept at the back of one's mind and brought forward at the right moment'. The Council, however, felt that 'it would be useful to the people of Northern Ireland to hear this kind of programme'.[40]

It was not until 10 October 1962 that a thirty-minute current affairs programme tackled the question of discrimination in employment. The occasion was the publication of Carter and Barritt's *The Northern Ireland Problem: a survey in group relations*. The BBC mounted a television press conference on what was seen to be a significant and possibly controversial book. Professor Charles Carter was pressed by J. E. Sayers of the *Belfast Telegraph:* 'Do you see an unwillingness in Northern Ireland to appoint Roman Catholics to public positions, or an unwillingness on the part of Roman Catholics to accept them?' Carter replied, 'There is a certain unwillingness to appoint them but there is also a strange ignorance on the part of the ruling party in trying to find those Roman Catholics who might fill the posts.' Mr Denis Barritt said that the purpose of their book was 'to encourage the majority to approach the minority open handed'.[41] This broadcast was not typical. Discrimination, to be explored by the Cameron Commission in 1968–9, was not usually the subject of programmes but the programme does indicate that some effort was made to tackle the most sensitive issues.

On radio in the course of the same year, 1962, a play, *The Renegade*, was performed, which dealt very frankly with the problem of mixed marriages in Northern Ireland. Dr Rudolph Erlich travelled to Belfast to lead a studio discussion between one Catholic and two Presbyterian clergymen on inter-church talks which had been going on in Edinburgh. Such broadcasts would have been inconceivable a decade earlier.

At the same time the BBC found the voice of sectarian extremism embarrassing, as when the Reverend Ian Paisley appeared on the regional news programme *Six O'Clock* in October 1962, and roundly attacked the Catholic Church. The occasion of the vituperation – the Catholic Church described as 'the harlot of Babylon' and the Pope as 'the anti-Christ' – was his own departure for Rome to protest against the attendance of representatives of the World Council of Churches at the Vatican Council. The BBC, Belfast, issued a statement after the broadcast, 'The BBC wishes to make it quite clear that it dissociated itself from certain remarks made in a recorded interview during the programme *Six O'Clock* and regrets any pain or offence caused to any members of the community.'[42] Paisley protested against the BBC's disclaimer and spoke of 'the storm of protests' which the BBC had received from people offended by the BBC statement of dissociation. The BBC had, according to its spokesman, received two telephone calls.[43]

In 1964, the BBC in Northern Ireland celebrated its fortieth anniversary and the occasion prompted a number of assessments in the press of its achievements to date. The *Belfast Telegraph* devoted a short leader to the occasion, in which it said that the BBC's

contribution to the life of the area has been particularly noteworthy on two fronts, the political and cultural. In Northern Ireland these two are often one, and the fact that radio has enabled both sides of what has been a divided community to share in the cultural heritage of each other, has done much to blur the lines of demarcation.

Sober arguments between opposing factions have never been a prominent feature of politics in these parts, but here again the BBC in its discussion programmes has done valuable service. It has succeeded in doing something more than broadcasting a simple repetition of the somewhat sterile Stormont exchanges, and still more can be done in the way of informed debate on public questions as people's ears become more open to the other man's point of view.[44]

In the mid-1960s the BBC in Northern Ireland began to explore more critically and more thoroughly many aspects of society in the region. The probing current affairs programme replaced the older fashioned objective, detached, documentary. *Topic* gave way to *Inquiry*. Subjects dealt with were social and economic: among many problems aired were housing, which was examined several times, loneliness, Christian Stewardship, cross-border attitudes to North–South co-operation and the development of North-Western Ulster.

This last *Inquiry* programme looked at the charge that successive Unionist Governments had neglected Northern Ireland west of the Bann. The Derry area had recently suffered the closure of one of its railway links with Belfast and had learned that the new university was not to be sited there. There was high unemployment in the region and strong allegations of neglect. The programme eschewed the political dimension: 'While the political element is important, it is the intention tonight to look beyond this in broader terms'. Participants the programme included John Hume, Stephen McGonagle and Brian Faulkner, Minister of Commerce. The programme indicated the level of investment there had been in the region, which it assessed as high but concluded that 'it is in overall planning and emphasis that the impression is left of unfair treatment in comparison to the other half of the province'. The style of the programme was typical of others. Political and sectarian dimensions of problems were played down or ignored.[45]

One significant development of the mid-1960s was the growing development of cross-border co-operation between broadcasters. On 31 December 1961 the Irish television service, Telefís Éireann, transmitted its first programmes. It was an historical occasion, for broadcasting in the Irish Republic had been freed from state control. Radio Éireann ceased to be one of the functions of the government

Department of Posts and Telegraphs and both media came under the control of a public body charged with the provision of a public service. Co-operation between the BBC and the new body was thus facilitated.

One of the first examples of co-operation was the establishment of a permanent link between Belfast and Dublin. This was essential to Telefís Éireann because it enabled the Dublin end to take programmes directly from Europe. In 1962, for example, when TÉ had been without the link, it had been obliged to have film from the Vatican City of the events surrounding the death of Pope John XXIII recorded in the BBC, Belfast, and rushed by chartered train to Dublin. The Programme Controller in Dublin, Gunnar Rugheimer, a Swede with extensive experience of Canadian broadcasting, had to devise a means of circumventing the Irish Post Office's plans to provide a micro-wave link through Anglesea to Dublin because that arrangement would take six or seven years to complete and would be inadequate in any case. Rugheimer could not ask the Post Office to provide capital for building an alternative but persuaded the BBC to build the link from Belfast to the border in return for a guaranteed permanent leasing. The BBC agreed but, Rugheimer remembered, 'The then national governor for Northern Ireland, Sir Richard Pim, took very great objection to this but was overruled by the rest of the Board of Governors.'[46] The BBC was facilitating a fellow member of the European Broadcasting Union and obtaining the means whereby television coverage of events in the Republic, especially sporting occasions, could be taken directly.[47]

The range of programmes carried subsequently was wide, in both directions. GAA football and hurling finals in Dublin were televised and shown on BBC1, although, in fact, films of the finals had been shown in 1961. The Irish Derby and other events in the racing calendar received coverage, as did rugby internationals. In return Telefís Éireann took coverage of the Orange processions on 'The Twelfth'. The broadcasters, north and south, co-operated in the televising of events in Armagh such as the funeral of Cardinal D'Alton and the enthronement of Archbishop Conway. In 1965 monthly meetings of executives from BBC Belfast and Telefís Éireann began;[48] one of the programme consequences was the showing to Northern Ireland viewers of two programmes made by Telefís Éireann. They were *Divided we Stand* and *The Heart of thy Neighbour*. 'A frank look was taken through Northern eyes at the South, and through Southern eyes at the North. Both were honest and hard-hitting, and it is interesting that they evoked nothing but praise and interest. A few years ago it is unlikely that "free speech" to this extent would have found ready acceptance.'[49] Broadcasters were playing their role in the era when Sean Lemass, the Irish Prime Minister, travelled north to visit the Northern Ireland Prime Minister Terence O'Neill, and O'Neill returned the call in Dublin. News bulletins reflected the growing cross-border interests of politicians and people.

In the course of 1963 the BBC Belfast extended its television facilities. Studio 8 was inadequate for more ambitious productions and something bigger was needed. This was found in Balmoral Hall, part of which was adapted so that a mobile, four-camera unit could be set up in it. The Hall was rented for most of the year and a variety of entertainment programmes were recorded before audiences there. The emphasis was on light and Irish music and two shows in particular, *Half Door Club* and *Ceili*, proved very popular.

The early 1960s also saw an expansion in a field of broadcasting which every Controller since 1924 had tried in vain to promote. In 1953 the number of registered listening schools in Northern Ireland had reached 500. Schools broadcasting was being noticed, although very many of the interested schools were in Belfast and other urban areas. In subsequent years the Education Officers for the North-West and the North of England devoted much energy to promoting schools' broadcasting in the region which was their added responsibility. Stephen Murphy and then Leslie Davidson set about persuading the educational service that BBC schools' programmes were an essential resource. The number of schools listening climbed steadily as a result. The pressures on the School Broadcasting Council to establish local production in Belfast became great and finally in 1960 the Council conceded. The three Northern Ireland representatives on the Council resisted the development to the very end, giving in with poor grace and demanding assurances that nothing controversial would ever be broadcast. A Northern Ireland programme committee was established and a producer, James Hawthorne, was appointed. The first local series *Today and Yesterday in Northern Ireland* was transmitted in the summer term, 1961. It was designed for children between ten and thirteen years of age in primary and secondary schools. 'The aim of the programmes is to help children find out more about their own country, its geography and history, about the different pursuits and skills of

Ulster people and something of their contribution to the United Kingdom, the Commonwealth and the world at large.'[50]

This schools' radio series was remade each year and the orders for the accompanying pamphlets provided an indication of their popularity. In 1961, 10,000 were ordered.

It was in 1965, however, that the decision was taken to prepare a series on modern Irish history. Irish historians were invited to prepare the scripts and the resulting *Two Centuries of Irish History* made a remarkable impact on teachers and on the public. It was a mark of the times and the timing that the series was welcomed unanimously and won extensive publicity north and south. It had taken almost twenty years for the original recommendation of the Northern Ireland Advisory Council to be realised.

In the mid-1960s there was a measure of euphoria in broadcasting circles. Rapprochement externally and internally in Northern Ireland seemed to have been achieved. One member of the Advisory Council, Sam Napier, could even speak in 1966 of 'integration' in Northern Ireland's society. He was expressing an opinion on the danger that local radio stations might make the community more inward looking. He argued that to date the BBC had made a substantial contribution to the integration already achieved and that he would not wish a backward step to be taken.[51]

In a short time Northern Ireland was to be plunged into conflict and civil strife. The question prompted is this: in its drive to develop a consensus, to extend the middle ground, had the BBC failed to alert the population to the real division which remained and to the extremes on both sides?

Robert Coulter, Assistant Head of Programmes at the time, answered the question in 1974:

It was partly inevitable in the circumstances, there having been a period when the freest of speech was not possible, when certain subjects were very 'dicey', seeing this beginning to ease and feeling that it was a positive move in the right direction, finding that speakers from opposite sides of the political and sectarian divide were willing to speak together, even with hindsight, one is tempted to think that was the natural thing to do: to get some public and open dialogue by people who were by tradition and reputation divided. In that sense it was positive but perhaps, one was seduced into thinking that having achieved that, the rest would follow.

The other thing that one can see as difficult, again with hindsight, is that if one talks about extremes on either side, a) they were not specially articulate beyond the area of their extreme views – they were not

201

particularly interested in social welfare goals or new educational practices, etc. The nature of extremists is to be completely dyed in the wool on their own subject and that is not what we wanted to explore; b) the extremes were not in our minds polarised the way one might say nowadays because a lot of the feeling about living conditions, about the lifestyle of the back streets of Belfast was common to both Protestants and Catholics, common to Derry, common throughout the Province. It was not a sectarian division in our minds and therefore, if one was exploring slum clearance, better educational opportunities, etc, we were not thinking in terms of sectarian division but whether we disguised in fact the growing undersurge, possibly we did, but certainly it wasn't conscious.

And so as one became more free to criticise mental health provision, employment opportunities, etc, one thought one was taking the whole people with you. At the same time in order to advance the process you had to win the trust, the confidence, of the people you cooperated with, the Stephen McGonagles, the Sam Napiers, the Brian Faulkners. You had to win their confidence in the process of broadcasting that you would not let them down, that you would not play them unfairly and therefore even that in itself made you progress along a middle line to some degree.[52]

The Crisis Breaks

Northern Ireland featured in network news bulletins many times in the course of 1966. The reports carried were those of incidents created by loyalist and republican diehards who were determined to demonstrate against moderating influences which appeared to be eroding the traditional dividing line between the communities. Each extreme publicly affirmed its fundamental commitment and in doing so raised tension. The tension at times produced violence and riots.

The Protestant loyalists were alarmed by the activities and pronouncements of the reformist Unionist Prime Minister, Terence O'Neill. Their opposition was expressed in many ways. For example, they did not approve of the official proposal to name a new bridge over the river Lagan after Queen Elizabeth; they wished it to be called after Lord Carson, the idol of hardline unionism. The outcome was confrontation and violent argument. Turning in another direction from which betrayal through compromise on principle was deemed to be emerging, the Reverend Ian Paisley led a truculent demonstration against the annual assembly of the Presbyterian Church in Ireland. His purpose was to halt the development of ecumenism – 'the Romeward trend of the Protestant churches'.

The republican and nationalist activists on their side welcomed 1966 as an opportunity to oblige the minority community to re-dedicate itself to the cause of ending partition, for it was the fiftieth anniversary of the Easter Rising of 1916. Large demonstrations and marches were organised throughout Ireland, including the north. Even moderate unionists found the commemorative activities provocative.

Television reporters and cameramen provided full coverage of all that went on and the news film was seen in Britain and overseas. The BBC's Board of Governors and its Director General, Hugh Carleton Greene, were made aware of the special broadcasting needs of Northern Ireland and responded by appointing an experienced newsman as Controller. It was a bonus that he was an Ulsterman. Waldo Maguire, of County Armagh farming stock, was a graduate of Trinity College, Dublin, and had served in the Army Intelligence Corps during the Second World War. He joined the BBC as a news sub-editor in 1945 and rose steadily to become editor of television news. In the two years before his despatch to Belfast, Maguire had been seconded to New Zealand to establish a television news service there.

Maguire was exhilarated by his posting to his native, newsworthy, region and was pleased with what he found there. Within a few weeks of his arrival he attended a meeting of the Regional Advisory Council at which recent news coverage was discussed. He praised the local news staff for 'the highly professional and objective way in which they had dealt with events'. 'The department,' he said, 'would continue to report as objectively and fairly as possible, bearing in mind the BBC's overall responsibility for ensuring that these reports were not liable to exacerbate public disorder.' The suggestion was put to Maguire that the image of Northern Ireland projected as a result of the news coverage on the network and throughout the world was a bad one. He replied that 'regrettably it was one's duty to report what was happening and if there were riots the world wanted pictures of them'.[1]

The new Controller also commented on related aspects of local production in a significant way. He criticised the nightly regional magazine on television, *Six-Five*, which he described as 'too soft and whimsical' and said he hoped 'a change in emphasis would make it more relevant to Northern Ireland and the present times'. Maguire was clearly not satisfied with the half of the programme which was prepared as feature material by general producers. As a hard news man he was pleased enough with the half prepared by the newsroom. It was surprising, however, that he pronounced himself satisfied with the local weekly current affairs programme *Inquiry* which he said was 'workmanlike'. He did not require that it should probe more deeply and tackle more significant issues. When, soon after, he was pressed by one member in a management board meeting to do something along these lines, he dismissed the advice.

In the weeks following the Advisory Council meeting there was much news. A new Protestant paramilitary organisation, the Ulster Volunteer Force, made its existence known by murdering a young Catholic barman. The men who committed the crime were caught and gaoled, and the UVF was proscribed by the Prime Minister, O'Neill. Then the Queen visited Northern Ireland, to name the Lagan bridge after herself. During her drive through the streets of Belfast her car was hit by missiles thrown by republican sympathisers. Finally, Ian Paisley was sent to gaol as a consequence of his earlier activities outside the Presbyterian Assembly.

The news team which covered these events was small. It had grown slowly since 1955 when one news-editor, C. L. Frankland, compiled the brief radio bulletins. In that year he was joined by Cecil Taylor who was to provide local television news. In a way that was typical of the time Northern Ireland had to make do with one man whereas other regions gained a journalist and a cameraman. Taylor had to learn to use a film camera. He was also set the task of producing independent and objective bulletins, for hitherto the bulletins 'sounded as if they were written night by night in the Government Press Office in Stormont'.[2]

When VHF radio was launched in the Region, another journalist was needed to prepare separate daily bulletins for it. Other appointments followed, including the first reporter to be drawn from the Catholic community. The need for specialists was at last recognised and Eric Waugh joined the BBC in 1962 as industrial correspondent. W.D. 'Billy' Flackes followed him in 1964 as political correspondent, satisfying a need to which the Stormont Committee of Privileges had drawn attention sixteen years earlier.

Towards the end of 1966 news coverage was again discussed by the Advisory Council. The claim was made that the network news had presented a distorted view of the atmosphere in Belfast before the Queen's visit and that this might have served to heighten tension. It was explained that Belfast had submitted a balanced report to London but that it was cut under pressure of time. This led the Council to press the issue of the danger of television influencing events by presenting a misleading picture of the situation. The Council was concerned that editorial control might create distortion but was on the other hand adamant that there should be no question of manipulating the news so as to protect the image of Northern Ireland. The Controller agreed: 'The presentation of Ulster's image was not really the concern of the news department; its duty was to report facts as objectively as possible, but nothing was done irresponsibly or unthinkingly.' Maguire added that he was always consulted by London departments who planned to produce programmes on Northern Ireland. The Director General had in fact reissued the directive which required that this be done and had said it was probable that in most cases any observations and objections by the Controller would be accepted and acted on. Maguire indicated that the editor of the nightly network current affairs programme *Twenty-Four Hours* was meticulous in referring relevant matters to him.

A speaker at the meeting expressed concern about the effects of giving publicity to extremist movements but was countered by another who felt that 'the BBC had rendered the community a service in revealing to a great number of moderately minded people, who had previously been asleep to the real situation, how extreme the extremists were and that was something that had to be done'.[3]

Thus it was that some of the issues which were to reverberate through the BBC and through the community at large in later years were raised and discussed in 1966. There followed, however, a period of nearly two years in which Northern Ireland lapsed back into oblivion and was almost unnoticed by network television.

Between the summer of 1966 and the summer of 1968 Broadcasting House, Belfast, pursued a determined policy of opening up broadcasting and of helping to improve community relations.

It was a time of civic weeks when the populations of whole towns were encouraged to come together in a variety of communal activities. The BBC paid particular attention to these festivals and mounted a series, *Kate at Eight*, which was designed to help promote them. The presenter, Kate Pratt, encouraged discussions of major community issues by bringing panels of local people before the cameras. The BBC also supported civic weeks by sending the Northern Ireland Orchestra to perform at some of them.

Political broadcasting was extended in a number of ways. Annual party political conferences were covered in some detail and for the first time a local election results programme was mounted. There was a monthly version of *Inquiry*, called *Gateway*, devoted to parliamentary and political activity and many other opportunities were offered to politicians to appear on television and radio. Ulster Television was producing at the time a hard-hitting and very successful early evening magazine, *Flashpoint*, and it set the pace for inquiry into local issues.

Progress was made in cross-border co-operation when a series called *Borderlines*, jointly produced with Radio Telefís Éireann, was launched. Speakers from both sides of the border discussed topics of common interest, with the series transmitted on the same day by both organisations. Within Northern Ireland, experiments were carried out which would have been inconceivable in earlier years. While coverage of the Orange Twelfth of July marches and of the Ancient Order of Hibernians' marches on 15 August was by now customary, a new departure in 1968 was the transmission in the evenings after the marches of special traditional music programmes which presented the ballads and tunes associated with the day. *Orange Folk* and *Green Folk* involved producing music which might have been expected to provoke a torrent of abuse from viewers. There was no public reaction and some favourable press comment. Likewise in 1967 Sam Hanna Bell produced a lengthy objective radio documentary called *The Orangemen* which received only praise.

There was a renewed effort to reflect the wider Irish culture in programming. *Ceili*, which had prompted criticism, became the more acceptable *Rinnce Mor*. The Clancy Brothers gave a concert in the Ulster Hall in March 1967 to celebrate the arrival of BBC 2 in the Region and the reception was so enthusiastic that BBC Northern Ireland was commissioned to make a Clancy series for BBC 2. Radio too had a variety of Irish folk music programmes.

There were stirrings of dissatisfaction and opposition in various sections of the unionist community. Spokesmen warned of the anti-unionist bias of both television services in Northern Ireland. They were particularly sensitive to the freedom with which nationalist politicians were allowed to state their opinions. The journal *The Unionist* indicated that Unionist MPs were contemplating a boycott of the BBC and UTV. Then *Twenty-Four Hours* did an item on the political and social problems of Derry and local unionists were enraged. The Imperial Grand Registrar of the Royal Black Institution declared that the BBC and UTV displayed 'a veiled sympathy with the anti-Partition conspiracy and in a subtle way colour news items in a manner which cannot fail to impair the Unionist image at home and abroad'.[4]

In the late summer of 1968 the civil rights movement began its campaign to achieve equal rights for all citizens in Northern Ireland. Attention was focussed in the first instance on an inappropriate allocation of housing in Caledon and then a march was organised in Coalisland. Both were reported on the BBC locally and nationally, but the real impact of media coverage was felt only on 5 October 1968. A march through Duke Street to the city centre of Londonderry had been declared illegal by the Minister of Home Affairs, William Craig, and the Royal Ulster Constabulary barred the way. The police then charged the demonstrators and in the course of the afternoon used water-cannons. Filmed reports featured prominently on the BBC network news. A former BBC employee living in Derry, however, alerted *Twenty-Four Hours* to the fact that Radio Telefís Éireann had got much more dramatic film of the events. The RTÉ film was shown on the BBC network and it proved sensational. In the following fortnight the demonstrations of sympathy with the civil rights activists and the demonstrations of outrage and anger of those who were opposed to them received the full attention of the Belfast newsroom. The Prime Minister, Terence O'Neill, found himself embattled, and travelled to London to discuss the situation with Harold Wilson, the British Prime Minister. In the Westminster House of Commons questions were raised about the situation and the impending visit. The Leader of the Unionist MPs, Captain Orr, implied that the questions were 'mischief making'. Wilson turned to him and remarked:

> Those who have tabled these questions and followed with supplementary questions have as great sincerity as the honourable and gallant Member. Without in any way seeking to trespass on the ground covered by the Government of Ireland Act, I say to the honourable and gallant Member that he is entitled to his view on the matter which he has just expressed. Up to now we have perhaps had to rely on the statements of himself and others on these matters. *Since then we have had British television.*[5]

That was on 22 October. Before the end of the year the crisis deepened with another civil rights march, this time in Armagh. The television cameras were there and the political pressure was kept up. O'Neill was obliged to produce a package of reforms. He was threatened from within his own party as a result but eventually won a vote of confidence. The BBC had a role to play in this too. The outside broadcasting unit was at Stormont to report on the package of reforms and to inform the world of the outcome of the vote of confidence. However, the event with the most media impact was to prove to be the People's Democracy march from Belfast to Derry over the New Year. On the way, it was confronted by Protestant extremists, most notably at Antrim and Burntollet. The 'battle' of

Burntollet provided film that was seen on the screens of many countries. Events in Derry afterwards were nearly as dramatic.

In January 1969 the Controller, Waldo Maguire, reported to the Regional Advisory Council:

> Our film cameramen and reporters have often had to work under trying and hazardous conditions, in the face of hostility, threats and sometimes violence from Protestant extremists who constantly try to prevent their activities being photographed or reported. I am very happy to commend the devotion to duty of our staff in such conditions ... On the whole, morale remained good, but the situation was a delicate one. Police co-operation was good, though no special protection was given by them to cameramen or journalists.[6]

This had had an unfortunate outcome on the occasion of the Armagh civil rights march. The loyalists under Paisley arranged a counter-march and made it very clear that cameramen and reporters would be in danger if they photographed what followed. A camera team was caught in the *mêlée* and a cameraman was seriously injured.

The open aggression shown to BBC men on the ground was paralleled by an unprecedented level of abuse in calls and in letters to Broadcasting House, Belfast. A substantial number of the letters expressed astonishment that the BBC 'as a government sponsored organisation' could allow such publicity to 'rebels and civil righters' and 'seditious organisations defying government authority' . . . 'giving Ulster a bad name'. Telephone calls accused the BBC of bias against 'the loyalists of Ulster'. The Advisory Council considered issuing a public statement that the obstruction and threats encountered by the BBC staff came from Protestant extremists. The Council decided against this course of action and wrote to the BBC Board of Governors instead, copying the letter to the Stormont Government. While the Council admitted that there were extremists on both sides, the thuggery came only from one side.

Telephone and letter protests did, however, come from the civil rights movement and its supporters declaring that the coverage was biased against them. They were somewhat at odds with the conclusion reached by the *Irish News:* 'Let's make no mistake about it . . the marches would not have mattered two pence if the TV cameras had not been there . . . the body blows of the truth have been hurting the Unionist Party, so their tactic is to try to discredit the BBC.'[7]

Political ferment continued in Northern Ireland through the spring and summer of 1969. The vilification of the BBC was sustained from all sides. The unionist establishment was to the fore, although in two cases prominent individuals, MPs Stratton Mills and Robert Porter, were obliged to withdraw their allegations and apologise publicly on threat of legal action.

It was ironic that when a rumour circulated that regional broadcasting was to be closed down because of the BBC's financial difficulties, the Belfast press rushed to the Corporation's defence. The *Belfast Telegraph* commented in in editorial: 'Northern Ireland with its unique history has a strong local identity which must not be allowed to disappear'. The *News Letter* in article entitled 'Hands off our BBC' outlined the history of the BBC in Northern Ireland over the previous forty years and more, listing 'memorable programmes expertly written and produced, to suit everybody from the intellectual to the man-in-the-street . . . In this off-shore region of the United Kingdom we have a special case for retaining our local BBC station . . . Northern Ireland has been referred to again and again as a cultural desert. We cannot afford to let them rob us of our main oasis.' The *Irish News* devoted a leading article to the subject: 'It would be tragic if the Belfast station with the sturdy independence and objectivity which it has revealed in its programmes in the last couple of years were to suffer any diminution of its powers or its programme output . . .'[8] As it happened, the rumour was unfounded.

In August, violence flared in Derry and erupted in Belfast soon after. On the nights of the 14th and 15th there was serious rioting. Many houses and larger buildings were set ablaze. Five people were killed and one hundred and twenty injured. The civil authority proved incapable of maintaining order and the army was called in.

It was a situation without precedent for broadcasters in the British Isles. Certainly some reporters and cameramen were familiar with similar scenes abroad, but coverage of civil disturbance on this scale at home presented the BBC with special problems. Waldo Maguire explained to the Regional Advisory Council,

. . . in the case of Northern Ireland, the effect of any broadcast is a factor which it would be irresponsible for the BBC to ignore. The agony of Ulster is the agony of our own listeners and viewers.

In the present atmosphere of hatred and fear, we have to recognise that the broadcasting of violently opposed views, passionately and offensively expressed, could have direct and immediate consequences on the streets of Belfast or Londonderry.

This, then, is the dilemma. While taking account of the fact that network news bulletins and programmes are being seen and heard in Northern Ireland, the BBC must not fail in its duty to the rest of the United Kingdom, to present the news fully and fairly, to explain the background to the violence, to provide a platform for the expression of all significant opinion.

There are two possible ways of getting out of this dilemma.

One is to produce the same kind of uninhibited programme which would be made if the shooting, rioting, looting and arson were taking place in a foreign country: and then ensure that it is not carried on Northern Ireland transmitters.

The other course is to modify to some extent the presentation of the broadcasts to give all the facts and opinions faithfully and comprehensively, but in a way designed to avoid extreme provocation. In practice, this means that parts of filmed or recorded interviews which include violently and offensively expressed opinion and allegations are cut out, and their substance included in the reporter's script; and that people liable to use highly inflammatory language are not asked to take part in 'live' studio discussions.[9]

Of these two options, opting out of network programmes was not favoured. It was only adopted once, in the case of a *Panorama* programme in July 1970, when East Belfast Protestants were heard on film calling on their neighbours to avenge the murder of their relatives by IRA gunmen.

The alternative, tempering coverage to avoid provocation, was adopted in its severest form for a short period of time: for two days between the worst of the rioting on 15 August and the restoration of order when the troops arrived on the streets of Derry and Belfast. Coverage within that period was carefully 'sanitised' to ensure all emotional outbursts, inflammatory and violent accusations were not screened. Instead the newsreader or presenter reported on what was said. The charge of censorship against the Controller first arose from this period of rioting and its aftermath. Years later, Martin Bell, one of the BBC reporters in Belfast at the time, said:

We made a mistake ... in 1969, in the August of that year when Catholics were burned out of their homes in the Falls by Protestants who attacked them from Shankill. The BBC reports then gave no indication of who these refugees were. They just spoke of refugees. The public was not to know whether they were Catholic or Protestant or who was attacking whom. That has subsequently been seen to be a grave mistake, and in eight years of reporting this thing, on and off, that was probably the only time when I was stopped by the powers above from saying what I wanted to say and what I have kept saying. Otherwise there is no censorship. There is a general sense of responsibility of the effect of what you report. If you get something wrong, you can very well be responsible for a riot – and you know it.[10]

Shortly after the events of August, Maguire wrote in justification:

. . . critics say the BBC should have said clearly who started the trouble and who carried it on. The plain fact is that the BBC did not know – and does not know. Our reporters report what they see and hear, and neither of our two reporters in the area at the time (the others were still in Londonderry) knew more than they broadcast. What we did do was to report faithfully the claims and counter-claims made by the two sides. It would be wrong for us to make a judgement. We shall report fully the findings of the Tribunal set up to do so.[11]

Martin Bell, however, clearly believed he knew what had happened.

Martin Bell was one of the extra reporters flown in from London to help the small Belfast newsroom which had been overwhelmed by the massive demands the local situation placed on it. The newcomers operated separately from an editorial point of view but they were at all times required to consult with the Controller. His justification of this was that they could not 'be expected to know the background to the complex and tortured situation in Ulster, they cannot know, in a country where appearance and reality are so often in conflict, who the key figures are, what the underground currents are, who can be believed and who can't, what the motives are behind a statement or action – the whole body of unpublished and unpublishable information that is accumulated by the Controller and his current affairs staff with their close contacts with both the Protestant and Catholic communities in this small province'.[12] Of course, Maguire's conviction was backed by a London directive to all staff. It had been reissued as recently as April by the new Director General, Charles Curran, who at the time had also stressed the need to ensure that BBC output did not avoidably exacerbate the situation.

The relationship between Waldo Maguire and the London staff, especially those working in the current affairs area, was unlikely to prove comfortable. To some extent Maguire was the victim of the past. For as Keith Kyle, political adviser to the BBC TV's current affairs departments, wrote in September 1969, 'Folk history lasts long in an organisation like the BBC.' The memory of the Whicker affair of a decade earlier, when half-a-dozen reports on Northern

Ireland had been suppressed, was far from dead and was quickly revived on the slightest hint that the Controller Northern Ireland was proving difficult. It was very unfortunate for Maguire because he was a reformer. Tony Smith, the editor of *Twenty-Four Hours*, implied what Maguire's role was when he said, 'I don't know any part of the world or any issue that was as difficult to deal with as Northern Ireland before Waldo Maguire arrived', and went on to add that since then his team had been as free to cover the region as any other crisis area.[13]

Points of difference inevitably arose between the London-based staff and the Controller. Maguire gave his own analysis of what they were:

Almost invariably they are about balance, or the likelihood of inflaming the situation. It is the duty of the Controller to keep reminding his London colleagues that there are Catholic and Protestant attitudes to almost every issue, and to urge them to give both. As one who has put many news and current affairs programmes on the air, the present Controller appreciates intimately the intense irritation and difficulty this can cause. The need to keep a story within the air time allocated to it, the problem of getting hold of the person to give the other view soon enough, the reluctance to commit the producer of the following day's edition to carry a reply: these are serious practical problems. Similarly, the wish to use the most colourful, articulate and forthright speaker possible is entirely right and natural in trying to make the most effective programme: it also causes delay and irritation to have to take into account the local view of the speaker's importance, his truthfulness, and his sense of responsibility.

The BBC, over the years, has insisted on the use of this machinery to ensure that producers of programmes on Northern Ireland will appreciate the intricacy and danger of the subjects they are handling, and that the Irish problem, which has complicated British politics for generations, cannot be solved in fourteen minutes by a production team that spends a few days in the Province.

The essential point, however, is that although the Controller in Northern Ireland must be consulted, and his advice considered, the final editorial decision is taken in London.[14]

The first hint of the friction to which the situation gave rise appeared in a feature in the *Observer*. It reported that two newspaper reporters who had been invited into Broadcasting House, Belfast, to give eye-witness accounts of the riots of 14 and 15 August for radio's *World at One* were turned away at the behest of the Controller: 'The BBC intended to see this crisis through by relying on its own staff reporters.' Maguire was described as 'the BBC's viceroy in Northern Ireland . . . a formidable Ulster Protestant'.[15]

It was, perhaps, significant that when Kevin Boyle, a member of the executive committee of the Northern Ireland Civil Rights Association, was quoted in the *Irish Times* as accusing the BBC of censorship and the Northern Ireland Controller as being responsible for it, the paper was obliged to disown the allegation as a result of legal action by the BBC.

The product of whatever processes of consultation and editing were necessary continued to reach the small screen and the microphone and to elicit disapproval from both sides in Northern Ireland society. Correspondents maintained an incessant bombardment of the newspapers and of Broadcasting House. In the *Irish News:* 'something will have to be done about the BBC . . . all along the bulletins and commentators show favour to the Unionist side.' In the *News Letter:* 'How much longer must we listen to People's Democracy and Civil Rights propaganda from the BBC? It is being poured out in every bulletin. Surely our BBC bulletins ought not to be a diary of the antics of the enemies of Ulster.'[16]

Towards the end of 1969 Lord Hill, the Chairman of the BBC, wrote:

> One of the hardest tests in the history of the BBC came in 1969, when we were broadcasting to the people of Northern Ireland at a time when argument had burst into the violence of stones, petrol bombs and firearms. At such times, those who are most hotly partisan do not want impartiality; they want news and views that support their own fiercely held opinions. In this difficult period, the BBC was assailed by both sides, creating at least a presumption that it had held the middle ground.[17]

In the course of 1970 the Provisional IRA emerged as a significant organisation and the BBC took note of its rise. *Nationwide* sent a team to the Republic of Ireland where it filmed a secret IRA training camp, showing part of what was claimed to be a force of 2,000 men undergoing military training. The decision to show the film was not taken lightly, and it was taken at the highest levels in the BBC. The transmission provoked controversy. Unionist MPs at Westminster were particularly critical of its showing in Northern Ireland, calling the decision to do so 'outrageous', 'appalling', 'alarmist' and 'irresponsible'. Some of them, however, welcomed its showing in Great Britain. Questions were asked in the Stormont Parliament and the Government asked for a special showing of the film in Broadcasting House, Belfast. The Prime Minister and most members of the Cabinet attended. Although the *Belfast Telegraph* and the *News Letter* were not in favour of the broadcast, most members of the Regional Advisory Council approved.

In January 1971 *Twenty-Four Hours* looked at the activities of the Provisional IRA much nearer home. Bernard Falk discovered that the Republican paramilitaries were behind a series of attacks on an army post in the Ballymurphy estate in West Belfast. In the programme he interviewed 'two senior officers of the Belfast Brigade', both wearing masks. They did not deny that they were involved in the attacks. Falk got them to admit that they presumed to provide order in an area where official law and order was non-existent.

The programme caused a storm of protest. The public showered Broadcasting House, Belfast, with abuse. The *Belfast Telegraph* and the *News Letter* strongly disapproved and published letters attacking the BBC. The Westminster MPs were once again to the fore, with Stratton Mills, pressing for the setting up of a 'watchdog committee', a concept which the Conservative Political Centre was currently fostering for wider purposes, Stanley McMaster, calling for an immediate inquiry and Robin Chichester-Clark, who happened to have been interviewed in a separate item on the same *Twenty-Four Hours* programme, protesting strongly to the Director General. Mills later asked the Postmaster General, Christopher Chataway, to instruct the BBC not to show anonymous IRA gunmen again. Chataway refused.

Members of the Regional Advisory Council were divided about the issues involved in showing the Ballymurphy film. Probably a majority of them, including people from both Protestant and Catholic communities, opposed the transmission. Their reasons for opposing were diverse. There was the harm done to community relations. There was the conviction that the reporter should himself have given an account of the role of the Provisionals and not interviewed them. The principle of allowing masked men from outside the law to appear was strongly questioned. Finally, there was a member who reported that since seeing the item many people whom he knew as liberal-minded had become hardliners, and they had asked him how British people would have felt during the war had disguised members of the Gestapo appeared on television and been

215

given the same treatment. One member of Council, Stanley Worrall, however, defended the interview. He won some support and the Controller said that he expressed the sentiments of the BBC. Worrall said the item

... represented a real and inescapable element in the situation in Northern Ireland, and though he would not approve frequent inclusion it would be a mistake to omit it entirely. For years, people whose business it was to incite hatred between the communities of the province, had been interviewed in many programmes and had been given endless opportunities to stir up suspicion and hatred, and when the result of some of this incitement was shown in hard practical terms among men who were anonymous and relatively humble compared with those who had been doing the inciting, there was horror and outcry about the law being broken. So long as these elements existed and were having an effect on the general situation, he considered it perfectly proper that from time to time – even though unusual methods might be involved in obtaining the information – the BBC should represent these elements and show them up for what they were. The BBC did not support them by showing them: it had seemed to him that the whole implication of the programme was that the BBC condemned them; the elements did exist and should not be swept under the carpet.[18]

Bernard Falk found himself in trouble in two quarters. In the BBC, he was carpeted for failing to follow through all the necessary consultative procedures with the Controller. More ominously, the Royal Ulster Constabulary announced its intention of investigating the interviews. If the police discovered the interviewees, Falk could be called into the witness box in court to identify them. Under the Criminal Law Act (Northern Ireland) 1967 it would be an offence not to do so. On 27 April 1971 Falk was asked to say whether one Patrick Leo Martin had appeared in the BBC programme on January 19. Martin was being charged with membership of the IRA and with acting with a view to promoting the objects of an unlawful organisation, the IRA, by taking part in a television programme. Falk refused to answer. His defence counsel made it clear that Falk had given his personal word never to identify the interviewees and, moreover, he was determined not to breach his journalistic code. One of the two presiding magistrates expressed sympathy with Falk and said, 'For some time past, it appears to us, this type of programme has been sponsored by television people such as the BBC and people like Mr Falk, as employees, find themselves in this sort of position. Unfortunately he has to carry the can. It's a matter which will have to be looked at that an employer can put an employee in this position.' The magistrates sentenced Falk to four days imprisonment and gave him leave to appeal. He abandoned the appeal and elected to serve the sentence.[19]

The Falk affair proved to be a turning point in the history of the BBC's coverage of the Troubles. Superficially, it may be viewed as an occasion when a London-based journalist got his 'come-uppance' in Northern Ireland. Falk had, after all, been made to realise a serious consequence of failing to consult the Controller Northern Ireland fully. His experience would prove a warning to all future 'visiting firemen'. The police had shown television journalists in no uncertain manner what could be the outcome of interviewing illegal paramilitaries on the screen. They may have been deliberately looking for an opportunity to do so, for at the time they were contemplating proceedings against another journalist who had also interviewed a Provisional. He, however, was locally based in Ulster Television and his interview was only transmitted in Northern Ireland, not through the whole Independent network. For whatever reason, no proceedings against him were instigated.

The senior executives in the BBC took the Falk affair very seriously. The jailing of an employee as a consequence of activities carried out in the course of his work for the Corporation was not a matter to be dismissed lightly. The executives, moreover, had been cited from the bench as the real authors of Falk's difficulties. Beyond that too was the fact that it had been made clear in court that a journalist in Falk's position could be prosecuted for a misprision of treason, for which the penalty would be very much more severe than four days in prison.

The outcome of the deliberations was a directive to programme staff prohibiting all interviews with the Provisional IRA without the prior personal permission of the Director General. Producers were required to seek that permission when an interview was being contemplated and no negotiations with the Provisional IRA were to be initiated until it was granted. Once permission was granted BBC personnel had to indicate to the Provisional IRA that all details of an interview would be disclosed if the police questioned the personnel afterwards.

For some this sort of procedure is a form of editorial control, for others it is a form of censorship. Their debate was sustained as the Northern Ireland crisis dragged on and Maguire necessarily remained at the centre of it, playing the role which he had been assigned by the BBC's Board of Governors and the Director General. Straight news reporters were seldom affected by his recommendations and often wondered what the arguments were all about. It was in the current affairs field, where reporters were required to explain the news, that clashes occurred. Waldo Maguire had a particular view of current affairs which was not shared by most of those who made the programmes. He could not accept that scoops and hard-hitting reporting were necessarily acceptable in the circumstances of Northern Ireland. He required coverage simply to reflect, not affect, the course of events. He was, of course, primarily concerned to reduce the negative impact of the media. Reporters must not exacerbate the situation. There came a time, however, when he applied his view more broadly than usual.

Tony Smith, the then editor of *Twenty-Four Hours*, subsequently described the occasion. It arose from a report prepared for the programme

> . . . on changing sentiment within the Ulster Unionist Party, shortly before the resignation of Mr Chichester-Clark as Prime Minister in Northern Ireland in February 1971. The report included film of a number of party meetings at which Chichester-Clark was roundly condemned, and in which Paisleyite sentiment within the party was shown to be widespread and unconcealed. The gist of the report was that Northern Ireland could well find itself in search of a new Prime Minister within a short space of time. The report was not shown on the persistent advice of the Belfast Controller, pending a series of changes, including most importantly some indication of the feelings of 'moderate opinion' within the Ulster Unionist Party. The whole point of the report was that moderate opinion was evaporating, and the later addition of an interview with a 'moderate' saying precisely that did not reconcile Belfast to the notion of transmitting the report. As the days passed the event predicted actually occurred, and the report was rendered valueless.[20]

The controversy between *Twenty-Four Hours* and Belfast over that incident became one about the very nature of current affairs programming. Visiting reporters accepted that local advice and criticisms from the Controller and his staff could be valuable but there was a growing feeling that Waldo Maguire did not share their principles and that what he stood for were the doctrines of a decade earlier. He seemed always to insist that each recognised political interest was represented in a programme and that each be accorded strictly equal time, with the commentary expressing no firm theme or conclusion. It was left open to the viewers or listeners, having heard the usual flatly contradictory arguments, to form their own opinions.

It was conceded that this approach might be what was wanted in Northern Ireland. It was strongly felt that it was not appropriate for the rest of the United Kingdom. If a report did not have a theme and there were so many conflicting elements in it that they cancelled each other out, the audience outside Northern Ireland rapidly lost its way and ended up no wiser than when it started.

Again, the suggestion could not be accepted that a programme dealing with controversial political matters ought not to coincide with a major political event in case the BBC should be suspected of wishing to influence the event itself. Rather, the current affairs journalist had to be free to decide that this point or issue was the one which it was important at this stage to bring to the public's attention. He might decide that this was so on the basis of information privately supplied or on his own 'hunch' about the way things were likely to develop. His journalistic judgement in the case might derive from the conviction that the point or issue in question was being neglected or that it was the political factor which had most gained in weight and interest at the time. If the current affairs journalist was not allowed to operate in this way, then the nature and purpose of his expertise was being denied.

There was a further suspicion that Maguire wished to assimilate the current affairs style of programming to that of news. He wanted the reporter to speak almost the whole piece to the camera and that the only other film should be short clips from interviews. The general purpose of the interviews should be to ensure that every point of view was covered. This was in complete contrast to the *Twenty-Four Hours* style which aimed to emphasise film, to reduce the amount of time the reporter faced the camera and to have as few clips from interviews as possible.

The old bogey of the Whicker banning was revived and at least one senior member of the *Twenty-Four Hours* team, Keith Kyle, began to think that either the BBC should accept a position in which programmes were made specifically for the non-Northern Ireland audience and not shown in the Region or that the team should pull out, seeing that it could not work in the way it was accustomed to everywhere else.

In the event neither course could be taken. The BBC was

219

determined to fulfil its obligation to cover the Northern Ireland crisis and to do it for all the United Kingdom indiscriminately.

The BBC staff in Northern Ireland were all affected by the crisis. Inevitably, no employee wholly escaped the attention which was focussed on the senior broadcasting service in the region. Reporters and cameramen, being obviously in the front line, seemed most at risk from violence. On 9 February 1971 however, a landrover carrying two BBC engineers and three construction workers was blown up by a landmine on the approach road to Brougher Mountain transmitter which lies close to the borderline between Tyrone and Fermanagh. All five men were killed instantly. The two engineers were Bill Thomas and Malcolm Hanson. Their deaths underlined for all staff the danger of their own situations.

Reporters and cameramen were subject to the hazards of mob violence from the beginning. They were beaten up, stoned, threatened and had their equipment damaged. When the shooting started, they began to live in even more serious danger.

In September 1971 the BBC staff magazine, *Aerial*, reported on what had happened to some members of staff:

> Cyril Cave, a local cameraman who lives in Belfast, and has been working in Londonderry, has probably been involved in more dangerous situations than anyone. 'I've been hit by just about everything,' he said, 'petrol bombs, paving stones and nail bombs.' He has been in hospital twice – once after a riot mob clubbed him over the head with a piece of wall and two weeks later after being knocked cold in a riot. He was dragged to shelter by the police behind an overturned burning lorry. Eric Pollen and sound recordist Frank Grey were beaten up by a crowd, their brand new camera car was completely wrecked and their equipment was stolen. Dick Macmillan was dowsed by a water cannon. London staff who have been injured include cameraman Peter Beggin who caught five pounds of paving stone on the side of his face; Bob Williams whose hearing was severely damaged when he was hit by a brick, and recordist Roy Benford who was attacked while covering the shooting of a sentry.[21]

The violence pressed in on all reporters and cameramen and affected their work:

> One of the problems that radio reporter Chris Drake . . . stressed was actually writing the news. 'If you say the wrong thing you could really stir up trouble. Everything has to be written again to make sure it cannot be misconstrued in any way. It's a rule never to speculate about anything.[22]

Trouble was, however, continually being stirred up. Local loyalist reaction to the coverage of the Troubles had always been vociferous. In August 1971 a deliberate attempt was made to organise it. A large advertisement was inserted in the *News Letter* which proclaimed, 'We as Ulster loyalists protest against the gross irresponsibility of the BBC and ITV in the reporting of the day to day trouble in Northern Ireland.' It continued:

> We question the right of the mass media to continually distort the news in favour of the terrorists and the politicians whose loyalties are to subversion and not to the constitution of the country. No time or expense is spared in interviewing the gunman, or travelling to the refugee camps for on-the-spot stories. Yet hundreds of Protestant families are without homes, having been evicted at the point of the gun, loyalist women and their children are living in fear, business premises have been burned and looted, and little of this side of the story is told.[23]

Readers were invited to sign on the dotted line and to collect signatures to 'demand a more balanced presentation of news'. By the end of a fortnight the organisers claimed to have collected 33,000 signatures and a deputation, led by Captain Austin Ardill, a former Unionist MP at Stormont, confronted the Controller Northern Ireland.

Maguire totally rejected the generalised and unsubstantiated allegations made in the advertisement and reiterated by the deputation. (Later, Maguire was to reveal that he had said he was surprised that only 33,000 people signed the petition.) He said he challenged the deputation to put a similar advertisement in the *Irish News* and he would guarantee that they would get almost as many signatures. When he was questioned by a reporter about this assertion, Maguire agreed that,

> most of our protests are now coming from the Protestant side. The most frequent protest we get is that we should just not let the opposition politicians on the air. About half of the letters I get state that Austin Currie, Gerry Fitt, Bernadette Devlin and John Hume should not be allowed to appear. The other main complaint is that we do not automatically put on someone to dispute with an opposition spokesman. Our attitude to that is that, in news, you report what is going on, what is newsworthy and you don't automatically go for an opposing opinion. But this balances out. All substantial bodies of opinion get a fair say.

When the same reporter asked about the degree of control

Maguire exercised over programmes to do with Northern Ireland, Maguire's answer was:

I am responsible to the Director General for everything that goes out originating in Northern Ireland. I am responsible for giving advice about all other programmes about Northern Ireland produced by our London staff but I should stress that I haven't the final say. The onus is on the producers of these programmes to take my opinion but my opinion, although I imagine a fair amount of weight is attached to it, isn't decisive. Further, I would say that it shouldn't be decisive. You cannot allow the tail to wag the dog. There is this safeguard. If the editor or producer of a programme decides not to take my advice, he must refer his decision 'up the line' to higher authority. Even then my advice can be overruled if it is thought that I am looking at the problem too myopically which indeed I might be. It is very easy to miss the wood for the trees.[24]

Current affairs producers might comment that the very process of consultation could delay the realisation of programme ideas to the point that they became irrelevant because the critical moment for transmission had passed. Maguire's answer to that was that the situation was so serious in Northern Ireland that no risks could be taken.

The intervention of the army in the Troubles slowly changed the political context within which the broadcast media worked. The level of interest of the greater British public in Northern Ireland rose. The Westminster Government and politicians in Britain became very much more concerned. When the initial honeymoon period passed and the army's relationship with the minority community deteriorated, the task of BBC reporters and cameramen became more difficult. In every clash between the army and the people of the Catholic ghettoes there were two accounts of what happened. Viewing audiences in Britain, like loyalist audiences in Northern Ireland, were prone to believe the army's case and dismiss all counter-claims. Reporters on the spot were never so sure and increasingly gave both accounts in their newsreports. The level of fury at this method of treating the situation rose steadily and the resulting demand that the BBC get on side became very loud. The difference now was that the attacks on coverage were not confined to Northern Ireland and the Unionist MPs at Westminster.

The course of events in 1971 was such that the friction between the army and the inhabitants of the Catholic ghettoes became even more embittered. Curfew, house searches and particularly the introduction of internment precipitated endless violence. The first soldier died in February and as the months passed there were others. The army shot and killed too. Attacks on BBC coverage of the riots and incidents reached a crescendo at the end of October.

On the evening of the 23rd the news carried a full report on an incident which had occurred in West Belfast. Troops were carrying out house searches in a street when a car entered it and drove very rapidly through it. According to the army account, as it reached the end of the street, the back window of the car was smashed by its occupants and shots were fired at the soldiers. The soldiers returned fire, killing the two women in the back seat. Keith Graves made his report from the street where it all happened. He found that local people completely denied the army's story that shots were fired from the car. Graves interviewed a resident and the driver of the car. Their accounts could not be reconciled with the army's but the editing of the piece left the last word to the officer in charge of the troops.

Questions were asked in the Westminster House of Commons about the incident. James Kilfedder, a Unionist MP at Westminster, wrote to the Chairman of the Board of Governors of the BBC, Lord Hill, complaining about the news coverage of the incident. Kilfedder suggested that such reporting undermined army discipline; he wrote of BBC reporters 'sniping in the back', and threatened to call for a television licence boycott in Northern Ireland in retaliation. Lord Hill's reply was a strong rejection of Kilfedder's charges. He deplored the accusation against BBC journalists and stated that their 'task is beset with difficulty which is increased by partisan attacks such as your letter'.[25]

Conservative and Unionist backbenchers were, however, roused and some eighty of them met the Home Secretary, Maudling, and urged him to exert pressure on the broadcasters. Julian Critchley hoped that Maudling would persuade the Chairmen of the BBC and of the Independent Television Authority 'to give instructions to editors that they should be extremely reluctant to use film of instant interviews, and that they should think more carefully about the hurt given by the broadcasting of extremist views. The reporting of the recent shooting of two women in the back of a car in Belfast was a typical example of the way things could go wrong. It was quite unfair on a confused and harassed major to subject him to tough questioning straight after the event.' Stratton Mills, Unionist MP, called for a code specifically related to current events in Northern Ireland. He suggested that this should be prepared by the BBC and

ITA in consultation with the Minister of Defence and should 'deal with the kind of semi-judicial inquiry by television which now takes place after every incident'. He believed that in practice the answer must be to do away with direct quotations after such incidents. Reporters should speak to as many eye-witnesses as possible, and then deliver a report for which they would be responsible.[26]

The majority of the backbenchers supported Critchley and Mills. A minority demanded outright censorship but Maudling was known not to favour it. At the same time in Northern Ireland, the Prime Minister, Brian Faulkner, said he would not go along with criticisms of unfair press and TV coverage. The GOC, Northern Command, Sir William Jackson, paid a tribute to the 'tireless and often dangerous' work of reporters and their 'balanced and reasonable' coverage of army affairs. Lord Carrington, the Secretary of State for Defence, was not critical and said it was 'absolutely right' for the British people to know what was going on in Northern Ireland and appreciate some of the difficulties facing British soldiers. Christopher Chataway, now Minister for Posts and Telecommunications, firmly rejected censorship in a reply to a question in the House of Commons.

It was against this background that the Home Secretary met Lord Hill and reported to him the character and intensity of the views expressed by the MPs. Lord Hill said he would consider them and reply. His letter of 23 November 1971 constitutes a strong defence of the BBC's coverage in Northern Ireland:

The BBC already undertakes a scrupulous editorial watch at all levels. We believe that if we went beyond that it would do nothing but harm and we would reject any such suggestion, from whatever corner it might come. Its immediate effect would be to destroy the credibility of all our reporting.

Lord Hill dealt with the criticisms that had been made of the BBC's reporting.

Most of the criticism has, in my view, been due to a failure to understand what the BBC is trying to do in Northern Ireland. We see it as our over-riding responsibility to report the scene as it is in all its tragedy to all the people of the United Kingdom. We do not side with the Catholics or the Protestants. The BBC and its staff abhor the terrorism of the IRA and report their campaign of murder with revulsion. Broadly the charges are that the BBC reporters and editors snipe at the army, and are 'soft' towards the IRA. The charges are untrue, and are deeply resented by our staff, many of whom do their work at great risk to themselves.[27]

On the evening before the despatch of the BBC Chairman's letter to the Home Secretary, a group of television and radio reporters including Jonathan Dimbleby met in London to discuss what some felt was the growing pattern of censorship within the BBC and the ITV systems. They asserted that the self-imposed 'code of conduct' which Mills and Critchley demanded already existed. One reporter said, 'It is not a question of censorship but of indirect and implicit pressures to steer clear of certain things.' At the meeting a number of instances of the results of those pressures were brought forward and a resolution was passed deploring the intensifying censorship.

The staff magazine *Aerial* tackled Desmond Taylor, Editor News and Current Affairs, about the charge of internal censorship. Taylor said, 'What staff don't seem to realise is that editorial responsibility is delegated to them by the Director General, but because of the difficulty of reporting in Ulster this responsibility is placed higher than usual.' He said that since April no one had been allowed to interview a member of the IRA without reference upwards to the Director General. He said the procedure was to protect the reporters and avoid errors of judgement. He dismissed as rubbish any suggestion that reporters were prevented from putting the Catholic view. 'We represent every shade of Roman Catholic opinion provided it hasn't a gun in its hand.' Taylor said that editorial control had been tightened after internment had been imposed in August 1971. It had eased for a while but at the time he was speaking – late November – every item on Ulster had to be heard by somebody senior before it went out. Taylor concluded by saying, 'The only right that has been withdrawn is the right of a reporter to interview a member of the IRA without permission. Also, instead of having a balance over a series of programmes we now try to get a balance in every programme.'[28]

The outcome of the controversy over BBC coverage in Northern Ireland in November 1971 was to strengthen editorial procedures within the BBC on all items to do with Northern Ireland. The immediate effect was on the BBC in London because the agitation had arisen among the Westminster government party's MPs. This was the first time that this had occurred. Previously the prime source of complaint and pressure had been among the members of the government party in the Stormont parliament or among the Unionist MPs at Westminster. The new situation brought a subtle change in emphasis. The network television and radio editors of news and current affairs were in the front line, and not the Controller Northern Ireland. His role was relatively diminished, although he still had to be consulted. The suspension of the Stormont Parliament on 30 March 1972 firmly shifted the centre of political pressure about Northern Ireland broadcasting to Westminster and the centre of response to the BBC in London.

During the month of November 1971 while Conservative pressure was being exerted on the BBC, preparations were going ahead for a major programme which would set before the public the range of solutions to the Northern Ireland problem which interested political figures had to offer. BBC Belfast had a very minor role to play in the project. The Controller, Maguire, had been one of the originators of the idea of a major talk-in but thereafter he played no part in the production. The format of the proposed programme derived its inspiration from the hearings of televised Senate Committees in the United States. There was to be a 'tribunal of inquiry' before which a range of 'protagonists' would present their solutions to the Northern Ireland problem. The 'tribunal' would be able to call on expert witnesses. The purpose was to review the range of proffered options but not to reach any consensus. The choice of the eight 'protagonists' was crucial. 'They were chosen to represent a balance of Protestant/Catholic, Loyalist/Republican, Right-wing/Left-wing views and to represent as faithfully as possible the wide spectrum of political views both North and South of the border.'[29]

It was the inclusion of two figures from the Republic, Michael O'Kennedy, a Government Minister, and Neil Blaney, a former Government Minister, which constituted the stumbling block for the Northern Ireland Prime Minister, Faulkner, and his Government. They refused to take part. Paisley indicated that his participation was dependent on a Unionist spokesman coming forward.

The Daily Telegraph disclosed the plans for the programme and took a strong stance against the 'insensitivity of the BBC'. Westminster Conservative and Unionist backbenchers manifested a rising storm of anger. Their main objection was that 'the official state radio and television service' would be providing a platform for Irish political personalities of extremist views from both sides of the border, notably Blaney and Bernadette Devlin. The programme would take 'the Province a step nearer to anarchy and civil war'.[30]

The Home Secretary, Maudling, intervened at an early stage, before the story reached the newspapers, and expressed his opposition. The BBC's Chairman, Lord Hill, was conciliatory to Maudling but firmly in support of the programme. The crux of the matter was, however, finding a Unionist speaker. Without one the programme could not go ahead. On 2 January 1972 three days before transmission, one was found, an obscure Unionist MP, John Maginnis. On the 4th, Maudling wrote to Hill saying he was utterly opposed to the programme because 'the form in which it had been devised could do no good and could do serious harm,' adding that he proposed to release his letter to the press.[31]

In the event *The Question of Ulster* was transmitted and the predictions of the Home Secretary and many other Conservative and Unionist politicians that it would have deleterious effects were seen to be both inappropriate and mistaken.

The Question of Ulster had a remarkably large audience in Northern Ireland, as well as in Britain and the Republic of Ireland. It is rightly regarded as a significant occasion when the BBC asserted its independence of government and successfully resisted considerable pressures. It was also an occasion which demonstrated that the fulcrum on which pressure over Northern Ireland broadcasting affairs had to be exerted had shifted to London from Belfast. That is where it was to stay.

In the summer of 1972 the Controller Northern Ireland took a short fishing holiday over the border in County Donegal. After a day boating on a lake he was not heard of for twenty-four hours. His disappearance made headlines in the national dailies, and it was feared that he had been kidnapped. In fact, he had had a stroke and was discovered by the lakeside. Waldo Maguire never returned to his post; after a period of sick leave, he took early retirement.

Eight men had been responsible for the destiny of the BBC in Northern Ireland before Maguire became Controller. All of them had to cope with the difficulties which the region posed but for none of them was the task so desperately demanding. He was a Controller who wished to open broadcasting fully to the communities in Northern Ireland and in that respect he achieved much. The exigencies of the deepening crisis in the region, however, cast him in an editorial role which can be misrepresented. An 'experienced political commentator', said in 1971 that it was a great mistake to make him out to be a sort of bogeyman. 'He has a responsibility for the security of his own staff who have to go back to their homes in Ulster every night. But I think he tends to assume the worst possible consequences will arise from any item. He does sometimes worry too much about what people in Ulster will feel about it.'[32] It was perhaps not surprising that Maguire worried, for from 1968 onwards he was personally the butt of persistent and often vicious invective. In one week he could be the target for the bitter venom of both the Paisleyite *Protestant Telegraph* and the Provisional IRA's *An Phoblacht;* at the same time he was probably being accused of betraying the middle ground. If broadcasting, and particularly television, has been the scapegoat for the political ills of Northern Ireland, then Waldo Maguire has suffered more than most from the unjust assessment involved.

8

The Time of the Troubles

In Maguire's time as Controller the editorial procedures were laid down which today apply to the handling of news and current affairs coverage of Northern Ireland. The various crises which have arisen over coverage since 1972 have merely led BBC executives to clarify those basic procedures.

The crises have been no different in kind from the one created in November 1971 by the Conservative and Unionist backbenchers at Westminster. They have featured the same politicians voicing the same objections. Why must the BBC serve the opponents of the State? The *British* Broadcasting Corporation should be part of the State's propaganda machine and the pursuit of the campaign against the republican paramilitaries should have priority over other considerations. The opposing extremists should be neither seen nor heard; for if they are, the exposure constitutes a propaganda advantage to them. Critical investigations into the conduct and practices of the armed forces, troops and police, engaged in the campaign against subversion are not only inappropriate but unpatriotic and treacherous. In general, film of republican demonstrations, such as parades and funerals, is unwelcome and interviews with republican paramilitaries are anathema.

Richard Francis, who succeeded Maguire as Controller in August 1973, had a very different view of the role of the BBC in Northern Ireland from that held by the right-wing MPs. He did not hesitate to expound his view when he was in Belfast and later when he was promoted to London as Director of News and Current Affairs. Francis, a Yorkshire man, whose involvement in the affairs of the Region began when he was executive producer of *The Question of Ulster*, had extensive production experience in television and a strong commitment to the belief that the broadcasting media have at all times an essential role in democratic society.

> I start from the presumption that the media have a very real contribution to make, in particular a contribution to the maintenance of the democracy

which is under threat, both by providing a forum where the harshest differences of opinion can be aired and by reporting and courageously investigating the unpalatable truths which underlie the problems of the Province. I have no doubt that if and when the communities of Northern Ireland reconcile their conflicts, it will be by understanding them and not ignoring them.

. . . what should the broadcasters be contributing to the public interest in the Ulster context? I can do no better than quote a *Times* leader of a couple of years ago advocating five things required of public service broadcasting:

1 the forestalling of rumour by the rapid reporting of events,
2 offering a source of news capable of commanding the trust of both communities,
3 exposing the views, passions and personalities of every party to the conflict for examination by all the others,
4 assisting people elsewhere in the United Kingdom to a better understanding of the Irish impasse,
5 uncovering abuses by the forces of authority, and providing a check against abuses by the very possibility of such exposure.[1]

Francis also addressed the inevitable Conservative and Unionist challenge:

In taking an independent and impartial position, we are sometimes asked whose side is the BBC on? The implication is that we should take sides, that in a situation lacking consensus the BBC should stand by the government 'in the national interest'. But which government? Which national interest? Often the government at Westminster has been at odds with Stormont. Often the Westminster government's point of view has been opposed, not only by undemocratic and violent organisations, but also by a majority of elected politicians in the province. Surely, the national interest must lie in solving the problem, and the public's interest in being given reliable information about the problem in their midst?

The experience in Northern Ireland, where communities and governments are in conflict but not in a state of emergency or a state of war, suggests a greater need than ever for the media to function as the 'fourth estate', distinct from the executive, the legislature and the judiciary. But if the functions are to remain separate, it must be left to the media themselves to take the decisions (within the limits of responsibility) as to what to publish, as to when, and as to how . . .[2]

Successive Westminster governments since 1971 have been most reluctant to accept the BBC as an autonomous member of the fourth estate at least as far as Northern Ireland coverage is concerned. The recurrent expressions of anger and outrage by ministers and MPs over programmes transmitted and not transmitted have been designed to induce an ever more rigorous process of self-censorship within the BBC in place of the overt censorship which government would have difficulty in imposing in time of peace.

When Richard Francis was Controller Northern Ireland he found that the political problems of broadcasting in the Region were not confined to meeting the pressures exerted by government ministers and politicians. In May 1974 he was confronted with a local *coup d'état*. In that month the Westminster Government allowed a loyalist group to overthrow the legally constituted government of Northern Ireland. The power-sharing Executive collapsed as a consequence of the stranglehold on the economy steadily exerted by the Ulster Workers' Council, with the help of the Protestant workforce in the electricity generating plants and the Protestant paramilitary organisations. Broadcasting played a critical part in the process. The Ulster Workers' Council had recognised that it would do so, and had made arrangements beforehand to launch its own radio service. This was not needed for, as one UWC leader stated, 'The BBC were marvellous – they were prepared to be fed any information. They fell into their own trap that "the public must get the news". Sometimes they were just a news service for us, we found that if the media was on our side we didn't need a gun.'[3]

Francis justified the BBC's performance during the strike on the grounds of public service and sustained the argument that the BBC could do nothing else because from the very first day the Executive proved ineffective. He personally pressed the ministers to come forward to answer the UWC's claims over the air. They would not do so and in effect forfeited their functions to the Workers' Council. The BBC was obliged to keep the public informed about what was going on and did so.

Robert Fisk, *The Times* correspondent in Northern Ireland at the time, examined the BBC's role in the UWC strike in his book, *The point of no return*. His analysis was based not alone on his own experience but on a thorough investigation of all the evidence available, including the BBC tapes of broadcasting during the period. Fisk shows that the BBC ran the strike as a straight news story from the moment it was called. 'The BBC's constant desire to furnish its audience with news, sometimes of a slender nature, made it seem as though all initiatives in Northern Ireland were being taken by the strikers. And the UWC, sensing the power they had thus acquired, began to use the BBC shamelessly.'

Francis would strongly challenge the implication that the BBC was duped and would argue that all news was cleared in the normal way. The BBC's journalists were, however, caught up in a relentless rush of events:

> Nearly all were Northern Ireland reporters, born and brought up in the Province and – for it needs to be remembered – there is not a scrap of evidence to suggest that they deliberately tried to bias their reports in favour of one side or another. What did happen, however, was that staff were forced by circumstances – principally the sheer amount of time devoted to live broadcasting – to abandon any attempt at examining the political and constitutional implications of the strike. They used up their talents in composing the unending stream of special news bulletins which detailed the location of road blocks, the political statements, the problems of the social services, the availability of bread and transport; constantly trying to keep this information up-to-date and searching for a new angle to make their summaries more informative, they could do no more than scratch the surface when it came to analysing the causes of the strike and the intentions of the men behind it. It was not their fault . . . that no attempt was made to probe the background, both social and political, of such a serious situation.[4]

It is difficult to suggest what alternative course the BBC might have taken. What is certain is that the news machine ran away with itself and all the participant reporters were intoxicated by the process.

When the Regional Advisory Council discussed the BBC's role in the UWC strike, the members were very aware that Northern Ireland had passed through a remarkable revolutionary or counter-revolutionary experience. There appeared to be a general feeling of inevitability about what had happened, particularly in relation to the BBC's role. One member, however, drew attention to recent statements by the Director General and by the Editor of News and Current Affairs in which they maintained the principle that the BBC was not in the least impartial about parliamentary democracy. The Director General had said that the BBC not only lived in a parliamentary democracy, it sustained and lived by it. The BBC in Northern Ireland, however, had clearly allowed local parliamentary democracy to be overturned with little comment. It might even have assisted in the process.

The consciousness that parliamentary democracy in Great Britain was not threatened undoubtedly permitted the BBC in Northern

Ireland to act out a fourth estate role. The BBC was in no sense an instrument of the Government of the region and when that Government failed, it was able to reflect the failure faithfully. It was no part of the BBC's function to save the Government. The Controller, Francis, once remarked to the author that the Corporation merely followed the pattern of political events dictated by external forces and if broadcasting incidentally assisted those forces, it was unintended and unavoidable. It had followed the pattern in 1968–9 when the civil rights movement set the pace and in a like manner in 1974 when the UWC determined developments.

On the occasion of the tenth anniversary of the UWC strike, in 1984, the BBC's Radio Ulster mounted a commemorative programme presented by Roy Bradford, a Unionist Minister in the ill-fated power-sharing Executive. The programme reviewed the course of the strike and suggested that its success was due in large part to the Labour Government's lack of commitment to what had been a Conservative political initiative. Whether this explanation is true or not, there is no doubt that the Labour Secretary of State for Northern Ireland, Merlyn Rees, did 'stand idly by' while the Executive fell.

Rees was not a loud-mouthed critic of broadcasters. Indeed when the BBC faced an outcry over the transmission of an interview with the Provisional IRA Leader, David O'Connell, in 1974, he remarked, '. . . if it makes people realise all over the UK that I am dealing with people who are out to kill for political reasons . . . it won't have done any harm'.

Rees' successor was quite different. Roy Mason assumed office in the autumn of 1976. He had strong views on how the campaign against the Provisional IRA should be conducted, and he believed that the media were playing a significant part in sustaining the violent situation. Within a few weeks of his arrival he was expounding to local journalists his conviction that a system of D-notices whereby the Government could impose blackouts on newspaper, radio and television coverage of certain events would soon bring an end to the Troubles.

On 6 November the BBC afforded Mason an opportunity to sound off about its own role. The occasion was a private dinner party given by the Board of Governors in the Culloden Hotel outside Belfast to mark the completion of a large extension to the BBC's premises on the Ormeau Avenue site. The guests included Mason, the GOC, the Chief Constable and the Lord Chief Justice. In the course of the evening they were invited to express their views about the BBC's performance in the region. Mason launched into a fierce attack on the Corporation. His starting point may have had more to do with an offence to *amour propre* than with his main argument. He protested that the local current affairs programme *Spotlight* had gone ahead with a critical profile of himself, in spite of his refusal to take part. He then asserted that the BBC gave a 'daily platform' to the Provisional IRA: that its coverage of Northern Ireland was 'appalling' and that it did not behave 'like a public service organisation'. He concluded by reminding his hosts that he was a member of the Cabinet which would decide on the new Charter and on the size of the licence fee.

The attack stunned the BBC Governors and executives present. Other guests took their cue from Mason and were equally disparaging. Kenneth Newman, the Chief Constable of the RUC, was alone in not joining the attack. The BBC's local Head of Programmes, Cecil Taylor, replied and in some measure was able to express the sense of outrage his colleagues felt. Within a few days all present had been circulated by the BBC with a document which retailed the charges which had been made, answering them in detail.

The affair, known in the BBC as 'the second battle of Culloden', was eventually leaked to the press in January 1977. It clearly showed that clashes between government and the BBC over Northern Ireland coverage need not be confined to periods when the Conservative party was in power.[5]

In March 1977 Roy Mason had cause to react to a programme which undoubtedly confirmed him in his view of the BBC. The *Tonight* current affairs team devoted an extended edition to an interview with a Fermanagh schoolteacher, Bernard O'Connor, who alleged that he had suffered grossly inhuman treatment at the hands of the RUC when he had recently been held by them for 168 hours. The interview in its transmitted, edited form lasted forty minutes and O'Connor was supported by another detainee who claimed that he had endured similar methods of interrogation. The police were asked to participate in the programme but declined to do so on the grounds that O'Connor's complaints were currently being investigated. The transmitted programme included a statement to this effect.

234

The programme produced a variety of angry reactions. The Secretary of State declared that it was one-sided and implied that the BBC had been duped into making it. The Chairman of the Northern Ireland Police Federation said that it was grossly unfair and had all the hallmarks of trial by television. The Conservative spokesman on Northern Ireland, Airey Neave, maintained that the programme had seriously damaged RUC morale and that 'in justifying it on grounds of "impartiality" the BBC had given the impression that they are not really on the side of the civil power in Northern Ireland'. Neave demanded to see the Chairman of the BBC and, meeting him, voiced his protest. Local politicians and Protestant churchmen joined in: the Fermanagh Unionist Harry West said the programme had been 'murderously irresponsible' and the Synod of the Presbyterian Church in Belfast passed a resolution deploring the fact that the transmission had gone ahead 'knowing full well that the police could make no reply pending investigation. The damage has been done which no correction or promise of discipline, if required, can undo'.[6]

The interview was conducted by Keith Kyle who had been introduced to Bernard O'Connor while the *Tonight* team was in Enniskillen preparing another programme. Kyle had been impressed by O'Connor and his story and had investigated the background carefully. He found that O'Connor appeared to be a respected citizen whose only active involvement in politics had been in his student days. Kyle felt . . .

a journalistic compulsion to make the story public without waiting for the lengthy, and probably stultifying, processes of the Complaints and Discipline branch of the RUC, to which O'Connor had presented a detailed statement on his release. I felt it was all the more urgent in that O'Connor's story, in the telling of which he displayed a remarkable facility for recall, in effect contradicted the most precise assurances which the then attorney General, Sam Silkin, was making before the European Court of Human rights at Strasbourg at that very time about the steps that had been taken to make it impossible for the type of inhuman treatment that had admittedly occurred in 1971 to be repeated.[7]

Kyle had another reason for wishing to have the programme transmitted promptly. He recognised 'that in the Catholic community in Enniskillen there was almost total scepticism among those who were aware that the interview with O'Connor had been filmed, and of my journalistic inquiries surrounding it, that the film would actually be transmitted'. The attitude of the minority community derived from the failure of the BBC in 1971 to expose the inadmissible interrogation techniques which had been practised on some of the recent internees. It had not been stated at the time that the BBC's inaction had been due to legal advice. The minority community would not have been impressed in any case had they known.

The O'Connor programme was transmitted with the support of the Controller Northern Ireland and his senior staff. After transmission, Kyle was required to submit a full memorandum to the Board of Governors justifying the programme and outlining his background investigations. His memorandum sparked off a review of Northern Ireland coverage by the Board and as a result the policy of the Controller Northern Ireland, Richard Francis, was endorsed and Keith Kyle's programme defended.

In a letter to *The Times* in response to the bitter criticism of the programme the Chairman of the Board, Sir Michael Swann, wrote:

> . . . I cannot describe our general stance better than in the terms of your leader of March 16. The BBC sees the duty of public service broadcasting in Northern Ireland as being to report and to reflect the conflict in all its manifestations. It sees both communities as part of its constituency, and to preserve its credit with both, it must not become the partisan of either!

Referring to Kyle's programme, Swann wrote that the Governors:

> . . . were in no doubt that it would have been wrong to suppress the material, believed to have been true by many citizens of Enniskillen (and which the programme makers themselves could find no reason, after meticulous inquiry, to disbelieve) . . . Delaying the broadcast by a few weeks might, they thought, have been justified. But the risk attached to any longer delay would have been the accusation of suppression from one of the constituent communities in Northern Ireland – and it is such a charge that leads directly to loss of trust and credibility.[8]

Kyle himself remained deeply concerned that the significance of the programme was lost in the row about it. Three years later, in 1980, after the conclusion of a civil action brought against the RUC by Bernard O'Connor, Kyle again raised, this time in the press, the question of inhuman interrogation procedures. The High Court judge read out a reserved judgement for two-and-a-quarter hours and awarded O'Connor exemplary damages of £5,000 plus costs. He did not believe all that O'Connor had said but, despite that, he believed enough of it to conclude that the police deserved to be rebuked.[9]

The programme highlighted another broad issue of a different kind. Its makers and the BBC had been subject to such a level of abuse that the effect could be to inhibit them from making further programmes which endeavoured to examine the grievances of the minority community in Northern Ireland. The journalist, Mary Holland, congratulated the BBC on the transmission – 'The BBC has resisted Mr Mason's bullying tactics with admirable spirit' – but went on to warn that such attacks as his, by politicians in power and out of power, induced a process of self-censorship among journalists:

> . . . If an article or a programme or an interview is going to provoke rage from Airey Neave, cries of IRA-lover from Mr Mason and 'flak' from the press, then everyone involved, no matter how courageous, from the researcher to the Controller instinctively reacts by thinking 'Oh God, can we face it?' . . .
>
> The *Tonight* team were reportedly distressed at the phone calls to the BBC calling them traitors. But this is not surprising. If Mr Mason says they are stirring it up, if almost nothing else appears in the rest of the press to support their story, how can the public know who is telling the truth? If Mason does succeed in bullying the BBC into a posture of docile co-operation or intimidating its staff into more rigorous self-censorship it will not help the situation in Northern Ireland, it will simply mean that the public is denied the information it needs to make a judgement on the issue . . .[19]

The impact of self-censorship on programming is, of necessity, difficult to assess. The impact of legal restrictions is less so. In 1976 the Prevention of Terrorism Bill passed through Parliament at Westminster and was enacted. In the course of the debates on the Bill it was suggested that there should be explicit clauses to inhibit broadcasters from aiding and abetting terrorists. The Bill was not amended in this sense. It was understood that it would not be necessary to do so.

In 1979 the BBC fell foul of the Government on two occasions and the Government determined to test the efficacy of the Prevention of Terrorism Act by referring both incidents to the Director of Public Prosecutions with a view to court proceedings. In July an interview with a member of the Irish National Liberation Army was transmitted on the *Tonight* programme. In the course of it the interviewee declared, 'We assassinated Neave because he was a militarist'. The sense of outrage which the programme engendered had not dispelled when the news broke in November that a *Panorama* team had recently filmed Provisional IRA men checking traffic which was passing through the village of Carrickmore in County Tyrone. There was a substantial difference between the two affairs. In the case of the interview all editorial procedures had been complied with and the decision to transmit had been made by the Director General with the support of the Board of Governors. In the case of the Carrickmore affair it was not clear how far editorial procedures had been followed but the film had not, in fact, been edited, much less transmitted. This was the situation when some Fleet Street papers released a grossly exaggerated version of what had happened in the County Tyrone village. The essential facts were that the *Panorama* team had crossed the border from the Republic where they had been making a programme. They had done so as a result of a telephone tip-off. They had followed the lead without clearing their intention with the Controller in Broadcasting House, Belfast, and so had ignored a procedural step. In Carrickmore, having spent some ten minutes filming cars being stopped, the team packed up and drove off to Belfast. They did not inform the security forces about what had happened. Similar film had been taken on a number of occasions elsewhere in Northern Ireland and it was not particularly remarkable.[11]

The story of Carrickmore was disclosed by chance. Weeks after the incident, a Dublin journalist visiting the County Tyrone village for another purpose was told what had happened. He wrote an account of it for his paper. The British press picked up his report and greatly embellished it. A dozen Provisional IRA men at most became one hundred and forty who took over the village, drilled in public, gave an elaborate display of a considerable armoury and offered to hold the village overnight if the camera crew wished them to do so for filming purposes. None of which was true.[12]

Questions were immediately raised in Parliament as a result of the press reports. The focus of attention and anger was the BBC and not the newspapers which had so effectively done the Provisional IRA's propaganda work for it. The Prime Minister, Margaret Thatcher, indicated that the BBC activities in Carrickmore would, like the INLA interview, be referred to the Director of Public Prosecutions who would examine them in the light of the Prevention of Terrorism Act.

The effect on the BBC was that there was a thorough internal investigation and once again editorial procedures were reviewed. Henceforward reporters and producers were required to seek permission from senior executives before they made contact of any kind with paramilitaries.* Previously the requirement had applied only when they intended to seek an interview.

In July 1980 the Attorney General, Sir Michael Havers, indicated in a parliamentary answer that he did not intend to prosecute the BBC television journalists involved in either of the incidents. The *Guardian* reported:

> The Attorney General's decision is likely to anger the substantial number of Conservative and Ulster Unionist MPs who believe that BBC journalists clearly broke the law and that an example should be made of them to discourage all journalists from reporting on the activities and attitudes of paramilitary groups.
>
> A report from the Director of Public Prosecutions to the Attorney General made it clear that there was enough evidence to bring a prosecution under Section 11 of the Prevention of Terrorism (Temporary Provisions) Act 1976, but he clearly decided that a court case would have caused an embarrassing row about press freedom.[13]

There was, however, an exchange of letters between the Attorney General and the BBC's Chairman which disclosed the implications of the Prevention of Terrorism Act for the BBC. Havers wrote:

> I should like to make it clear that I have no wish to see any form of censorship on reporting of events in Ireland and I accept that your organisation as well as others involved in broadcasting and the press have a duty to report on these events and their background. The public should know them and understand, as far as possible, how they have come about. However, I believe that these two incidents went far beyond this and constituted little more than propaganda exercises by terrorist organisations to which your staff have willingly given their support. In both cases, they went to considerable effort to contact persons whom they believed to be connected with known criminal offences and had every reason to believe would be connected with further offences. Indeed, in my view, the road-block incident at Carrickmore was itself a criminal offence as an act of terrorism. In both cases your staff had taken steps to obtain information of a nature which might have assisted in the apprehension or prosecution of terrorists or might have prevented further acts of terrorism. In neither case did they attempt to contact the

* Full text in Appendix IV.

239

appropriate authorities to pass on the information acquired and only did so eventually and reluctantly under pressure . . . Any interview with a person purporting to represent a terrorist organisation is potentially a source of information of the nature referred to in Section 11 of the Act arising not only from the actual contents of the interview but also from any negotiations leading up to and the actual arrangements for it.[14]

Sir Michael Swann expressed grave concern about this last sentence: for it . . .

could be read as meaning that the police should be informed, at every turn, of the letters, phone calls or meetings with go-betweens which are, I have no doubt, necessary if a journalist is ever to acquire information from known or suspected terrorists. If this is really what the law says, then all reporting of who terrorists are and what they say would, in practice, be halted abruptly.

Sir Michael Swann had earlier in the letter declared:

We reject absolutely the suggestion that our staff willingly gave their support to any propaganda exercise by the IRA or INLA. Indeed, in the case of Carrickmore there was in fact no publication by the BBC.[15]

The Prevention of Terrorism Act, as it applies to broadcasting, has not subsequently been tested in the courts because no interviews with terrorists and almost no film of their activities have been transmitted since 1981. The effect of the Act is almost certainly equivalent to the directive which the Fianna Fáil government issued to the Irish broadcasting service, Radio Telefís Éireann, forbidding the service to broadcast interviews with subversives or film of their activities.

Late in 1980 the BBC was confronted with a new dimension to the Northern Ireland situation. Republican prisoners in the Maze Prison went on hunger strike for the first time. It was a form of protest which was calculated to win maximum news coverage. Apart from its intrinsic interest to the media, the hunger strike provided the pretext for a variety of sympathetic demonstrations which were newsworthy. As the health of the hunger strikers began to decline seriously, they were assured of attention in every news bulletin.

Adverse reaction to the news coverage was soon expressed. It was a revival of a phenomenon which had been a notable characteristic of the period from 1968 to 1972 when Broadcasting House, Belfast, received a constant and sometimes heavy flow of telephone calls and letters protesting about news and current affairs programmes which dealt with the Troubles. This had eventually eased off because, as

Richard Francis suggested, 'apart from wearying of the problems, Ulster people have come to recognise that the broadcasters are going to tell them how it is and some of the things they will hear they will not like'.[16] The hunger strikes of 1980 and 1981, however, provided a sustained provocation to unionists. The sheer amount of coverage – in every bulletin and at the top of most bulletins – incensed loyalists and even people who were by no means extreme in outlook. The callers complained bitterly of excessive coverage and that the BBC was being seen to give support to the protesters, to be recruiting for the Provisional IRA and to be helping to create martyrs. It was frequently asserted that the media were keeping the Troubles going. A question which was asked again and again was: why were the victims of the Provisional IRA not given equal prominence with the strikers?

On 30 October the BBC felt impelled to mount a studio discussion of the coverage of the hunger strike. Richard Francis returned from London, where he had become Director of News and Current Affairs, to take part. The fifteen-minute discussion on *Scene around Six* excited considerable interest and viewers were annoyed when it was ended so that the transmission could return to the network. Some phoned in to express their support for the critics of the BBC's coverage. There were those who said, 'The idea that you can make things go away by ignoring them is childish'. There was one caller who asked, 'Where did you get your members of the public from? There's not one from a nationalist area.' In all there were twenty telephone calls during and immediately after the programme.

The coverage of the ancillary demonstrations in Belfast drew a particularly harsh public attack from the Unionist MP Robert Bradford. 'It is totally irresponsible to give the H-block protest the constant media coverage without which their protest would die. Nothing breathes more life into the criminals' cause than television coverage of their friends disrupting commercial life in Belfast stores.' He alleged that there were 'Republican manipulators in the BBC' and claimed that 'the motive for carrying news of the protest was to give maximum publicity to the supporters of those convicts who were guilty of vile murders and crimes'. The BBC rejected Bradford's allegation and claim, saying that they were 'as offensive as they are untrue'.[17]

A couple of weeks later the Belfast Hunger Strike Committee complained of inadequate coverage of the strike. It seems to have organised a telephone campaign: over eighty calls were received in Broadcasting House, Belfast, all making the same point. As a result the Northern Ireland News contained the following item:

The BBC has been accused of not giving enough coverage of the H-blocks hunger strike. The allegation comes from the Belfast Hunger Strike Committee, who say in a statement that demonstrations and pickets have been ignored and press statements not carried. They say this is thinly veiled censorship and claim the BBC has been promoting a pro-Government line. For the BBC, a spokesman says the Corporation has not been promoting any political line. The BBC had not departed from the principle of informing the public as fully and accurately as possible of events of significance in the community. The spokesman added that they found it not insignificant that on the one hand they had been criticised for giving the hunger strike too much publicity and now, on the other, for not giving it enough.[18]

It is noteworthy that the same Northern Ireland News had opened with a lengthy account of the condition of Seamus Mullan who had that day completed twenty-six days on hunger strike.

Shortly after, the Vice-President of Sinn Fein, Gerry Adams, issued the following statement:

It would seem that in spite of its frequently and strenuously declared editorial formula of impartially reporting events of public interest that the BBC is more bound by loyalties to its British Government Broadcasting Charter than by notions of impartiality when it comes to reporting protests on the hunger strike issue.

An H-block march in Dublin on 22 November, estimated as at least 12,000 strong by other establishment media sources, was ludicrously cited by the BBC on Saturday evening as 4,000 strong, and protests the following day in Crossmaglen, Armagh, Lavey and Turf Lodge – estimated by other media as 3,000, 2,000, 4,000 and 800 strong respectively – were ignored by the BBC altogether. This policy of non-coverage and misrepresentation, which has been blatantly pursued by the BBC throughout the twenty-seven days of hunger-strike, can be clearly seen to result from political dictat rather than any alleged 'lack of public interest' as the hunger strike issue continues to preoccupy and embarrass Thatcher's Government in the face of public concern and condemnation of its stance, both at home in Ireland and internationally.[19]

Adams had a point when he attacked the figure given for attendance at the Dublin march. The BBC had underestimated the numbers. It was resolved that in future the newsroom would distance itself from such estimates and simply quote the figures given by the police and the demonstrators. Adams, however, had been misinformed about the failure to report the smaller demonstrations.

The first hunger strike ended on 18 December 1980 when the strikers called it off. It was to prove in many respects a rehearsal for the second. The BBC's role as messenger reporting the course of events increasingly alienated the majority community while it clearly failed to satisfy the active extremists in the minority community.

The second hunger strike differed in two important respects from the first. In the course of it one of the strikers, Bobby Sands, stood successfully as a candidate in a Westminster by-election and subsequently he and a number of his fellow strikers died. These differences accentuated sharply the news interest of the situation. They likewise accentuated the reaction to the news coverage. Local, unionist, expression increased in bitterness but this time the more vociferous attacks on the BBC were made in Westminster and in the British national dailies.

On 15 May 1981 Lord Ellenborough opened a debate in the House of Lords: 'BBC news items seemed oriented towards the IRA rather than their victims'. Lord Monsen asked whether the Government would make representations to the BBC to ensure that its television news and current affairs programmes gave at least as much coverage to the victims of IRA atrocities and their families as was recently accorded to the IRA hunger strikers and their sympathisers. Lord Monsen: 'On the evening of May 5, BBC 1 devoted approximately sixteen minutes of its main 9 p.m. news bulletin to the death of a hunger striker and BBC 2 *Newsnight* allocated no less than thirty-three out of fifty minutes to this event. At least three quarters of those chosen by the BBC to comment on this matter were broadly sympathetic to the hunger strikers whereas, for example, the young mother brutally murdered by the IRA in Londonderry a few weeks previously while collecting census forms received little attention or sympathy by comparison. This is deplorable.'[20] The debate continued with other Lords making similar points.

The BBC was obliged to comment on what had been said:

Like every other branch of the media the BBC has felt bound to do its fundamental duty and reflect what has clearly been an exceptionally critical period in Northern Ireland. We believe our coverage has been broadly right.

We recognise that what we report is, to many people, deeply disturbing

243

and that inevitably the messenger tends to attract some of the odium of the message. We shall, of course, continue to monitor carefully the content of our news coverage working extremely closely with the BBC Northern Ireland.

The BBC's Director General, Sir Ian Trethowan, addressed the problems involved in an article in *The Times:*

> . . . criticism of the media has been particularly sharp over the coverage of the hunger strikers, above all Bobby Sands. One crucial point which many of the critics missed was the significance of the Fermanagh and South Tyrone by-election. Whatever the reasons for Sands being the only Catholic and Republican candidate, electors were free to abstain, or spoil their papers, if they did not wish to support him. Instead, over 30,000 of them voted him into Westminster, and so transformed the situation. When last did an elected MP starve himself to death? When last did someone starving himself to death receive a procession of eminent international emissaries? The irritation of many viewers at being shown so much about Sands was entirely understandable, but however much they disliked it, the Sands affair became an international event which had to be reported to the British public.[22]

Trethowan's argument provoked a somewhat intemperate response from Paul Johnson in the *Spectator:*

> The truth is the BBC, as at present constituted and led, has no positive commitment to legality. It sees itself as a kind of independent observer, morally neutral as between those seeking to enforce the law and those doing their best to destroy it . . . it acknowledges no obligations to the state, no duties to Britain.[23]

Elsewhere, in the *Sun,* Johnson stated:

> The duty to act lies with the Government. Ministers already possess, or can easily obtain, perfectly adequate powers to control the coverage of events in Northern Ireland. I suggest that they immediately impose a ban on all open air TV filming and live coverage throughout the Province . . . if, as I believe, fading Ulster from the TV screens leads to an immediate decrease in the level of violence, then we should think seriously about drawing up a permanent and enforceable code of conduct, for TV coverage.[24]

The debate continued when the hunger strike was over. On 21 September 1981 *Panorama* presented a programme which the television critic of the *Daily Telegraph* summarised as follows:

> Last night's film, which sought painstakingly to be unbiased, presented a

chilling resumé of the immediate consequences of the hunger strike. Besides provoking an upsurge of violence and death, it had enlisted moderate Catholic sympathy for the Provisionals and prompted a big increase in American-Irish support. It had also, of course, given the Provisionals a political base with Owen Carron's election for Fermanagh . . .[25]

The critic complimented the BBC. 'It was encouraging last night to find that the BBC at least has faith in the ability of the people of this old democracy to judge sensibly for themselves, however sensitive the issue.'

The reaction of some in Northern Ireland was somewhat different. 'Outraged loyalist politicians and angry Ulster viewers last night attacked the BBC *Panorama* programme,' reported the *News Letter*. James Kilfedder, MP, called the broadcast 'a propaganda coup for the IRA which will result in more innocent deaths.' Kilfedder demanded an immediate investigation by BBC executives of the programme and asked for equal air time for a programme which would show some of the Provisional IRA's victims and express the views of the 'decent, law abiding citizens of Ulster'. The Official Unionist Party protested to the BBC's Director General. In a letter to Sir Ian Trethowan, Jeremy Burchill, chairman of the Party's legal committee wrote, 'The IRA have engaged in their suicide campaign in the Maze Prison in an attempt to gain publicity for their evil cause. The BBC have given them what they crave.'[26] The BBC's Controller Northern Ireland rejected the complaints out of hand. 'There was nothing in the programme to suggest a friendly or co-operative attitude towards the IRA. The IRA were strongly challenged by a tough investigative team which came up with some disturbing information.'[27]

The hunger strikes of 1980 and 1981 were commonly perceived to have polarised the two communities in Northern Ireland. The propaganda victories won by the Provisional IRA increased the bitterness and frustration of the unionist population, and the determined resistance of the Conservative Government to granting any concessions to the strikers, which had received a powerful groundswell of unionist support, caused the minority community to consolidate in determined opposition to British rule.

On the unionist side the BBC was perceived as one of the means by which the Provisional IRA had gained its propaganda triumphs. It had ensured that the 'other side' was seen and heard. It had betrayed, once again, in doing so, its 'British' role. While its sins, as perceived by loyalists, were sins of commission, its sins on the republican/nationalist side were sins of omission. As a British institution its failure to report specific incidents was clearly censorship in the British interest and its interpretation of events was dictated by its antipathy to republican/nationalist objectives.

These opinions of the BBC in both communities might be presumed to have reflected the hardening of attitudes. Press coverage, especially of the reactions of politicians, and the correspondence and telephone calls to the newspapers and to the BBC, would tend to confirm this analysis. If it is true, there would appear to be a limited basis for the credibility of the BBC in Northern Ireland. Yet in the days of violence surrounding the deaths of Bobby Sands and the other hunger strikers, the *Sunday Times* conducted an opinion poll which showed surprisingly that support for the idea of power-sharing was 'still powerful in the province'. Some 62% of the population approved of it and that included a 53% majority of Protestants. 'It is arguable,' the *Sunday Times* stated, 'that the main political parties in Northern Ireland are standing in the way of what the voter actually wants to happen.'[28]

Although suspicion of opinion polls is probably universal, there is no doubt that the *Sunday Times* findings represented a corrective to common perceptions at the time. They suggested that the communities might have found, through the experience of the Troubles, some basis for consensus in Northern Ireland even in the most difficult of times.

The BBC's public policies in Northern Ireland presume such a consensus and endeavour to build on it. It is obviously difficult to do so in the light of the profound suspicions in the two communities, each of the other and both of the BBC.

The minority community's suspicions are of a 'British' institution which aligns itself with the unionist/Protestant majority. In the political sphere and in the present long-running crisis this involves profound scepticism about the way in which the minority's points of view and especially its grievances are presented, or more specifically, are not presented, on television and radio. The doubts extend to every dimension of the BBC in Northern Ireland. The employment policies of the Corporation and its programme policy in respect of the Irish language are two most sensitive areas.

There is a perception among Catholics that the BBC in Northern

Ireland has always been a Protestant/unionist institution. It is a view which the journalist, Peter Lennon, writing in the *Listener* in 1983 expressed and will have reinforced: 'within a very short time of my arrival in Belfast a very curious scarcity became apparent: in my pilgrimage of Northern Ireland broadcasting executives I was not meeting any Catholics'.[29]

In the past there was real substance to the Catholic view. Before the Second World War Catholics were only employed as artistes in the Belfast studios but then it could also be said that very few Ulster Protestants were employed on the full-time programme staff. The BBC in London seems to have adopted the strategy of employing English and Scottish personnel as a means of dealing with the divided society. After the war local people were recruited, but for a decade they were only Protestants. Thereafter, the policy of liberalisation which affected programme policy also affected recruitment policy. Catholics were employed and their numbers increased slowly. A few were employed in Broadcasting House by 1968.

The situation then changed and the Fair Employment Agency was able to report in November 1983:

> The Agency was satisfied that the Corporation took a realistic view of recruitment requirements in Northern Ireland and that the methods they employ contribute to equality of appointment within the Corporation.
>
> Bearing in mind that the Agency examined only the recruitment aspects of the Corporation's employment procedure and no detailed exercise had been carried out on the composition of the present workforce, the Agency was, nevertheless, satisfied with what it had found. The Corporation has declared an equal opportunity policy and its procedures are designed to provide fair selection for jobs.[30]

There is one area of programme policy in which a persistent lobby would claim discrimination has been practised. Programmes in or about the Irish language before 1981 were confined to one series. Songs were sung in Irish from time to time but that was all and it certainly didn't satisfy the lobby.

The promotion and propagation of the Irish language is one of the more controversial cultural issues in Northern Ireland. Many in the majority community regard the Irish language as a foreign language. Some, more kindly disposed, recognise it as a dying language whose revival can only be divisive and therefore consider that it had best be left to its fate. By some in the minority community, however, the capacity and the determination to speak Irish is regarded as the true

247

criterion of Irish identity. While Irish speakers have been at pains to deny that the revival movement is necessarily associated with a political stance, there is no doubt that for the greater part of this century most of the enthusiasts have been associated with the nationalist movement and many with its republican wing. As a consequence, in the conflict between the communities unionists have not merely exhibited a scant regard for the Irish language and its revival, but have tended to categorise those who use it and those who propagate it as subversives. Within the minority community it is difficult to determine its true status. The very fact that it is an issue in the conflict tends to enhance commitment to it.

When a group of committed Ulster speakers compiled a report in 1978 on 'Ulster Irish on Ulster Radio and Television' they were faced with the problem of determining how many people in Northern Ireland know Irish, can speak it and use it in their daily lives. These questions had not been asked in any census since well before partition. The group, therefore, could only furnish some disparate data. From the Gaelic League classes in Ulster it was calculated that 2,500 fluent speakers had been produced in the previous decade. The League's monthly magazine sold 1,800 copies per issue. The group were able to say that there were at least one hundred families in Northern Ireland who used Irish as their language of everyday life. These facts are scarcely impressive in audience terms. The group had a much stronger case when it came to young people in formal education. Statistics from the Department of Education show that between 1,700 and 2,000 pupils take General Certificate Ordinary Level in Irish each year and about 5,000 to 6,000 children from Northern Ireland attend summer schools in the Irish-speaking areas of Donegal each year. A serious demand for school broadcasts could be made on the basis of these figures.[31]

It is clear that only a small minority within the 500,000-strong minority has an active interest in the Irish language. It is argued, however, that the language is at the heart of Irish culture and if a policy of cultural pluralism is to be advanced then programmes in Irish are essential. The case has also been made on grounds of parity: the BBC should treat Irish in the same way as it treats Scottish Gaelic or Welsh.

The Irish language lobby first approached the BBC in the 1930s and its requests were dismissed on the grounds that programmes in the language would have limited appeal: the potential audience was so small. The same response was given again and again in the 1950s and 1960s. Sean O Boyle, who had made an outstanding contribution to Irish folk music programmes on the BBC, drew attention to the neglect of the language when he served on the Regional Advisory Council. He pointed out that a very serious weakness of the popular broadcasts on Ulster dialects given by the Reverend W. F. Marshall was his ignorance of Irish. It was not until 1971 that O Boyle got a chance to present a radio series about the language, called *The Two Voices*.

In the programmes he aimed to show how the cross-fertilisation of Irish and English had benefitted both cultures in Ulster. He quoted from many sources in the Irish language, ancient and modern, and was able to illustrate the wealth of prose, poetry and songs which had become a common heritage. O Boyle's basic argument in *The Two Voices* was: 'The Planter and the Gael live cheek by jowl: their two cultures must not remain forever in opposition, there is no question of accepting one and rejecting the other.'

It was not until a decade later, in 1981, that a regular Irish language series began on BBC's Radio Ulster. It is entitled *Anois*, in English 'Now', and is a magazine programme. It contains music, interviews, reviews of books and plays, short stories and scripted talk. The presenter of *Anois* is Gerard Stockman, Professor of Irish in the Queen's University, Belfast.

The *Andersonstown News,* published in the heart of Catholic West Belfast, responded to the news that the BBC was to launch the Irish language series with an aggressive leader:

We believe this is an important announcement on two accounts. First of all it signifies an awareness by the broadcasting authorities here that the cultural imperialism practised by them for decades has become unacceptable to the nationalist population and has to be modified before the accusation of cultural discrimination is taken to the International Court of Human Rights or some similar body. Therefore, it is important that we understand that this 'change of heart' by the BBC has been brought about, not by an eagerness to do the right thing, but rather by the fear that its 'cultural Nuremberg' may not be far off.

If the BBC thinks that a thirty minute programme at some off-peak hour will satisfy the appetite of the culturally-starved nationalist people of the Six Counties, it is badly mistaken. We have been offered an hors d'oeuvre; let's hope that the main meal will not be long in coming.

The second point to arise out of the decision to broadcast in Irish is the way that it was brought about. Although the BBC stated that the decision was taken without any outside pressure, this newspaper knows that that was not the case. The people mainly responsible for the decision were members of the Irish Language Movement who put together a well-researched and well-presented document on the Irish Language in the Six Counties which highlighted the BBC's blatant discrimination against Irish culture in general and the Irish language in particular. We understand that the document was so devastating that it would have been difficult for the BBC to have ignored it.[32]

In a society which promoted pluralism, the various cultural traditions would be respected. Each would be represented in broadcast programming. There would be no room for exclusive attitudes, no facile dismissal of other traditions as forms of 'cultural imperialism'. A necessary step towards the achievement of such a pluralistic policy in broadcasting was the creation of a power-sharing executive in the field of programme policy planning. In 1981 the BBC's Northern Ireland Region took that step. Under the BBC's new Charter of that year the Region acquired a Broadcasting Council.

The Broadcasting Council for Northern Ireland determines policy for all regional production and is answerable to the public for it. The Council is responsible for the staff involved in such production. It is required, of course, to work within the budgets allocated to it from London. These are far more generous than they would be if they were dependent on the income from the licence fees collected in the region. Scotland, Wales and Northern Ireland are all heavily subsidised from BBC central funds.

The Broadcasting Council is chaired by the 'national' Governor, who, like other members of the BBC's Board of Governors, is a Government appointee. The members of the Broadcasting Council on the other hand are chosen by a panel appointed by the BBC's General Advisory Council which is itself appointed by the BBC. The panel is required to sound opinion in Northern Ireland and to consult cultural, religious and other interests before it makes its selection. The Council must be broadly representative and is confined to between eight and twelve members. Inevitably, of course, such a Council will provoke criticism. It is likely to consist predominantly of middle-class, professional people as are many similar public bodies. It will, however, always be drawn proportionately from the two communities of Northern Ireland and although its disposition may be to occupy the middle ground, its members must obviously be open to the lobbying of special interest groups in their own communities.

The Broadcasting Council replaced the Advisory Council which had existed since 1947. It was a reform which the Stormont Government could have made at any time in over twenty years. It had been tempted to do so in the period from 1968 to 1972, when unionist dissatisfaction with the BBC led to demands for a Government takeover. The Stormont Government was aware, however, that although it would provide a list of nominees to the proposed executive council, they would have to be broadly representative of the population of Northern Ireland. It was therefore not enthusiastic about the reform because it would have meant power-sharing. The council's power would in any case not have affected network production and moreover the overall allocation of the budget for Northern Ireland would necessarily have remained with the BBC in London.

In 1975, after the Stormont Parliament had ceased to exist, the BBC's Regional Advisory Council was asked to consider if it would recommend that an executive council be established in Northern Ireland to manage local programme affairs. The Council was much influenced in reaching its conclusion by the arguments of the Controller, Richard Francis. He remained profoundly suspicious of the power of whatever government operated in Northern Ireland to nominate the shortlist of possible members of the executive council. Stormont had gone, the Westminster ministers of state were there now, but what might follow? Even if this dimension changed and the members were not political nominees, it would be likely that the political majority would insist on a majority of their kind on the council. 'Consequently, there would always be a danger that the minority would entertain suspicions about the BBC itself.'

Francis was certain that any move to establish an executive council would be interpreted as a move to limit the BBC's autonomy in Northern Ireland.

> . . . the independence of our broadcasting service in Northern Ireland has depended to a considerable degree on the Region being an integral part of the BBC, in resisting political pressure, in the exercise of editorial judgements applicable to the UK as a whole. This has been crucial in the maintenance of impartiality . . . In Northern Ireland, where political consensus is so hard to achieve, the need for the primary broadcasting service to be an integral part of a national institution independent of political influence is arguably greater than anywhere else.[33]

251

The Advisory Council was persuaded and recommended no change.

Within five years there was a volte-face, but not by the Advisory Council. It was not consulted. A new BBC Governor for Northern Ireland and a new Controller decided, after a period in office, that the reasons which had been advanced for not having an executive council were not compelling. A representative body could work amicably because the Advisory Council had done so for more than thirty years. The process of selection of members for the council could be similar to that for Scotland and for Wales and so exclude the influence of any future regional government. The time was opportune because there was no devolved government in existence and therefore there were no local politicians in power to influence the issue. The BBC Governor for Northern Ireland, Lady Lucy Faulkner, and the Controller, James Hawthorne, therefore set about lobbying in the necessary quarters, so that when the BBC was granted its new charter in 1981, provision was made for a Broadcasting Council for Northern Ireland.

Hawthorne was personally keen on the arrangement. He had been Director of Television in Hong Kong before taking up the Controllership and in the colony had been subject to the direct pressure of politicians and men of influence. He believed that a broadcasting council could shield the professional broadcasters. His earlier experience as a schools' producer in Northern Ireland had convinced him that the School Broadcasting Council performed an invaluable role. He had every reason to believe that a council with more general responsibilities would serve broadcasting no less well.

The Broadcasting Council for Northern Ireland, which began operating in the autumn of 1981, represents an experiment in devolution and in power-sharing. It is too early as yet to make a serious assessment of its performance, but it can be said that the members have looked at questions involving Irish language programmes and have also fully supported the development of drama production in the Region for the networks. Since its inception, the Council has not been confronted with a major political crisis and therefore has not been required to reflect on coverage through news or current affairs.

Devolution in the field of schools' broadcasting preceded devolution in regional programme production. In 1978 the Northern Ireland School Broadcasting Council was established. Prior to that date, local production of schools' programmes had been subject to the advice of a Northern Ireland committee of the School Broadcasting Council for the United Kingdom. The new body is autonomous and is representative of a wide range of interests in the region's educational service.

To date the most sensitive issue which it has handled is the question of programmes for schools in Irish. The argument for such programmes had been taken to its predecessor, the Northern Ireland committee, during the 1960s and 1970s. The committee, which had also been representative of the educational service, investigated the claims of the lobby through a survey of Irish language teaching in 1970. After careful consideration, it decided that Irish language programmes could not be placed high on its list of priorities. It was already promoting series in Irish history and in Irish geography and these were being used in both Protestant and Catholic schools. If the committee was to accede to the Irish language lobby's demands then resources would be used for a series which would only be used in Catholic schools. This would be an inequitable use of limited resources. Additional series should be devoted to curriculum areas which were of value to the schools on both sides of the religious divide.

The Irish language lobby persisted, however. In 1978 its case was reconsidered by the new School Broadcasting Council for Northern Ireland. The Council decided to place high on its list of priorities a series to support the teaching of Irish. A working party recommended that a new series, 'Irish Studies', should be prepared and launched in a three-year cycle. It would be designed for junior pupils in secondary schools and would consist of four resource units in Irish geography, Irish history, Irish literature and Irish language. 'The Irish language content is to be recorded by native speakers in the Ulster dialect: programmes will provide practice in specific grammatical structures and will include cultural elements to develop an awareness of Irish heritage: music, song, folklore, literature, place names, family names, traditional crafts.' In 1983 an Irish language producer was appointed by the BBC to carry out the project. The first ten programmes will be transmitted in the spring of 1985 and ten new programmes will be added in each of the years 1986 and 1987.

There is perhaps some irony in the fact that the Republic of Ireland's government department of education abandoned all financial support for school broadcasting, including Irish language programmes, a decade ago. The action was dictated by the need for cutbacks in public expenditure following the international oil crisis of 1973–4. There were, however, contributory factors such as a lack of official conviction in the effectiveness of school broadcasting and a diminishing commitment to the Irish language on the part of the government.

This diminishing commitment reflected changes in the cultural attitudes of people in the Republic. There has in fact been a growing disparity between the two parts of Ireland in cultural matters. The Republic has lost its insularity while Northern Ireland has been driven in on itself. Brian Friel, Ulster's – indeed Ireland's – most distinguished living dramatist, stated the position as he saw it in 1973:

> The North has been retarded for so long – for the past fifty years – that people on both sides have become frozen in their attitudes. But the rest of Ireland has moved on. The Catholics in the North have little in common with the Catholics in the Republic, and the Protestants in the North have nothing in common with the Protestants of the South. The people of the North, Catholic and Protestant, have more in common with each other than with anyone else. They are divided by similarities.[34]

The confrontation and conflict between the two Northern communities has sharpened the need for each to preserve and assert its identity. The minority has found it particularly easy to attribute to the British regime the forces which are eroding its traditional culture. Elsewhere in Ireland the same 'alien' forces do not have such a focus.

The British Broadcasting Corporation is, as a consequence, subject to loud and often bitter demands that it grant greater access to expressions of the minority's culture. There is every reason to believe that it will increasingly do so.

Conclusion

The prime tasks of the BBC in Northern Ireland have grown to be the provision of a comprehensive, accurate and credible news service and of frequent, regular, current affairs programmes which aim to explain what is reported in the news. The difficulties which these tasks present are great. The constraints on the activities of journalists are many, as the foregoing account has made clear.

There is a war going on, at least as far as the combatants and those who actively support them in the opposing communities are concerned. A very significant dimension of that war is the propaganda battle. Both sides facilitate journalists by providing press and public relations services but neither side exhibits any enthusiasm when confronted with people determined to penetrate beyond the handouts and the up-front explanations. Investigative journalism is a hazardous occupation in Northern Ireland, as a recent attempt to assassinate a journalist illustrates.

The state, through the law, has increasingly narrowed the parameters within which investigation can take place. Journalists who endeavour to explore and present the perspective and arguments of those who actively oppose the state are in danger of prosecution.

In these circumstances the BBC has evolved 'Standing Instructions and Guidance' for its journalists,* editorial procedures which have been developed through experience of the Northern Ireland situation. They may be represented as further constraints on journalists. They may, on the other hand, be regarded as protective mechanisms devised to preserve the Corporation's increasingly limited field of manoeuvre. The danger of internal procedures is that they inhibit action and encourage self-censorship. The public interest is best served by those who assert their determination to find out, whether they be journalists in the field or in executive positions. The

* See text in Appendix IV.

maintenance of the greatest possible measure of autonomy *vis-à-vis* the state and the most powerful pressure groups within it represents a traditional ideal among broadcasters and journalists alike. It has not always been pursued with determination in Northern Ireland. It is essential in the interests of the informational needs of the democratic process that it should be.

Of course, even when news coverage in Northern Ireland is achieved, there is no guarantee that it will reach the greater audiences the BBC serves. The often remarkable contrast between local news bulletins in Northern Ireland and those from the radio and television networks is a fact of which Northern Ireland listeners and viewers are acutely aware. They feel the fact that news items are attenuated or dropped in London inhibits understanding and responses from the population of the other island. Richard Francis, when he was Controller Northern Ireland, adverted to the problem in 1977:

> . . . where the network news can go wrong over Northern Ireland is by doing too little; news values are relative, and disruption in the province (two bombs and one killing a day on average last year) is no longer exceptional. But when shootings and explosions destroying whole businesses in the UK's eighth largest city go unreported on the network news and in the national dailies – as happens more and more frequently – when a small incendiary in Liverpool rates a headline before the assassination of a prominent Ulster industrialist; when a bomb in a north-west London pillar-box rates the same amount of film as the destruction of Belfast's central parcel sorting office . . . then perhaps we are no longer concerned for the real values of our society!

Of necessity, reduced news coverage means that less current affairs programming is required to explain it.

Francis was afraid of a different consequence:

> If the violent activities of terrorists go unreported, there must be a danger that they may escalate their actions to make their point. If we don't seek, with suitable safeguards, to report and expose the words of terrorist front organisations, we may well be encouraging them to speak more and more with violence.[1]

There is no doubt that both communities in Northern Ireland feel that reduced coverage on the networks is not in their interests, although they may well differ over the emphasis they would wish to see placed in fuller news bulletins and over the nature of the political responses which they would hope for in the light of them.

BBC news coverage of Northern Ireland is nowadays provided by news teams in Belfast and, to a lesser extent, current affairs programming about the region originates there. There are few reasons for arguing that the BBC in Belfast has been responsible for a more cautious approach to news and to current affairs programming. Quite the contrary, not only do news values limit what the networks use of local reporting, but there is reason to believe that the close proximity of Westminster to BBC headquarters makes it more hesitant in what it uses and explains.

As the Northern Ireland crisis persists, the need for the British public to be made aware of it and, more importantly, to be helped to understand it, is more and not less essential.

The Belfast news and current affairs department today is a considerable operation. It now has an establishment of fifty-five professional journalists, including some on contract and not on staff. It has the only BBC newsroom outside London which is serviced twenty-four hours a day, every day. The history of the BBC in Northern Ireland over the years of the Troubles is not, however, just the story of an expanding newsroom. Other dimensions of broadcasting have developed too. The viewers and listeners of the region have an almost obsessive interest in local news but they are also extremely keen on entertainment programmes. In the worst of times people not only switched from news bulletin to news bulletin but were obliged to find recreation in their homes, chiefly from television and radio. The BBC has responded to this situation. It has been stimulated to do so not only because of its public service commitment, but also because it has had to meet the challenge of independent television and radio.

There has been a substantial rise in production and this has required increased staff and increased accommodation. In the late 1960s BBC Belfast was producing some 200 hours of television and 700 hours of radio per year. In the broadcasting year 1983–4 this became 340 hours of television and over 3,000 hours of radio.

The overall effect of this expansion has been that BBC Northern Ireland has achieved a service on a par with Scotland and Wales. This represents a transformation in its position. For long an impression existed in the BBC that Northern Ireland was an embarrassment to the Corporation, 'a half region', an anomaly which existed for political reasons but for no good cultural reasons. As a consequence Northern Ireland was at the end of the line when it came to the provision of new equipment and resources. The Belfast staff have felt that the post of Controller has been filled with senior men whom head office wished to put out to grass, punctuated from time to time with a 'high flier' who needed a short spell of experience in a difficult region. Denis Johnston dubbed Northern Ireland 'the kitty region' into which the BBC dropped its 'left-overs' and its charity. The outcome of 1968–84 has been to change all that. Fifteen and more years of violence have thrust Northern Ireland into the forefront of the BBC governors' and executives' attention. It has achieved the status of a full region with the resources and structures needed to sustain it as such. The Broadcasting Council for Northern Ireland and the School Broadcasting Council for Northern Ireland have been established with executive powers. Both bodies between them determine policy in all local programme making. Both are intended to be properly representative of the two communities in the region. Their decision-making will undoubtedly reflect their composition. Already there are clear indications of new departures. The whole process has been described as the 'Ulsterisation' of the BBC. Some commentators have attributed political significance to it but this is very doubtful. BBC staff in Northern Ireland at all levels see it as the region coming into its own and achieving, at last, parity with Scotland and Wales.

It should perhaps be remembered, however, that there are limits to what can be achieved in local programme production. These are determined by the resources available which are now, as they have always been, greatly in excess of the revenue collected from the population of the Northern Ireland region. Network subsidisation permits a level of development which would not otherwise be possible. This is almost as true in Scotland and Wales as in Northern Ireland.

Even with this help, local production has always represented a small fraction of the programmes transmitted by the BBC in Northern Ireland*. (The fact that most programming had to be provided by the Belfast studio in the early months, in 1924 and 1925, was not intended but was due to technical difficulties which limited simultaneous broadcasting from other stations.) There is no doubt that so long as the BBC goes on broadcasting to the people of the region the vast bulk of the programmes will be from the network. This is especially true of television.

* See Appendix II for details of a random week's production in 1938, 1952 and 1968.

Broadcasting, as concerned in these islands, is primarily a means for entertainment. There is no way in which a population of one and a half million could provide itself with the amount and standards of entertainment which are available from the BBC network.

Those who perceive this dominance of the airwaves as a form of 'cultural imperialism' would do well to remind themselves that elsewhere in the island of Ireland BBC programmes figure dominantly in the television provision and, in any case, the words of the first film censor in the Irish Free State may be singularly apposite: 'It is not Anglicisation which I fear, but Los Angelisation.' BBC network production at its best offers windows in sound and vision on the metropolitan, international and cosmopolitan scenes to the enclosed, narrow, provincial society of Northern Ireland.

In one sphere of cultural life, music, the local BBC has, from the beginning, endeavoured to provide access to the wider world outside the region. It maintained the only full-time permanent orchestra in the region during the greater part of the last sixty years. The pre-war BBC Northern Ireland Orchestra and the post-war BBC Northern Ireland Light Orchestra not only provided music on their own account but, in addition, their members were enabled under the terms of their contracts to constitute the professional core of the Belfast Philharmonic Orchestra and the later City of Belfast Orchestra. In the course of the 1970s the BBC, in co-operation with the Arts Council of Northern Ireland, sought to create a full-time independent symphony orchestra which would absorb the BBC's local orchestra. In 1980 this was achieved and the BBC undertook to subsidise the new combination, the Ulster Orchestra, with £1,000,000 spread over ten years.

While the music department of Broadcasting House, Belfast, has thus brought orchestral music in the great Western tradition to the people of Northern Ireland, it has also sought to promote local music and musicians. Members of the department, notably in recent years Edgar Boucher and Havelock Nelson, have been major stimulators of musical life in the region. In 1974, for example, on the occasion of the fiftieth anniversary of the BBC in Northern Ireland, Boucher devised *Four Centuries of Music in Ireland*, a series of concerts which offered a comprehensive survey of Irish music in all its forms.

These musical activities have only a marginal relevance to the sectarian/political divide in Northern Ireland. Serious music finds its audience indiscriminately among both communities. The same is true of popular music.

259

Popular music of every kind – folk, pop, country and jazz – is broadcast on Radio Ulster, which was the first of the BBC's national regional services. It was launched in 1975 with the intention that it would eventually provide a complete day-long schedule of locally originated programmes. By 1984, seventy-five hours per week were being transmitted and it is proposed that this will become twelve hours a day in 1985–6. Popular recorded music provides the substance of the programming but its main strands are news bulletins and information sequences which are of special significance during the present Troubles. The flexible formats of the programmes are easily adapted to more extended hard news coverage when necessary.

Radio Ulster was established in anticipation of the arrival of independent commercial radio in the region. It is required to compete with Downtown Radio. The outcome, as elsewhere, is cheap, easy-to-listen-to, programmes. Unfortunately, the locally-produced programmes on Radio Ulster tend to be less demanding than those on Radio 4 which they are replacing.[2] Although the BBC does insist on a much higher ratio of speech to music than its commercial rival in Northern Ireland, there is no doubt that the competition between local radio stations everywhere has led to the emergence of a broadcaster's form of Gresham's Law – bad programmes tend to oust good programmes – and musical wallpaper rules.

After one year Downtown Radio claimed that within the VHF area which it covered 68 per cent of people listened to it once a week, compared with 45 per cent for Radio Ulster. Downtown admitted that many listeners still turned automatically to the BBC for news. The BBC disputes the size of the disparity between the percentages but its research confirms that people regard the BBC as the authoritative source for news and current affairs programmes.

Patterns of listening and viewing in Northern Ireland are undoubtedly class-related as they are throughout the United Kingdom. The working classes, the Registrar General's social categories C and D, are more likely to turn to independent radio and television than to the BBC. It would be interesting to discover if political disposition accentuates this tendency in Northern Ireland: to find out if the alienation of the Protestant working classes, many of whom perceive the British Broadcasting Corporation as un-British, if not actually anti-British, and if the antagonism of their Catholic counterparts who perceive the Corporation as un-Irish,

260

when not positively anti-Irish, leads both to switch to the commercial channels to any greater extent.

Whatever the perceptions the opposed communities may have of the BBC, the BBC in its local production does not fail to reflect and confront the division. Two fields of programming in particular are thus engaged: the religious and the drama departments.

Religious broadcasting in Northern Ireland has long since advanced beyond the transmission of services from the major denominations. The annual conferences of the churches are reported, discussions between church and laymen on the controversial issues which divide the churches are mounted, church leaders are frequently interviewed and phone-ins are encouraged. The issues between the churches are fully aired and at the same time the ecumenical drive is satisfied by joint activities as in religious music programmes. The head of the religious department from 1955 to 1979 was a Presbyterian minister, the Reverend Moore Wasson and from 1979 has been a Catholic priest, the Reverend James Skelly. Clergy from the major denominations work together in a full-time capacity within the department.

Drama production in Broadcasting House, Belfast, has undergone a profound change since the mid-1960s. Since then all production has been for the network, whether on radio or on television. As a consequence the standards of the plays and of the productions have had to be higher. The producers have increasingly drawn on all Ireland for scripts and the plays presented have explored the more sensitive and significant issues in Irish and particularly Northern Irish society. A succession of talented radio producers began with Ronald Mason in the early 1960s and included Robert Cooper in the late 1970s and early 1980s. They belong to a tradition which dates back to Tyrone Guthrie in 1924. One type of drama from those early days has, however, been abandoned long since: the Ulster kitchen comedy has not been favoured since the early 1960s. Most modern Ulster drama has a more serious intent. The list of local dramatists who have established reputations through radio and latterly through television is long and includes such names as Joseph Tomelty, Janet McNeill, Graeme Roberts, John D. Stewart, Sam Thompson, Stewart Love, Stewart Parker, Maurice Leitch and Graham Reid. The outstanding Ulster dramatist is Brian Friel. He writes for the stage but most of his plays have been produced for broadcasting.

261

In recent years the BBC radio drama department in Belfast has received up to three hundred new plays from all over Ireland each year. These have to compete for the five hundred new drama slots on BBC network radio each year. Between 1977 and 1984 Robert Cooper was commissioned to produce well in excess of one hundred plays from Belfast. Cooper's observations on the Ulster playwrights among those who have had their plays produced, as compared with the others from the Republic, are that they 'are often more open and hard hitting in their zeal for observing our thoughts and behaviour. Far from Ulster being in danger of losing its identity, they are striving to build up a more accurate picture of it, sorting out our ideas and placing them in perspective.'[3] The standard of the plays and of their productions has been sufficient to ensure that there have been quite a few award winners among them. As a result of the success of local radio drama, the BBC has been tempted to develop its own television drama production. The first full-length play produced was *Catchpenny Twist* by Stewart Parker, transmitted in 1977 and again in 1978.

The difficulties which Broadcasting House, Belfast, faces in this enterprise are great. For a variety of reasons television drama is more expensive to produce in Northern Ireland than in any other region of the BBC. Yet the gamble is regarded as worth it. It means the talent of the region can be reflected in productions by the region for the network. It is a way of presenting an aspect of the creative vitality of the two communities in Northern Ireland to British audiences. The trilogy by Graham Reid, *Too Late to Talk to Billy, A Matter of Choice for Billy* and *A Coming to Terms for Billy* represents the standard which it is hoped to maintain.

The drama enterprise is one of those developments which the new Broadcasting Council has been encouraging strongly. It is a means by which the problems of the people of the region can be explored and by which greater insight may be given to and gained by the audiences into themselves and into the nature of the society in which they live. This represents one way in which the BBC may play a constructive role in Northern Ireland's divided society.

In the course of the past sixty years, the BBC has adopted three strategies in succession for coping with that divided society. In the pre-war period, the BBC ignored the division and sought to prevent any of its manifestations from impinging on programmes. This was an abdication of social responsibility. In the post-war world, the

262

pursuit of such a strategy proved impossible. The BBC then sought to be the means of bringing both sides of society together. The feeling that this should be done without provoking vociferous and possibly violent reaction from the unionist majority meant that the positive aspects of community relations were emphasised and the negative underplayed. A consensus emerged which had a false basis. When the civil rights movement attempted to give it a real basis, the BBC's strategy became irrelevant. Broadcasting House, Belfast, threw over the incubus of having always to placate local unionist feelings and there then emerged the third and current strategy which requires the broadcasters to reflect the whole of society in Northern Ireland as it is, in its negative and its positive aspects. Within the constraints imposed by the law, BBC Belfast is increasingly endeavouring to do this. The price of the strategy is that neither community is satisfied, for each manifests exclusive political and cultural attitudes, and harbours the ultimate determination that the other side will not be seen or heard. If there is middle ground, then that is where the BBC in Northern Ireland endeavours to stand.

The BBC in Northern Ireland may stimulate and review the political process, but the problems involved are not those *of* the broadcaster, except in so far as he or she is a private citizen. They remain, however, pressing problems *for* the broadcaster.

Appendix I

In the early days of broadcasting the fare offered by the Belfast and Dublin stations was remarkably similar, as indeed were the schedules of most European stations. An evening's programmes consisted for the most part of live music of the more serious kind. To this was added a number of informative talks designed to improve the audience. The following example of a day's programmes from 2BE and 2RN was chosen at random. The lists of programmes are as they were published in the *Irish News* on 19 March 1926. From the earliest days this paper provided its readers with the day's programmes of both stations and also those from London.

It is noteworthy that 2RN's programmes were not notably more Irish than those from 2BE. This feature was markedly changed when the republican party, Fianna Fáil, won power in Dublin in 1932.

BELFAST STATION

11.30 – 12.30	Gramophone records
3.00 – 3.30	School transmission: Mlle Heritier, French conversation; Arthur Malcolm, English verse reading
4.00 – 4.15	Miss Noel Brown, MA, *Three Literary Portraits: (3) Maria Edgeworth*
4.15 – 5.15	Belfast Radio Trio
5.15 – 5.20	*Children's Letters*
5.20 – 6.00	*For the Children* (relayed from Glasgow*)
6.00 – 6.53	Dance music (relayed from London)
6.53 – 7.00	Summary of wireless papers (relayed from London)
7.00 – 7.10	Weather forecast and news (relayed from London)
7.10 – 7.25	Mr Percy Scholes, music critic (relayed from London)
7.25 – 7.40	Musical Interlude (relayed from London), consisting of Weber Pianoforte Sonatas, interpreted by Charles Kelly: V – 2nd Sonata Op. 39 in A Flat (d) Rondo; 3rd Sonata, Op. 49, in D minor (a) Allegro Feroce.

* This was unusual. The children's programme was normally produced by 2BE itself.

7.40 –	8.00	D. A. Chart on 'The Rise of Ulster Industry'
8.00 –	8.55	Portion of Concert by the Belfast Philharmonic Society, relayed from the Ulster Hall. Stiles Allen, soprano; Tudor Davies, tenor; Harold Williams, baritone. The Society's chorus and orchestra, conducted by E. Godfrey Brown. Scenes from The Saga of *King Olaf* (Elgar)
8.55 –	9.05	Talk from studio on *Enigma Variations*
9.05 –	9.30	*Enigma Variations* from Ulster Hall [The programme from 8.00 – 9.30 was relayed to all Scottish stations]
9.30 –	10.00	*Week's Feature* (relayed from London)
10.00 –	10.10	Weather forecast and news (relayed from London)
10.10 –	10.25	Mr J. G. F. Fryer, Ministry of Agriculture Talk (relayed from London)
10.25 –	10.30	Local news
10.30 –	11.00	Dance music (relayed from London)
11.00		Closedown

DUBLIN STATION

7.30 –	7.45	Talk on 'Early Civilisation in Western Europe', Mr F. E. Stephens, BA
7.45 –	8.00	German lesson, Miss Olga Von Wenckstern
8.00 –	8.10	Songs, Mr A. J. Ireland (baritone) – 'Eldorado' (R. Mathew); 'Little Boy Blue' (Nevin); 'A Memory' (Goring)
8.10 –	8.20	Songs, Miss Sidney Jameson (contralto) – 'Obstination' (M. Fontenailler)
8.30 –	9.00	Half hours with great composers, second of series, RIAM – Allegro con brio from Sonata in C minor (Beethoven). Mrs MacDonagh (violin) and Miss M. Haimer (piano). Songs, Miss Josephine Curran – 'The Walnut Tree' (Schumann), 'Starry Summer Night' (Debussy). Piano solo, Miss M. Haimer – 'Waldes-rauchen' (Liszt), 'Vivace' from Sonata in G – Mrs MacDonagh (violin), Miss M. Haimer (piano)
9.00 –	9.10	Gaelic Songs, Nora Ni Mhathghamhna. *'Bean dubh a Glenna'*, *'Bruac na Carrige Baine'*, *'Cnoncainn Aerach Chill Mhuire'*
9.10 –	9.30	Choir of the United Free Church of Scotland (conductor, Mr L. G. Banton). 'Bound for the Rio Grande', 'Shenandoah', (Sea Shanties), Curwen, 'Billy Boy'. Full choir – 'O Hush Thee, My Babie' (Sullivan), 'Scots Wha Hae' (arr. Bell), 'The Road to the Isles' (Kennedy Fraser)

9.30 –	9.40	Station Orchestra
9.40 –	9.50	Songs, Mr A. J. Ireland (baritone) – 'Thou art risen, my beloved' (Coleridge-Taylor). 'In the Silver Moonbeams' (arr. Somerville). 'I Married a Wife' (Traditional)
9.50 –	10.00	Songs, Miss S. Jameson
10.00 –	10.01	Weather forecast
10.01 –	10.30	Barry's Orchestra

Appendix II

The memo which the Controller Andrew Stewart issued in 1949 to all programme staff in Broadcasting House, Belfast, is the most important statement on regional policy to originate in Northern Ireland. It is as follows:

PROGRAMME POLICY

In Northern Ireland, as elsewhere, the BBC regional organisation has two main functions:

1 To operate the Northern Ireland Home Service by drawing fully on the resources of the Region and, in the main, on other BBC Home Services. The programmes should reflect the character and taste and inform the thought of listeners in Northern Ireland.
2 To supply the BBC with Northern Ireland programmes.

The division of the territory of Ireland between Northern Ireland, which is part of the United Kingdom, and the Irish Republic, which is an independent state, adds another function:

3 To supply the BBC with general Irish programmes where appropriate as a practical expedient.

This division of territory raises problems which are unique in the BBC, and the following points will guide Programme Sections on (1) above.

Music
While Ulster music and musicians are the first charge, the body of Traditional Irish music is common to the whole island and therefore available to North, as well as South, as part of the living body of music of Western culture, so fully represented in BBC programmes.

Drama
The work of Ulster playwrights should have first call upon attention and help. Plays by other Irish authors, in which character or situation could emerge in Ulster, should be considered on merit, as should plays with close Ulster parallels from other parts of the United Kingdom, or from other countries. As in the other BBC Regions, the search for and development of actors should proceed with the search for scripts.

Features

Should treat Ulster themes, with special regard for the character and interests of the large population on the land and in country towns.

Talks

Should examine general contemporary problems where Ulster thought can add to understanding. The main responsibility is to the social economic and political affairs of the people of Ulster: farming and country life are important. In literature and criticism they will compass writing with which Ulster has affinities, employing outside speakers where appropriate and on merit.

News

Should report fairly upon happenings and affairs in or affecting Northern Ireland, giving due weight to matters of importance and real interest, avoiding the irresponsible and the merely sensational in presenting a balanced day-to-day summary.

Religious broadcasting

Should attempt to serve and represent fairly the various forms of Christianity practised in Ulster.

Children's Hour

The guidance given above will apply to the appropriate parts of *Children's Hour*.

General

Employment with the BBC in Northern Ireland arises from the fact that Northern Ireland is within the United Kingdom, throughout which broadcasting is conducted under Charter by the BBC. To ensure that each natural and historical region of the United Kingdom contributes and receives appropriate programmes, the BBC maintains a Regional organisation. Programme staff in the Northern Ireland Region, therefore, have two fundamental duties:

a The search for and presentation of programmes in Northern Ireland for the NI Home Service

b A professional orientation to the BBC and British broadcasting in providing programmes for the BBC as a whole and in observing BBC policy and standards.

These predominate over consideration of programmes from other sources, e.g., matter derived from some personal aptitude or qualification, such as proficiency in seventeenth-century Italian music or American swing or Scandinavian twentieth-century drama, is secondary, as is matter, including Irish matter, from outside the United Kingdom.

The Northern Ireland Region is, however, the BBC's workshop in Ireland: therefore, other Services will prefer to have some of their Irish programmes produced in Northern Ireland rather than by London

Departments. This is a sensible use of BBC Regional resources, in so far as it results in the best handling of the programmes. On occasion the NI Home Service may be used to try out such Irish programmes for other BBC Services: such occasions should be recognised as serving this special BBC purpose, and not as departures from NI Home Service policy (see (2) and (3) above).

In brief we will put first things first, and the first things for Staff here are the search for and imaginative treatment of Ulster matter at a high standard of professional excellence for the NI Home Service.

Il faut cultiver nôtre jardin.

1 March 1949   Andrew Stewart

Appendix III

Local production has varied in quantity over the sixty years. Apart from the exceptional first months when 2BE was limited in the amount of programmes which it could take SB from other stations, the bulk of programmes transmitted to the audience in Northern Ireland has always been from the network. This is obvious when the schedules are examined.

A week's locally produced programmes from three years: 1939, 1952 and 1968 are listed here. The weeks were chosen at random. The summer months were avoided because local production has always dropped during that period.

1939

NORTHERN IRELAND REGIONAL PROGRAMME

Sunday 5 March 1939

11.30 – 12.00	This Symphony Business. George Nash wants to know. James Denny explains. The BBC Northern Ireland Orchestra
6.35 – 6.50	Gramophone records. Debussy: Petite Suite
6.55 – 7.50	A Religious Service from Carlisle Memorial Church, Belfast
8.45 – 8.50	Week's Good Cause. Appeal for the Home for the Blind, Cliftonville
9.35 – 10.00	*Elephant Shooting.* A short story written and read by Lord Dunsany. (Broadcast on all regions)

Monday 6 March 1939

5.00 – 5.15	Contribution to *Children's Hour.* 'Patterkins and the Lamb': a short story for the smaller listeners, by Ann Rivers
6.00 – 6.45	The Band of the Royal Ulster Constabulary, with Hugh Mart, baritone
6.45 – 7.00	*Problems and Prices:* an agricultural review

7.20 – 7.30	Northern Ireland news, weather forecast and farmers' bulletin
7.30 – 7.50	The Use of Leisure – 'Education for Leisure'. A discussion with A. J. Tulip, John Hewitt and L. E. G. Laughton
7.50 – 8.30	The BBC Northern Ireland Orchestra with music by Delibes, Drigo and Coleridge-Taylor
8.30 – 8.45	*Farmers' Work and Worry*, a talk by Peter Fitzpatrick. The topic was grass silage

Tuesday 7 March 1939

11.15 – 11.40	Launching of the new Royal Mail Steamer *Andes* by Vicountess Craigavon. Commentary by Raymond Glendenning
5.30 – 6.00	Contributions to *Children's Hour*. 'Try this one', games problems. 'Important to us', Graeme Roberts reviews news of the month in Northern Ireland
7.20 – 7.30	Northern Ireland news, weather forecast and farmers' bulletin
7.35 – 7.50	*Famous Irish Trials: (5) The Yelverton Marriage Case.* Compiled by H. Montgomery Hyde
7.50 – 8.30	*Wanted – a tune.* Schubert or Gershwin? Berlin or Brahms? played by the BBC Northern Ireland Orchestra and James Moody's Dance Band
8.30 – 9.00	*Ulster Weekly.* A radio magazine for listeners, by listeners
9.40 – 10.00	Darts. Final of Down & Antrim League. Commentary by Raymond Glendenning

Wednesday 8 March 1939

5.30 – 6.00	Contribution to *Children's Hour*. 'Tuning up': BBC Northern Ireland Orchestra and two children asking questions
7.20 – 7.30	Northern Ireland news, weather forecast and farmers' bulletin
7.30 – 7.45	*Monday Night at the Ulster Hall.* J. O. Corrin talks about the music to be played at next Monday night's concert at which Gigli will be soloist. Illustrated with gramophone records
7.45 – 8.15	*Round the Fire.* A sing-song from Lisnabreeny Youth Hostel, Castlereagh, Belfast

Thursday 9 March 1939

5.00 – 6.00	*Children's Hour.* A competition for ten-year-old children. Questions and answers
7.20 – 7.30	Northern Ireland news, weather forecast and farmers' bulletin
7.30 – 7.50	The Harp Quintet
7.50 – 8.00	Topical Talk by John Irwin
8.00 – 8.15	*The Winter Evening.* Two speakers
9.35 – 10.00	*Dwellers in the Glens.* Raymond Glendenning takes the microphone 'unobtrusively into the lives of the people of the Glens'.

Friday 10 March 1939

5.00 – 5.15	Contribution to *Children's Hour.* Songs by the Coleraine Linnets Choir
7.20 – 7.30	Northern Ireland news, weather forecast and farmers' bulletin
7.30 – 7.45	*Accent on Rhythm,* a further selection of dance tunes, some old, some new, arranged by James Moody
7.45 – 8.30	BBC Northern Ireland Orchestra. Music by Glazunov, York Bowen, Walton O'Donnell and Ravel
8.30 – 9.00	Sing-song at the 'Dug-Out' supper of the British Legion (Northern Ireland area)
9.45 – 10.00	'More Junk': a talk by George Nash

Saturday 11 March 1939

2.45 – 2.55	Interlude of gramophone records
2.55 – 4.30	Rugby Union International. Ireland v Wales. Commentary by H.B.T. Wakeham from Ravenhill Park, Belfast
4.30 – 5.00	Two Bands – Argyle Temperance Flute Band and the Lisburn Temperance Silver Band
7.00 – 7.20	*Ulster Garden:* a discussion
7.20 – 7.30	Northern Ireland news, weather forecast and farmers' bulletin
7.30 – 7.40	Association Football. Eyewitness account of match between Irish League and the League of Ireland by Harold Risk
7.40 – 8.15	The Northern Ireland Singers in music from Mozart's 'Cosi fan tutte', 'The Beggar's Opera' and Handel's 'Solomon'. Singers accompanied by Frederick Stone
9.40 – 10.00	*Leek and Shamrock.* Illustrated eyewitness account of this afternoon's rugby international

1952

Sunday 5 October 1952

7.45 – 8.30	Harvest Thanksgiving Service from Roseyards Presbyterian Church, Stranocum, Co Antrim, conducted by the Rev Moore Wasson
10.30 – 11.00	*The Arts in Ulster*, a monthly review. Literature: David Kennedy; Drama: James Boyce; Painting: C. E. Brett; Music: John Cowser. Chairman, J. J. Campbell

Monday 6 October 1952

12.00 – 12.25	James Moody accents the rhythm with Winnifred Davey and Peter Alister and two guest artists
6.15 – 6.20	Northern Ireland news
6.30 – 6.55	*Irish Rhythms* with BBC Northern Ireland Light Orchestra, conducted by David Curry
6.55 – 7.10	For Northern Ireland farmers: Deep litter management

Tuesday 7 October 1952

7.15 – 7.50	BBC Northern Ireland Light Orchestra conducted by David Curry
6.15 – 6.20	Northern Ireland news
6.40 – 7.00	*The McCooeys*. The story of a Belfast family, written by Joseph Tomelty and produced by Sam Denton
7.30 – 7.45	Hymn singing by St Thomas' Parish Church Choir, Belfast

Wednesday 8 October 1952

6.15 – 6.20	Northern Ireland news
10.45 – 11.00	Music for two pianos played by Joan and Valerie Trimble

Thursday 9 October 1952

6.15 – 6.20	Northern Ireland news
10.00 – 10.20	Folk Music. The subject of Irish folk music is given an airing in a discussion between Sean O Boyle, Jerry Hicks, Sean Dynan and Sam Denton

Friday 10 October 1952

6.15 – 6.20   Northern Ireland news
6.30 – 6.40   *Sporting Preview.* Events in Ulster over the weekend.
7.00 – 7.30   *The Singing Blackbird,* a play for broadcasting by Joseph Tomelty. The action of the play takes place somewhere in Northern Ireland. Produced by James Mageean
7.50 – 8.00   *The Week at Stormont.* A report on recent Northern Ireland parliamentary debates

Saturday 11 October 1952

1.55 – 2.15   Ulster Bank. Ravenhill Temperance Flute Band
3.40 – 4.30   Rugby Football. A commentary on the Ulster v Lancashire match at Ravenhill Park, Belfast, by Sammy Walker. Summaries by Ernest Strathdee
5.00 – 5.55   *Children's Hour* – 'Irish Stew'. 'Button Brown': another episode in the life of the Brown family by John D. Stewart. 'The Wee Ginty Engine': a story by Anne Quekett. 'When I was a Child': a series of talks by speakers well known to young listeners. This week's speaker: Michael Murphy
6.15 – 6.20   Northern Ireland news
7.00 – 7.25   *Ulster Sports Report.* Introduced by Ronald Rosser, produced by Charles Freer
7.25 – 7.45   *The McCooeys.* The story of a Belfast family (to be repeated on Tuesday)

1968

BBC RADIO 4

Saturday 9 November 1968

7.10 – 7.15   Northern Ireland news
8.10 – 8.15   Northern Ireland news
6.25 – 6.30   Northern Ireland news
6.30 – 7.00   Ulster sports results
7.05 – 7.30   *Ulster Garden* visits Londonderry. Members of the City of Londonderry and District Horticultural Society put questions to Eric Mayne, Dick Grubb and Norman Martin. Chairman, Crosbie Cochrane

BBC RADIO 4

Sunday 10 November 1968

11.45 – 11.48   Northern Ireland news headlines

Monday 11 November 1968

6.00 – 6.20	*Scene around Six:* news, topical features from city and country
11.37 – 11.40	Northern Ireland news headlines

BBC RADIO 4

Monday 11 November 1968

7.10 – 7.15	Northern Ireland news
8.10 – 8.15	Northern Ireland news
12.55 – 1.00	News and weather for Northern Ireland
5.55 – 6.00	News and weather for Northern Ireland
6.25 – 6.45	*Round up:* the day's news and views in Northern Ireland
11.15 – 11.45	*Music Room:* a series of programmes by artists from Ulster. Schumann's Song Cycle *Dichterliebe,* Op. 48 Sung by Eric Hinds, accompanied by Havelock Nelson
11.45 – 11.48	Northern Ireland news headlines

BBC TELEVISION

Tuesday 12 November 1968

6.00 – 6.20	*Scene around Six*
9.55 – 10.15	*Anything goes.* BBC cameras set out to find the people, places and events that interest Ulster today
11.35 – 11.38	Northern Ireland news headlines

BBC RADIO 4

Tuesday 12 November 1968

6.55 – 7.00	Weather and Northern Ireland fatstock prices
8.10 – 8.15	Northern Ireland news
12.55 – 1.00	News and weather for Northern Ireland
5.55 – 6.00	Weather and Northern Ireland news summary
6.25 – 6.45	*Round up*
11.45 – 11.48	Northern Ireland news and headlines

BBC TELEVISION

Wednesday 13 November 1968

10.25 – 10.45	*Ulster in Focus:* programme for Schools. 'Linen – facing the challenge'

| 6.00 – | 6.20 | *Scene around Six* |
| 11.25 – | 11.28 | Northern Ireland news headlines |

BBC RADIO 4

Wednesday 13 November 1968

7.10 –	7.15	Northern Ireland news
8.10 –	8.15	Northern Ireland news
12.55 –	1.00	News and weather for Northern Ireland
5.55 –	6.00	News summary and weather
6.25 –	6.45	*Round up*
11.45 –	11.48	Northern Ireland news headlines

BBC TELEVISION

Thursday 14 November 1968

2.30 –	2.50	*Ulster in Focus* – repeat of Wednesday's school programme
6.00 –	6.20	*Scene around Six*
6.20 –	6.40	*Match Play.* The second series of a TV quiz-cum-golf game (Knock, Belfast v Castlerock)
6.40 –	7.05	*Transworld Top Team* – International top of the form. Belfast v Toronto
9.55 –	10.20	*Look Who's Talking.* Harry Thompson takes a live look at this week's Ulster scene: comment, discussion and entertainment
11.20 –	11.23	Northern Ireland news headlines

BBC RADIO 4

Thursday 14 November 1968

7.10 –	7.15	Northern Ireland news
8.10 –	8.15	Northern Ireland news
9.35 –	9.55	For schools – James Hawthorne discusses inductive and deductive reasoning
9.55 –	10.15	For schools – 'Irish History: Unionists'
5.55 –	6.00	News and weather for Northern Ireland
9.30 –	10.00	*Ulster Opinion,* monthly discussion on what's happening in Ulster
11.55 –	11.58	Northern Ireland news headlines

276

Friday 15 November 1968

6.00 – 6.20	*Scene around Six*
11.20 – 11.23	Northern Ireland news headlines

BBC RADIO 4

Friday 15 November 1968

6.00 – 6.05	Weather and Northern Ireland fatstock prices
7.10 – 7.15	Northern Ireland news
8.10 – 8.15	Northern Ireland news
9.55 – 10.15	For Schools – *Today and Yesterday in Northern Ireland* – Aircraft Makers
12.55 – 1.00	News and weather for Northern Ireland
7.00 – 7.30	*Country Window* produced by Sam Hanna Bell. 'What we hope to do in Country Window', Sam Hanna Bell said when introducing this monthly series in April 1967, 'is to tell town people and country people something about our Ulster countryside'.
11.15 – 11.45	*Ulster Band* – Ballycoan Pipe Band. Northern Ireland Senior Champions for 1968

Appendix IV

The impact of the Northern Ireland problem on the BBC as a whole is most readily seen in the special editorial procedures which apply to all programming which has to do with the island of Ireland. These procedures date back to 1937 when, as a result of a complaint from the Regional Director for Northern Ireland about a programme on 'The Irish' from the North Region, the network Programme Board ruled in its minute No. 576 that 'whenever any department or Region was about to produce a programme involving a subject, of which another department or Region possessed knowledge and experience, there should be preliminary consultation between them'. The Regional Director's intention was to prevent programmes being produced which might prove offensive to public opinion in Northern Ireland. He was particularly concerned about programmes which dealt with the independent Irish state, Irish identity or Irish culture and which by intention or implication seemed to call in question the right of Northern Ireland to exist. His successors were exercised by the same concern.

During the Second World War the ruling of 1937 was elaborated and strengthened. A succession of directives was issued by the BBC's Head Office which required all departments of the BBC to consult with the Northern Ireland Regional Director on all programme proposals to do with Ireland and Northern Ireland. (See Chapter 4 above). The Director effectively became the censor of all such production from 1940 to 1944. In the post-war period the directive was modified and consultation with the Controller Northern Ireland became a matter of courtesy but soon programmes from the network precipitated such angry reactions from the Unionist Government and population that the directive had to be strengthened. The crises over programmes occurred again and again and the Director General on each occasion reissued the directive. Political crises had the same effect because it was felt that unionist opinion would then be very sensitive.

When the Troubles began in 1968–9, the directive was in force but, as the years have passed, it has been revised substantially in the light of the experience of covering civil disturbance and armed insurrection. In the present situation the directive has become a series of standing instructions and guidance. They are included in the BBC News and Current Affairs Index (Second Edition, 1984). The title of the section is: *Coverage of Matters affecting Northern Ireland**:

> It is the responsibility of those receiving these instructions to ensure that they are made known to everyone working in this area. Heads of Departments are responsible for the correct communication of their departmental proposals to Network Controllers and CNI, and where necessary to ADG, and for the effective discharge of these instructions. It must not be assumed that the advice and co-operation given to a Network producer by Northern Ireland staff implies responsibility for the programme in its final form; that overall responsibility remains with the Network output department.

Section I

Standing Instructions

1. Referring up through Line Management

The BBC's system of delegated responsibility puts the onus on individual programme-makers to judge when to refer upwards in case of doubt or difficulty with regard to policy or the law. The normal process of referral through line management to Network Controllers is especially important in dealing with programmes affecting Northern Ireland. Network Controllers will refer to their Management Directors and ADG as appropriate.

Programme making is often itself a public activity and usually so in Northern Ireland. Our activities are under close and often partisan observation; they may lead, at any stage in the making of a programme, to public, political or paramilitary reaction. Referral enables senior and experienced professionals in the BBC to weigh the editorial value of programme material against the physical, political and legal risks in a sectarian environment affected by terrorism.

* The following is a key to the initials used in the document: DG Director General; ADG Assistant Director General; CNI Controller Northern Ireland; HPNI Head of Programmes Northern Ireland; ENCANI Editor News and Current Affairs, Northern Ireland; HRNI Head of Radio Northern Ireland.

279

2. Referring to Northern Ireland Staff

(a) Controller Northern Ireland must be consulted and his agreement sought to all programme proposals having a bearing on Ireland as a whole and on Northern Ireland in particular.

He does not have a right of veto, but in cases of disagreement the proposal shall be suspended until it has been referred to ADG and finally, if necessary, to DG for their ruling.

CNI will be the first point of contact on network programme proposals other than news and same-day programme items. In his absence HPNI, ENCANI and HRNI will deputise, in that order.

HPNI will be the principal point of reference for the continuous process of consultation and advice in detail.

(b) ENCANI is the first point of contact in all day-to-day matters of coverage for network radio and television news bulletins and sequences.

ENCANI will nominate a senior member of his staff for consultation in his absence. In matters of particular sensitivity regarding the content of news programmes, ENCANI will consult ADG, as will the Editors of Television and Radio News.

Daily current affairs programmes, which work closely with regional newsrooms, will also for practical reasons refer to ENCANI as the first point of contact on any same-day coverage. Their longer-term projects however require consultation with CNI.

(c) Consultation is a two-way process requiring the fullest possible disclosure of the programme proposal, upon which CNI can form an opinion; it is also a continuing process. After the first consultation at the outset of the proposal, CNI is to be kept informed about its progress and consulted about any significant change, incident or problem which may occur. He also needs to be informed of the transmission date envisaged and of the context in which it is being transmitted.

3. Referring proposals to interview Members of Terrorist Organisations and those who are or may be associated with such Organisations.

In these cases the producer or editor making the proposal will make it first to his Head of Department who will refer to ADG and notify the network Controller and CNI. Interviews with individuals who are deemed by ADG to be closely associated with a terrorist organisation may not be sought or transmitted — two separate stages — without the prior permission of DG.

Section II

Principles and Practice – Reporting Northern Ireland

It is recognised that in the peculiar circumstances in Northern Ireland and the Irish Republic the news reporter, or those engaged in making a programme which has been endorsed in the BBC's consultative processes, may be confronted by the unexpected.

He may find he has a 'lead' which takes him into the unknown and into areas of risk. He may find he has no time to refer back to his editor or that it may be dangerous to use a telephone. He may judge the 'lead' to be a propaganda trap for him, his programme, for the BBC; or he may judge that he should follow it through. It is the instinct of the journalist to find out, and nothing in this revised instruction is intended, in these rare but real circumstances, to inhibit the reporter from finding out.

The reporter must weigh the circumstances and the possible consequences. The responsibility for publishing what he discovers lies with his editor: the reporter cannot promise publication. He should inform his editor of any unexpected circumstances at the earliest opportunity.

The purpose of this revision is not to inhibit the proper pursuit of our journalism, but to clarify procedures in the light of case histories studied by News and Current Affairs Editors since the Standing Instructions were first written in 1971. These directions should not therefore be read as restrictions. They are the framework in which our journalists are free to work in a difficult, contentious and dangerous area, backed by the fullest possible authority of the BBC.

References

PREFACE

1. Two examples were the Peace Conference delegation received on 22 August 1969, and the loyalist delegation received on 27 August 1971. The loyalist group came to protest against TV coverage of Northern Ireland and as evidence of public support for their protest they showed 33,000 signatures, which they had collected, through an advertisement in the Belfast *News Letter*.
2. R. Cathcart, 'The Independent Television Authority as an internal influence on programmes: a case history', a paper presented to the Fourth Symposium on Broadcasting Policy. Proceedings published by the University of Manchester, 1972.
3. R. Cathcart, 'The Mass Media in Twentieth Century Ireland', to be published in F. X. Martin, F. J. Byrne and W. Vaughan, 'The New History of Ireland' (Oxford, 1986), vol. 7.
4. For example, A. Smith, 'TV Coverage of Northern Ireland', *Index on Censorship*, 1, no. 1 (Summer 1972), 15 – 32.
5. R. Cathcart, 'BBC Northern Ireland: 50 Years Old', *Listener*, 92, no. 2372 (12 September 1974), 322–4.
6. A. Briggs, *The History of Broadcasting in the United Kingdom* (London, 1961–79), vols. 1 – 4.

INTRODUCTION

1. A fact recalled independently by both Mungo Dewar, who arrived in 1926 to organise the administration of 2BE after the Station Director had been dismissed, and Henry McMullan, who was active in a part-time capacity in the station in the 1920s before he joined the BBC in 1931. Interviews by the author, 1974.
2. G. C. Beadle, *Television: a critical review* (London, 1963), p. 24.
3. C. A. Siepmann, 'Report on the Regions – 460, Supplement on Northern Ireland', September 1936. This document and all subsequent BBC documents, unless otherwise stated, are in the BBC Archives Centre, Caversham.
4. *Northern Whig*, 31 January 1936.
5. *Northern Whig*, 1 February 1936.

6. Special Supplement on the BBC, *The Times,* 14 August 1934. The article on Northern Ireland is unsigned but was undoubtedly written by the Regional Director, George Marshall.

7. Siepmann, op. cit.

8. G. Marshall to Controller of Programmes, 26 July 1937.

9. R. McCall, 'The BBC in Northern Ireland: a note for the Chairman and members of the Board of Governors', 28 May 1958.

10. Belfast *News Letter,* 13 January 1959.

11. '"You can't get Bouquets all the Time", Ulster told', *Northern Whig,* 14 January 1959; Belfast *News Letter,* 14 January 1959.

12. Peter Black, *The Mirror in the Corner* (London, 1972), p. 125.

13. Annan, *Report of the Committee on the Future of Broadcasting,* HMSO (London, 1977), p. 270.

14. W. Maguire, 'Northern Ireland Crisis', in the staff journal, *Ariel,* 14, no. 9 (September 1969), 1 – 2.

15. R. Hoffman, 'Northern Ireland faces up to its Problems', *Ariel,* 14, no. 10 (October 1969), 10 – 11.

16. W. Maguire in a broadcast talk given in the series, *Assignment in Britain,* Radio 4, 23 August 1970.

CHAPTER 1: BROADCASTING COMES TO BELFAST

1. Circular letter 34609/22 from GPO dated 15 May 1922, signed J. J. De Wardt, PRONI Com. 21/12 PO 1846.

2. *First, second and third interim Reports and the final Report of the Special Committee to consider the Wireless Broadcasting,* Stationery Office (Dublin, 1924), p. 318.

3. Ibid., p. 321. For general background, R. Cathcart, 'Broadcasting: the early Decades', in B. Farrell (ed.), *Communications and Community in Ireland,* to be published in Cork, October 1984.

4. S. Watt, Ministry of Home Affairs, to Secretary, Ministry of Commerce, 6 September 1922. PRONI Com. 21/12 PO 1846.

5. D. Marconi, *My Father, Marconi* (London, 1962).

6. W. J. Baker, *A History of the Marconi Company* (London, 1970); H. A. Boyd, *Old Ballycastle, and Marconi and Ballycastle: two Lectures delivered on the occasion of the Town's Civic Week, 17th – 24th August, 1968* (Belfast, 1968); *Irish Radio Journal,* 2, no. 28 (9 January 1926), 1215 for an account of the Kingstown experiment.

7. *Irish Radio Journal,* 1, no. 1 (December 1923), 14 – 15. Father Ryan, CM, in 'My Wireless Experience' describes radio experiments which he conducted in Castleknock College, Co. Dublin.

8. Asa Briggs, *The Birth of Broadcasting* (London, 1961), p. 47.

9. *Belfast Telegraph,* 22 October 1945.

10. Circular letter 34609/22 from GPO dated 15 May 1922, signed J. J. De Wardt, PRONI Com. 21/12 PO 1846.

11. GPO Press Notice 96 'Wireless Broadcasting', 18 May 1922, PRONI Com. 21/12 PO 1846.

12. J. C. W. Reith, *Broadcast over Britain* (London, 1924), p. 61.

13. Secretary, Ministry of Commerce, note in file, dated 17 April 1923. PRONI Com. 21/12 PO 1846.

14. *Irish Radio Journal*, 1, no. 1 (December 1923), 22; 1, no. 2 (January, 1924), 48; 1, no. 9 (June, 1924), 372 – 3. This last surveys a controversy about the nature of the Northern Radio Association (Ireland).

15. Feature by N. Inglis as President of the Northern Radio Association (Ireland), *Northern Whig*, 15 September 1924.

16. Minutes of Board Meeting of BBC, 14 November 1923.

17. Brown, GPO, to BBC, 18 January 1924; BBC to GPO, 23 January 1924; GPO to BBC, 29 January 1924. BBC Archives, File 700 Technical General, Wavelengths.

18. *Irish Radio Journal*, vol. 1, no. 4 (March 1924), 133. In September 1924, the correspondence columns of the *Northern Whig* and the Belfast *News Letter* had letters complaining of the interference from 2BE.

19. GPO to BBC, 5 March 1924. File 700 Technical General, Wavelengths.

20. *Belfast Evening Telegraph*, 25 March 1924.

21. *Irish Radio Journal*, 1, no. 13 (August 1924), 396.

22. Godfrey Brown to Stanton Jefferies, 30 August 1924, quoted in Miss Edwin's summary history of the BBC in Northern Ireland, 1924–37. File 462.8 Northern Ireland.

23. *Radio Times*, 24 October 1924.

24. Belfast *News Letter*, 15 September 1924.

25. *Northern Whig*, 16 September 1924.

26. Belfast *News Letter*, 8 August 1924.

27. A. Burrows, Director of Programmes, to Major Scott, Station Director, Belfast, 5 September 1924.

28. J. C. W. Reith, *Broadcast over Britain* (London, 1924), pp. 112–13.

29. *Belfast Evening Telegraph*, 15 September 1924.

30. Extract from Godfrey Brown's contribution to programme of reminiscences, '2BE Calling!' transmitted on 21 March 1936.

31. *Dublin Evening Telegraph*, 16 September 1924.

32. Ibid.

33. *Northern Whig*, 18 September 1924.

34. *Irish News*, 16 September 1924.

35. *Reith Diaries*, 1924, pp. 57 – 8. Copy of the original in BBC Archives.

36. *Radio Times*, 28 November 1924.

37. *Northern Whig*, 23 November 1924.

38. *Irish Radio Journal*, 2, no. 12 (15 May 1925), 865.

39. *Irish Radio Journal,* 2, no. 16 (15 July 1925), 948–9 and 952.
40. *Radio Times,* 12 December 1924.
41. Tyrone Guthrie, '2BE Calling 1924', in *The BBC in Northern Ireland, 1924 – 1949.* A silver jubilee booklet (Belfast 1949).
42. Minute Book of the Religious Advisory Committee, Belfast, 1924–34, 3 November 1924.
43. Ibid., resolution passed 2 February 1925.
44. *Irish Radio Journal,* 2, no. 3 (15 January 1925), 676–7.
45. Minute Book of Educational Advisory Committee, Belfast, 1924–8, 4 December 1924.
46. *Irish Statesman,* 31 January 1925.
47. *Irish Radio Journal,* 2, no. 13 (1 June 1925), 886.
48. *Irish News,* 15 March 1926.
49. *Irish News,* 20 March 1926.
50. J. G. Stobart's report on visit to Belfast, 1 December 1925.
51. The suggestion was to be implemented by a group of loyalists forty-seven years later in the Belfast *News Letter,* 12 August 1971.
52. *Northern Whig,* 26 June 1926; *Irish News,* 26 June 1926; additional information in *Irish Radio Journal,* 2, no. 54 (10 July 1926), 1835.
53. *Irish Radio Journal,* 2, no. 54 (10 July 1926), 1828.
54. Sir Gerald Beadle in an interview with the author, 15 May 1974. This, and other interviews mentioned later, were recorded for use in, and as background to, 'Belfast Calling', a 50th anniversary programme, NI Radio 4, 18 September 1974.
55. Miss Edwin's summary history of the BBC in Northern Ireland to 1937. File 462.8 Northern Ireland; D.H. Clarke to Managing Director, 22 October 1926.

CHAPTER 2: 2BE CONSOLIDATES

1. G. C. Beadle, *Television: a critical review* (London, 1963), p. 23.
2. Sir Gerald Beadle in an interview with the author, 15 May 1974.
3. G. C. Beadle to Director General, 1 March 1927.
4. Asa Briggs, *The Birth of Broadcasting* (London ,1961), pp. 360–84.
5. *Irish Radio Journal,* 2, no. 46 (15 May 1926), 1638–9.
6. Goldsmith's draft reply to G. C. Beadle with Reith's note, as filed 16 March 1927. File R13/366/1.
7. *BBC Year Book,* 1928, p. 181.
8. *BBC Year Book,* 1930, p. 111.
9. *BBC Year Book,* 1929, p. 91.
10. PRONI File Com. 21/12 PO 1846.
11. *BBC Year Book,* 1928, p. 181.
12. *First, second and third interim Reports and the final Report of the Special committee to consider the Wireless Broadcasting,* Stationery Office (Dublin, 1924), pp. ix–x.

13. *BBC Year Book*, 1931, p. 146.
14. *Daily Express*, 28 June 1930.
15. Belfast *News Letter*, 6 May 1931.
16. Belfast *News Letter*, 21 May 1931.
17. Belfast *News Letter*, 16 October 1929.
18. Belfast *News Letter*, 21 October 1929.
19. *Northern Whig*, 6 April 1931.
20. *Manchester Guardian*, 18 March 1931.
21. Belfast *News Letter*, 20 March 1931.
22. *Northern Whig*, 21 March 1931.
23. Belfast *News Letter*, 24 March 1931.
24. Belfast *News Letter*, 27 March 1931.
25. Belfast *News Letter*, 28 March 1931.
26. Sir Gerald Beadle in an interview with the author, 15 May 1974.
27. *Northern Whig*, 31 October 1931.
28. Belfast *News Letter*, 3 January 1929.
29. *Northern Whig*, 23 January 1929.
30. *Northern Whig*, 3 November 1931.
31. *Northern Whig*, 31 October 1931.
32. *Northern Whig*, 23 November 1931.
33. J. C. Stobart's Report on visit to Belfast, 4 November 1926.
34. Asa Briggs, *The Golden Age of Wireless* (London, 1965), p. 307.
35. Belfast Station Director to Director of Programmes, Head Office, 10 September 1929.
36. Assistant Director of Programmes to Belfast Station Director, 20 September 1929.
37. *Irish News*, 17 March 1930.
38. *Radio Times*, 6 February 1931, p. 337.
39. *BBC Year Book*, 1928, p. 181.
40. Extract from recorded interview played in 'Belfast Calling', a 50th anniversary programme, NI Radio 4, 18 September 1974.
41. Minutes of Educational Advisory Committee, Belfast, 1924–8, 14 December 1926.
42. *Irish News*, 2 April 1927.
43. Minutes of Educational Advisory Committee Belfast, 1924–8. Beadle's report on 22 March 1927.
44. *Northern Whig*, 3 April 1931.
45. J. C. Stobart's Report on visit to Belfast, 4 November 1926.
46. 'Talking to the World: H.R.W. visits the Belfast Broadcasting Station', *Sunday Independent*, 10 January 1930; the same correspondent wrote a similar piece but with interesting additions in *Irish Motoring* (22 December 1928), p. 449.
47. Belfast *News Letter*, 21 March 1928.
48. Belfast Station Director to Controller, Head Office, 5 May 1930.

49. Belfast Station Director to Controller, Head Office, 22 October 1930.
50. Belfast *News Letter,* 12 November 1927.
51. Belfast *News Letter,* 9 December 1930.
52. Minutes of Control Board Meeting, 8 May 1928.
53. G. C. Beadle, *Television: a critical review* (London, 1963), p. 24.
54. Asa Briggs, *The Golden Age of Broadcasting* (London, 1965), pp. 293–339. The story of the struggle to establish regional broadcasting deserves more extended treatment than Briggs could afford in his work. The Archives reveal the major role played by Beadle. A meeting held in Head Office on 11 July 1932, to discuss regionalism, under the chairmanship of the Director General, proved a turning point. File: Regional Broadcasting 460, 1923–39.
55. Northern Area Director to Director General, 4 May 1928: '. . . it is very gratifying to have in one's area a station which is so ably run . . .'; entry on Beadle, G. C. in *Who's Who in Broadcasting,* London, 1933: '. . . he was recalled by the BBC to take over the very difficult job of directing the station at Belfast. This duty he carried out to such uniform efficiency that . . .', etc.
56. Belfast *News Letter,* 9 September 1931.

CHAPTER 3: TOWARDS A REGIONAL SERVICE

1. *BBC Year Book,* 1934, p. 235.
2. J. Costman, 'Regional Broadcasting', *BBC Quarterly,* 2, no. 3 (October, 1947), 160.
3. Ibid.
4. *BBC Year Book,* 1934, p. 235.
5. *Northern Whig,* 4 September 1929.
6. *Northern Whig,* 3 May 1930.
7. Belfast *News Letter,* 1 October 1932.
8. J. C. W. Reith, *Broadcast Over Britain* (London, 1924), p. 36; Andrew Stewart, Controller NI 1948–52, in an interview with the author, 1973.
9. Belfast *News Letter,* 1 October 1932.
10. *Northern Whig,* 17 March 1933.
11. Belfast *News Letter,* 21 March 1933.
12. Belfast *News Letter,* 21 March 1933.
13. Belfast *News Letter,* 23 March 1933.
14. Belfast *News Letter,* 23 March 1933.
15. Belfast *News Letter,* 23 March 1933.
16. Belfast *News Letter,* 22 March 1933.
17. Belfast *News Letter,* 21 March 1933.
18. *Radio Times,* 19 January 1934, p. 204. A defence of the programme with short account of the controversy which followed its transmission.
19. Marshall's report on the programme contained in the Director

General's Report to the Board of Governors, 14 February 1934. Ref. R1/3/13.
20. *Northern Whig*, 27 December 1933.
21. *Northern Whig*, 29 December 1933.
22. *Northern Whig*, 30 December 1933.
23. *Northern Whig*, 30 December 1933.
24. *Northern Whig*, 30 December 1933.
25. Belfast *News Letter*, 1 January 1933.
26. Belfast *News Letter*, 30 December 1933.
27. *Northern Whig*, 1 January 1933.
28. *Northern Whig*, 4 January 1933.
29. Belfast *News Letter*, 1 January 1933.
30. Belfast *News Letter*, 28 December 1933.
31. *Northern Whig*, 28 April 1934.
32. Belfast *News Letter*, 24 April 1934.
33. *Northern Whig*, 1 May 1934.
34. Marshall to DG, 14 May 1946.
35. An interesting account of the circumstances of this interview is given in Northern Ireland Regional Director to Asst. Controller (Programmes), 15 November 1935.
36. *Northern Whig*, 21 October 1935.
37. *Northern Whig*, 28 October 1935.
38. *Northern Whig*, 30 October 1935.
39. *Northern Whig*, 31 October 1935.
40. *Northern Whig*, 1 November 1935.
41. *Northern Whig*, 6 November 1935.
42. *Northern Whig*, 9 November 1935.
43. *Northern Whig*, 1 November 1935.
44. *Northern Whig*, 30 October 1935.
45. Belfast *News Letter*, 1 October 1932.
46. Director of Regional Relations, Report on visits to Scotland and Belfast, 29 March 1933.
47. *Northern Whig*, 2 October 1934.
48. *Irish News*, 2 November 1934.
49. G. Marshall, 'Broadcasting in Northern Ireland', *Radio Times*, 20 March 1936, p. 7.
50. Marshall quoted in the DG's Report to the Board of Governors, 8 May 1935.
51. Regional Director's quarterly talk, 30 December 1935; also Marshall's feature in the Belfast *News Letter*, 20 March 1936.
52. *Northern Whig*, 31 December 1935.
53. Ibid.
54. J. B. Clark, DES to Controller (P), Liaison between NI and The Free State, 23 December 1935.
55. Ibid., penned footnote by Controller (P).

56. J. B. Clark to Programme Director, Northern Ireland, 2 January 1936.
57. J. B. Clark to Dr T. J. Kiernan, 6 January 1936.
58. *Daily Mail,* Irish edition, 15 Janaury 1936.
59. *Evening Standard,* 17 January 1936.
60. Programme Director Northern Ireland to Director of Empire Service, 13 February 1936.
61. *Northern Whig,* 31 January 1936 and 5 February 1936.
62. Belfast *News Letter,* 7 February 1936.
63. Programme Director NI, to DES, 19 February 1936.
64. Belfast *News Letter,* 4 February 1936.
65. *Irish News,* 28 May 1936.
66. *Irish News,* 4 December 1936.
67. C. A. Siepmann, 'Report on the Regions – 460, Supplement on Northern Ireland', September 1936.
68. Northern Ireland Regional Director to Controller (Admin.), 24 November 1937.
69. Ibid., appendix.
70. Marshall in the DG's Report to the Board of Governors, 23 February 1938.
71. Belfast *News Letter,* 29 March 1938.
72. *Irish News,* 30 March 1938.
73. Marshall in the DG's Report to the Board of Governors, 25 May 1938.
74. Belfast *News Letter,* 5 April 1938.
75. Belfast *News Letter,* 26 April 1938.
76. Marshall in the DG's Report to the Board of Governors, 25 May 1938.
77. Ibid.
78. Belfast *News Letter,* 5 April 1938.
79. *Irish Press,* 2 Janaury 1937.
80. *Irish News,* 29 March 1937.
81. *Daily Mail,* Irish edition, 6 February 1937.
82. *Northern Whig,* 24 April 1937.
83. *Belfast Telegraph,* 24 April 1937.
84. Marshall in the DG's Report to the Board of Governors, 8 June 1938.
85. Marshall in the DG's Report to the Board of Governors, 28 June 1939.
86. *Northern Whig,* 8 July 1939.
87. *Irish Press,* 13 June 1939.
88. Controller (Programmes) to Belfast Station Director, 14 November 1933.
89. Northern Ireland Regional Director to Assistant Controller (Programmes), 14 January 1938.
90. Northern Ireland Regional Director to Controller (Programmes), 28 July 1937.
91. J. Salt replying on behalf of North Regional Director to Northern Ireland Regional Director, 3 August 1937.

92. Northern Ireland Regional Director to Controller (Programmes), 11 March 1938.

93. Controller (Programmes) to Northern Ireland Regional Director, 14 March 1938.

94. Marshall in the DG's Report to the Board of Governors, 13 April 1938.

95. Belfast *News Letter*, 19 March 1938.

96. Marshall in the DG's Report to the Board of Governors, 26 April 1939.

97. Programme Director Northern Ireland to Director Overseas Service, 8 June 1938.

98. Controller (Programmes) to Northern Ireland Regional Director, 15 June 1938; also DOS to NIRD, 14 June 1938.

99. *Daily Express,* Irish edition, 9 July 1937.

100. *Irish News,* 13 October 1936.

101. *Irish News,* 8 September 1938.

102. *Northern Whig,* 4 October 1937.

103. Belfast *News Letter,* 17 September 1937.

104. In an interview with the author, 1974: this passage was used in 'Belfast Calling', programme to celebrate 50th anniversary of the BBC in Northern Ireland, 18 September 1974.

105. *Reith's Diaries,* entries for 14 and 15 December 1933.

106. *Belfast Telegraph,* 5 January 1935.

107. *Belfast Telegraph,* 15 April 1939.

108. *Belfast Telegraph,* 22 April 1939.

109. An early example of an appreciative notice is to be found in the *Strad,* August 1931.

110. Marshall in the DG's Report to the Board of Governors, 12 June 1939; for additional background, R. Cathcart, 'Some aspects of School Broadcasting in Ireland', *Northern Teacher,* 10, no. 6 (Summer 1973), 3 – 7.

111. *Irish News,* 10 December 1938.

112. In an interview with the author, 1974.

113. Report in the *Kinematograph Weekly* (10 December 1933), referring to broadcast sermon transmitted on 7 December 1933.

114. D. O'Raghaille, *A Listener's Opinion: Improvements needed in Radio Éireann* (Tralee, 1944), p. 27.

115. In an interview with the author, 1974.

116. In an interview with the author, 5 May 1983.

117. Ibid.

118. In an interview with the author, 1974.

119. Ibid.

CHAPTER 4: THE WAR YEARS AND AFTER

1. DPP to Controller (Programmes), 12 September 1939.

2. Ursula Eason in an interview with the author, 5 May 1983.
3. HLD to SE(s), 21 December 1939.
4. Ursula Eason in an interview with the author, 5 May 1983.
5. Lord Craigavon, 'Ulster's Part in the War', *Listener,* 23, no. 578 (8 February 1940), 266.
6. Ursula Eason to DPP, 11 January 1940; details suggested in Ursula Eason, Acting Programme Director, Northern Ireland, to ADPP, 15 February 1940.
7. *Glasgow Herald,* 18 March 1940.
8. R. A. Rendall to Northern Ireland Regional Director, 26 January 1940; NID to R. A. Rendall, 29 January 1940: This memo is annotated by J.P.C.
9. Miss K. Fuller to AC (O), 16 February 1940.
10. Director-Overseas, J. Clark, record of telephone conversations, 16 February 1940; R. A. Rendall's record of telephone conversation with Home Office, 20 February 1940.
11. Northern Ireland Director to Controller (Programmes), 18 March 1940.
12. Controller (Programmes) to Heads of Departments, 19 April 1940.
13. C. Conner, Overseas Director, to Northern Ireland Director, Marshall, 4 May 1940.
14. Marshall, NID, to C. Conner, HO, 7 May 1940.
15. Directive from Empire Division of MOI, in memo from WRPD, 17 May 1940.
16. Northern Ireland Controller to Controller (Programmes), 18 July 1940.
17. Turnell to Controller (Programmes), 30 July 1940.
18. Northern Ireland Director to Controller (Programmes), 29 November 1940.
19. Northern Ireland Director to DPP, 2 December 1940.
20. Controller (Programmes), B. E. Nicholls, Programme Directive, no. 47, 17 December 1940.
21. Director, Broadcasting Division, Ministry of Information, to Controller (Programmes), 20 November 1940.
22. L. Wellington, Director of Broadcasting Division, Ministry of Information to Controller (P), 8 December 1940.
23. A. Stewart, Broadcasting Division, Ministry of Information to Godfrey Adams, BBC, 10 January 1941; also Memorandum from Empire Division, 15 January 1941.
24. Ursula Eason to DPP, 17 January 1941; Northern Ireland Director to ADPP, 21 January 1941.
25. *Northern Whig,* 14 March 1941.
26. Controller (Programmes) to Adviser for Home Affairs, 21 July 1941.
27. Northern Ireland Director to Controller (Prog.), 18 March 1941.
28. *Irish Times,* 18 March 1941.

29. Gilliam to Val Gielgud, Director Features & Drama, & AC(P), 18 February 1941.
30. Ibid., footnote in pen appended by Gielgud.
31. Northern Ireland Director to Controller (P), 3 March 1941.
32. Salman to Director of Talks, 22 February 1941.
33. 'Irish Magazine': proposals submitted by H. L. Fletcher, 6 May 1941.
34. Ursula Eason to C(H), HO, 23 May 1941.
35. Remarks added to a memo from North American SD to ETD, 28 May 1941.
36. J. M. Andrews to F. W. Ogilvie, DG, 10 July 1941. File: Policy – Éire, 1930–43.
37. Marshall to DG, 22 July 1941.
38. F. W. Ogilvie to J. M. Andrews, 2 August 1941.
39. J. M. Andrews to F. W. Ogilvie, 6 August 1941.
40. Marshall to DG, 7 August 1941.
41 .Pat Hillyard and Francis Worsley, Report on visit to Dublin to Controller (Programmes), 5 September 1941.
42. Ibid; B. E. Nicholls, Controller (Programmes), to Marshall, 15 September 1941.
43. J. M. Andrews to Marshall, 18 September 1941.
44. Marshall to Controller (Programmes), 18 November 1941.
45. Controller (Programmes) to Asst. Director of Variety, 8 January 1942.
46. Controller (Programmes) to Marshall, 17 March 1942.
47. Letter addressed to 'Donald', D. F. Boyd, from Denis Johnston, 6 September 1941; also NID, Marshall, to ASNE, 9 September 1941.
48. John Irwin to R. A. Rendall, Director of Empire Service, 21 September 1941.
49. Marshall, NID, to Assistant Controller, Overseas, 8 December 1942.
50. J. Betjeman to B. E. Nicholls, 4 October 1941.
51. Assistant Senior News Editor to A. P. Ryan, Senior News Editor, 12 September 1941.
52. Controller (Programmes) to Howard Thomas, 13 January 1942.
53. A. P. Ryan, Senior News Editor, to E. Rawdon-Smith, Dominions Officer, 26 January 1942.
54. Controller (Programmes) to Marshall, NID, 27 February 1942.
55. J. M. Andrews to Marshall, 16 March 1942.
56. Controller (Home), Sir Richard Maconachie, to NID, 23 March 1942.
57. Marshall to NLD, 28 September 1943.
58. Marshall to Controller (Programmes), 25 May 1943.
59. Marshall to NLD, 28 September 1943.
60. Marshall to Controller Overseas Service, 23 October 1943.
61. Controller Overseas Service, J. B. Clark, to Marshall, 27 October 1943.
62. Marshall to Director General, 15 November 1943.
63. J. M. Andrews to Marshall, 27 January 1943.

64. Marshall to Andrew Stewart, Scottish Programme Director, 19 August 1943.
65. A. P. Ryan, Controller (News), to DG, 15 June 1943.
66. Ursula Eason to DPP, 11 February 1943.
67. Ursula Eason, Northern Ireland Programme Director, to Controller (Programmes), 29 July 1941.
68. Ursula Eason, NIPD, to DPP, October 1942.
69. DPP to Ursula Eason, 23 October 1942.
70. Val Gielgud, Director of Features & Drama, to Assistant Programme Planning, 27 January 1943.
71. Marshall to Controller (Programmes), 22 April 1943.
72. *Northern Whig*, 30 July 1943.
73. *Northern Whig*, 2 August 1943.
74. *Northern Whig*, 30 September 1943.
75. *Northern Whig*, 24 September 1943.
76. *Northern Whig*, 18 April 1946.
77. *Northern Whig*, 23 August 1943.
78. *Northern Whig*, 26 August 1943.
79. *Northern Whig*, 24 August 1943.
80. *Irish News*, 19 October 1943.
81. *Irish News*, 23 November 1944.
82. Assistant CN to A. P. Ryan, Controller News, 5 July 1944.
83. John Irwin to HNAS, 'Projected Programme on North American Service', 13 September 1945. File E1/953.
84. Senior Controller, B. E. Nicholls, to Heads of Department, 15 August 1946.
85. Marshall to Controller Overseas Services, 26 August 1946.
86. C. Conner, Director of Overseas Programme Services, to Controller Overseas Services, 17 January 1947.
87. C. Conner to J. B. Clark, Controller Overseas Services, 31 January 1947.
88. J. B. Clark, Controller Overseas Services, to Senior Controller, 15 February 1947.
89. Marshall to R. Beattie, 30 July 1945.
90. Marshall to Rev J. W. Welch, Director of Religious Broadcasting, 20 October 1944.
91. *Belfast Telegraph*, 25 October 1945.
92. *Irish Times*, 8 November 1945.
93. *Irish News*, 28 March 1947.
94. Marshall quoted in the DG's Report to the Board of Governors, 24 March 1948.
95. This comment was reported in the Belfast *News Letter*, 13 February 1948. Such publicity for Advisory Council sessions was not to occur again.

96. Director of Home Broadcasting, B. E. Nicholls, to Marshall, 11 March 1948.
97. Marshall to B. E. Nicholls, 16 March 1948.
98. Marshall to D.G., 31 August 1946.
99. Godfrey Talbot to Editor (News), 31 July 1947.
100. *Irish Times,* 31 October 1946.
101. Rev J. W. Welch, Director of Religious Broadcasting, to DG, 28 May 1946.
102. Belfast *News Letter,* 4 June 1948.
103. *Irish News,* 9 November 1946.
104. *Irish News,* 28 March 1947.
105. *The Times,* 5 April 1948.
106. *Irish Press,* 3 April 1948.
107. Marshall quoted in DG's Report to Board of Governors, 2 June 1948.

CHAPTER 5: THE PROFESSIONAL TOUCH

1. Recounted by Andrew Stewart in an interview with the author, 1973.
2. Andrew Stewart, Broadcasting Division, Ministry of Information, to Godfrey Adams, BBC, 14 May 1940.
3. Stewart to Director of Spoken Word, 2 September 1948 and reply from Controller Talks, to Stewart, 10 September 1948.
4. Stewart to Director of Home Broadcasting, 2 September 1948.
5. Stewart's report to the Board of Governors for the period 8 November 1948 to 26 January 1949.
6. George Barnes, Director of the Spoken Word, 'My Visit to Northern Ireland – 10/11 November 1948', to the Director General, 16 November 1948. File: Television Development in Northern Ireland, 1952–54.
7. In an interview with the author, 1973.
8. Stewart in an interview with the author, 1973.
9. Details given by Dr E. W. Boucher in an interview with the author, 3 January 1984.
10. Stewart to Director of Home Broadcasting, 7 December 1948.
11. K. A. Wright to Head of Music, 25 July 1949.
12. Horace Dann to Head of Music, Northern Ireland Light Orchestra – Morning Music – 26 July, undated but undoubtedly 26 July 1949.
13. Kenneth Baynes to Head of Music, 30 August 1949.
14. Northern Ireland Advisory Council minutes, 11 February 1953.
15. S. H. Bell, 'The Microphone in the Countryside' in *The BBC in Northern Ireland, 1924–49,* a Silver Jubilee publication (BBC Belfast, 1949).
16. In an interview with the author, 1974.
17. S. H. Bell, 'The Microphone in the Countryside', op. cit.

18. Northern Ireland Advisory Council minutes, 8 February 1951.
19. In an interview with the author, 1974.
20. Stewart's Report to the Board of Governors for the period 29 February to 8 May 1952.
21. Quoted from the draft of the report for 1949 presented to the Board of Governors.
22. H. McMullan, 'The McCooey Family', *BBC Year Book*, 1951, pp. 64–5; see also a feature: Norman Phillips, 'Two million Irish switch on for the McCooeys', *John Bull* (24 October 1953).
23. George Barnes, Director of the Spoken Word, to Director of Home Broadcasting, 7 April 1949.
24. Ibid.
25. Stewart, Report on interview with the Prime Minister, 4 January 1949, to Director of the Spoken Word.
26. *Belfast Telegraph*, 22 January 1949.
27. *Belfast Telegraph*, 26 January 1949.
28. Stewart to Director of the Spoken Word, 26 January 1949.
29. Ibid.
30. Stewart's Report to the Board of Governors for the period 8 November 1948 to 26 January 1949.
31. *Irish News*, 21 October 1948; Stewart's Report to the Board of Governors for the period 16 June to 19 September 1949.
32. Stewart's Report to the Board of Governors for the period 10 November 1950 to 23 January 1951.
33. PRONI Com 69/12, BBC representative on committee of inquiry.
34. Ibid., footnote penned at the end of memo.
35. *Northern Whig*, 24 August, 31 August and 7 September 1949.
36. Recommendations of Beveridge Committee, PRONI CAB 4/840.
37. Note by the Prime Minister, B. Brooke, to Cabinet on the BBC in Northern Ireland, 2 March 1951, PRONI CAB 4/840.
38. As recounted by Andrew Stewart in an interview with the author, 1973.
39. Northern Ireland Advisory Council minutes, 8 February 1951.
40. Belfast *News Letter*, 18 July 1951.
41. *Sunday Independent*, 18 May 1952.
42. *Northern Whig*, 12 June 1952.
43. Ursula Eason in an interview with the author, 5 May 1983.
44. Sam Hanna Bell in an interview with the author, 1974.
45. Ursula Eason in an interview with the author, 5 May 1983.
46. Stewart to Director of the Spoken Word, 24 October 1952.
47. H. McMullan, 'Within our Province', *BBC Year Book*, 1950, p. 55.

CHAPTER 6: THE ATTEMPT TO CREATE A CONSENSUS

1. Conner's Report to the Board of Governors for the period January to April 1953.

2. Marriott to Director of the Spoken Word, 24 August 1953.
3. Marriott to Director of the Spoken Word, 25 August 1953; also Marriott to Director of the Spoken Word, 25 September 1953.
4. Controller's Report to the Northern Ireland Advisory Council, 30 April 1953.
5. Controller's Report to the Northern Ireland Advisory Council, 25 April 1955.
6. Murphy, Education Officer, NW Division, Manchester, to Controller Northern Ireland, note undated, but early May 1953.
7. Ibid.
8. T. W. Moody and J. C. Beckett (eds.), *Ulster since 1800: political and economic survey* (BBC London, 1955); *Ulster since 1800: a social survey* (BBC London, 1957).
9. Controller's Report to the Northern Ireland Advisory Council, 29 January 1954.
10. Recording of the 100th edition of *Your Questions*.
11. Asst. to C. P. Television to Director of Television Broadcasting, 30 March 1954; Jacob, Director General, as reported in Board of Management minutes, 5 April 1954.
12. Belfast *News Letter*, 29 March 1954.
13. Ibid.
14. Ibid.
15. Acting Film Booking Manager to CP Television, 6 April 1954.
16. Director General, Sir Ian Jacob, to Prime Minister Brookeborough, 7 April 1954.
17. Brookeborough to Sir Ian Jacob, 13 April 1954.
18. Director General to Director of Television Broadcasting, 7 April 1954.
19. Controller's Report to the Northern Ireland Advisory Council, 30 April 1954.
20. *Northern Whig,* 12 Janaury 1959.
21. In an interview with the author, 1974.
22. In an interview with the author, 1974
23. McCall's Report to the Board of Governors for the period January to March 1957.
24. Controller Northern Ireland, R. McCall, to Director General, 31 March 1958.
25. *Northern Whig,* 10 January 1959.
26. Ibid.
27. Belfast *News Letter*, 12 January 1959.
28. Belfast *News Letter*, 12 January 1959.
29. *Belfast Telegraph,* 14 January 1959.
30. Belfast *News Letter*, 14 January 1959.
31. McCall to Grace Wyndham Goldie, 14 January 1959.
32. H. McMullan in an interview with the author, 1974.

33. Northern Ireland Advisory Council, 24 April 1959.
34. *Northern Whig*, 27 April 1959.
35. *Northern Whig*, 28 April 1959.
36. *Northern Whig*, 29 April 1959.
37. *Northern Whig*, 1 May 1959; the Director General's statement on the affair and various comments at the BBC's General Advisory Council meeting in the Controller Northern Ireland's Report to NIAC, 23 October 1959.
38. Northern Ireland Advisory Council minutes, 23 October 1959.
39. In an interview with the author, 1974.
40. Northern Ireland Advisory Council minutes, 8 February 1957.
41. *Northern Whig*, 11 October 1962.
42. *Northern Whig*, 6 October 1962.
43. *Northern Whig*, 8 October 1962.
44. *Belfast Telegraph*, 21 October 1964.
45. 'Allegations of neglect in North-West Ulster', *Inquiry*, transmitted 17 December 1965.
46. G. Rugeheimer in an interview with the author, 27 November 1972.
47. Paper on Northern Ireland Development presented to the Northern Ireland Advisory Council, 3 July 1964.
48. Northern Ireland Advisory Council minutes, 14 January 1966.
49. Controller's Report to the Northern Ireland Advisory Council, 8 October 1965.
50. Controller's Report to the Northern Ireland Advisory Council, 21 April 1961.
51. Northern Ireland Advisory Council minutes, 15 April 1966.
52. Robert Coulter in an interview with the author, 1974.

CHAPTER 7: THE CRISIS BREAKS

1. Northern Ireland Advisory Council minutes, 24 June 1966.
2. In an interview with the author, 17 April 1984.
3. Northern Ireland Advisory Council minutes, 30 September 1966.
4. Controller's Report to Northern Ireland Advisory Council, 13 January 1967.
5. Parliamentary Debates, HC, 22 October 1968 Cols. 1088–9.
6. Controller's Report to Northern Ireland Advisory Council, 3 January 1969.
7. *Irish News*, as cited in the Controller's Report to the Advisory Council, 18 April 1969.
8. *Belfast Telegraph*, 26 May 1969, Belfast *News Letter*, 12 June 1969, and *Irish News*, 7 June 1969.
9. Controller's Report on 'BBC and The Northern Ireland Crisis' to the Northern Ireland Advisory Council, 3 October 1969.

10. Martin Bell in Seminar report on 'Terrorism and the Media', in *Ten Years of Terrorism*, Royal United Services Institute for Defence Studies (London, 1979), pp. 92–3.
11. Controller's Report to NIAC, 30 October 1969.
12. Ibid.
13. K. Kyle, 'The Ulster emergency and the BBC's impartiality', *Listener* (4 September 1969), 298.
14. Controller's Report to NIAC, 3 October 1969.
15. *Observer*, 17 August 1969.
16. *Irish News*, 21 August 1969; Belfast *News Letter*, as cited in the Controller's Report to the Advisory Council, 3 October 1969.
17. *BBC Handbook*, 1970, p. 9.
18. Northern Ireland Advisory Council minutes, 2 April 1971.
19. *Belfast Telegraph*, 27 April 1971.
20. A. Smith, 'TV Coverage of Northern Ireland', *Index on censorship*, 1, no. 2 (Summer 1972), 25.
21. *Ariel*, no. 1 (10 September 1971).
22. Ibid.
23. Belfast *News Letter*, 12 August 1971.
24. Belfast *News Letter*, 27 September 1971.
25. *Daily Telegraph*, 26 October 1971; *Daily Telegraph*, 29 October 1971.
26. *Daily Telegraph*, 17 November 1971.
27. Lord Hill, Chairman of the BBC, to R. Maudling, Home Secretary, 23 November 1971, as reprinted in *BBC Record*, December 1971, also *The Times*, 24 November 1971.
28. *Ariel*, no. 7 (3 December 1971).
29. R. Francis, 'The Question of Ulster', *Ariel*, no. 10 (21 January 1972).
30. *Daily Telegraph*, 28 and 29 December 1971.
31. Lord Hill, *Behind the Screen* (London, 1974), p. 221; *The Times*, 5 January 1972.
32. *Observer*, 21 November 1971.

CHAPTER 8: THE TIME OF THE TROUBLES

1. R. Francis, 'Terrorists on Television', a speech to the Broadcasting Press Guild, 12 July 1979. *The Times* leader referred to is from the 16 March 1977 edition.
2. R. Francis, 'Broadcasting to a Community in Conflict – the experience in Northern Ireland', a lecture at the Royal Institute of International Affairs, 22 February 1977.
3. R. Fisk, *The Point of no Return* (London, 1975), p. 127.
4. Ibid., p. 137.
5. *Daily Mail*, 6 January 1977; *Guardian*, 7 January 1977 and *Observer*, 23 January 1977.

6. Keith Kyle, 'Bernard O'Connor's Story', *Listener* (10 March 1977); *Guardian*, 4 March 1977; *Morning Star*, 5 March 1977; *Irish Times*, 10 March 1977; *The Times*, 11 March 1977; *Observer*, 13 March 1977.

7. Keith Kyle, 'The O'Connor Case: Police interrogation in Ireland – a judge's view', *Listener* (10 July 1980).

8. *The Times*, 22 March 1977.

9. Keith Kyle, op. cit.

10. Mary Holland, 'Mason plays it rough', *New Statesman* (11 March 1977).

11. *Observer*, 11 November 1979; *Guardian*, 10 November 1979 and an important letter by Vincent Hannah in *Guardian*, 12 November 1979; *The Times* and *Daily Telegraph*, 16 November 1979.

12. *Daily Star*, 9 November 1979; *Daily Telegraph*, 9 November 1979; *Daily Express*, 9 November 1979.

13. *Guardian*, 12 July 1980.

14. Sir Michael Havers, Attorney General, to Sir Michael Swann, Chairman of the BBC, reproduced in *BBC Record*, August 1980; *The Times*, 2 August 1980.

15. Sir Michael Swann, Chairman of the BBC, to Sir Michael Havers, Attorney General, reproduced in *BBC Record*, August 1980; *The Times*, 2 August 1980.

16. R. Francis, 'Broadcasting to a Community in Conflict – the experience in Northern Ireland', a lecture at the Royal Institute of International Affairs, 22 February 1977.

17. Belfast *News Letter*, 7 and 8 November 1980.

18. Northern Ireland news bulletin, 22 November 1980.

19. Sinn Fein press statement supplied to BBC, 24 November 1980.

20. *The Times*, 15 May 1981.

21. *Sunday Telegraph*, 17 May 1981.

22. Ian Trethowan, 'Should the Terrorists be given Air Time?', *The Times*, 4 June 1981.

23. Paul Johnson, 'The IRA's best Friend . . .', *Spectator* (13 June 1981).

24. *The Sun*, 18 June 1981.

25. *Daily Telegraph*, 22 September 1981.

26. Belfast *News Letter*, 22 September 1981.

27. *Belfast Telegraph*, 22 September 1981.

28. *Sunday Times*, 8 June 1981, pp. 15–17.

29. Peter Lennon, 'Broadcasting Problems in Northern Ireland', *Listener* (23 June and 30 June 1983).

30. Report of investigations into the recruitment practices of the BBC in Northern Ireland, Fair Employment Agency, Belfast, November 1983.

31. 'Ulster Irish on Ulster Radio and Television', a report by a study group, Belfast, September 1978.

32. *Anderstown News,* 4 April 1981.
33. R. Francis, 'Note on a Broadcasting Council for Northern Ireland', 14 March 1975. R. Francis, 'A note on what "one-BBC" means to Northern Ireland', 14 March 1975.
34. *Radio Times,* 15 February 1973.

CONCLUSION

1. R. Francis, 'Broadcasting to a Community in Conflict – the experience in Northern Ireland', a lecture to the Royal Institute of International Affairs, BBC, 1977.
2. R. Francis, 'Is cheap radio driving out the good?', *Listener* (28 June 1984).
3. Colin Ross, 'From Teaboy to Top Man – the dramatic rise of Robert Cooper', *Belfast Telegraph,* 10 December 1980.

Index

302

304

306